RUNNING UPHILL

Congressman James F. McNulty Jr. (D-Ariz.)

RUNNING UPHILL

*Recollections of a
Congressman from Arizona*

Jim McNulty

Edited by Alex Witzeman

Whitewing Press / Tucson

Whitewing Press
P.O. Box 65539
Tucson, AZ 85728-5539

Distributed by the University of Arizona Press, Tucson

Library of Congress Control No. 2003096168
ISBN 1-888965-06-1 (cloth)
ISBN 1-888965-07-X (paper)

CONTENTS

FOREWORD

FOR OVER A HALF-CENTURY Jim McNulty has added a strong dose of Irish wit and humor to Arizona's social, cultural, and political life. His panache has made life more interesting for all of those who have had the good fortune to cross his path. Together with his wise and lively wife, Jacquie, he has been a mainstay in the political and cultural life of Arizona for decades.

We first met at the University of Arizona in 1947 where we were among the flood of veterans who entered college after World War II thanks to the emancipating effects of the GI Bill. These students had been to war, were certain of their own minds, and they sometimes found themselves in conflict with the administration of the University. Things soon began to change at the University of Arizona, and after graduation, things began to change in the Arizona Democratic Party.

As students, McNulty and I were both interested in government and he became part of my inner circle of friends as I began my adventures in Arizona politics. He favored me with his staunch support, and in 1960, we locked arms to help a young Irish Senator from Boston "steal" the votes of the Arizona delegation to the Democratic National Convention. The nomination of Jack Kennedy was one of my life's great ventures, and it was a turning point in Arizona politics. McNulty was one of the young Democratic activists who helped to make it happen and he is in a unique position to tell the tale.

Jim's life experiences provide a fascinating look at the Arizona of the last half of the twentieth century. In his memoir, McNulty offers a forthright and honest analysis of the political process and takes us on an unforgettable journey through Arizona's modern political history. I recommend his memoir to students of politics and the law, particularly those with a healthy sense of humor.

STEWART L. UDALL
U.S. Secretary of the Interior, 1961–69

FOREWORD

IN 1982 CONGRESSMAN MORRIS K. UDALL told me about his friend Jim McNulty of Bisbee, Arizona, who was running for Congress. Mo introduced me to Jim and I liked what I saw. He was both smart and down to earth, he had a great Irish sense of humor, and his political views were a good fit with my own. I agreed to fly out to Tucson to appear at a fundraiser for the young Democratic candidate.

That event was the beginning of a friendship that has lasted for twenty years. McNulty served his term in good order and was unusually well-liked by his peers in the House of Representatives, just as he had been during his five years in the Arizona State Senate. He was known as a true gentleman and was a stranger to malice, an unusual trait in any legislative body. Jim was defeated in 1984. Happily, however, he kept voluminous notes of his term in Washington, which are reproduced in this memoir.

Jim McNulty's career in law and politics clearly marks him as an outstanding American. His insights into those professions may raise a few eyebrows, but they are honest and rooted in long experience. McNulty earned the respect of his legislative colleagues on both sides of the aisle with his integrity, his hard work, and his ability to make people smile. He has brought those same talents to the writing of this political memoir. The result is a candid analysis of Arizona politics and politicians in the last half of the twentieth century by a man who toiled in the political mines himself for nearly forty years.

BILL BRADLEY
U.S. Senator (D-New Jersey), 1979–95

EDITOR'S PREFACE

THROUGHOUT HIS LEGAL AND POLITICAL CAREERS, Jim McNulty recorded his experiences and observations in essays, journals, op-ed pieces, letters, formal interviews, and speeches. Fortunately for historians, he retained most of this material, as well as a wide variety of papers from his careers in politics and law. The material was donated to the University of Arizona Library early in 2001 and it is maintained there among the many other fine manuscript collections. His writings over the years have provided much of the content for this memoir. The other materials in the McNulty Collection have provided a rich source of additional historical detail and also have been invaluable in verifying the facts of many of the events recounted here.

Most of the narrative that follows, however, has been taken from more than twenty hours of interviews I conducted with Jim beginning in July 2001 and concluding in April 2002, which were supplemented with numerous telephone and in-person conversations to clarify and expand the various stories. In the preparation of this memoir Jim also wrote a great deal of new material. Jim's comments in an interview done by Jack August in 1986 for the Evo DeConcini Oral History Project at the Arizona Historical Society in Tucson also provided some insightful observations that have been adapted for use here.

Whenever possible, archival newspaper reports and documents from the McNulty Collection were used to corroborate dates and facts as well as to provide additional perspective and detail on the events being described. Thomas E. Sheridan's marvelous book, *Arizona: A History,* was our primary source for checking relevant local historical facts. It also provided some revealing details on episodes from Arizona history such as the struggle over the Right-To-Work laws and the violent strike in Clifton-Morenci in 1983.

The initial impetus to begin this project came from Jim's son, Michael McNulty, not from Jim himself. I believe that Jim's innate modesty prevented him from seeing his personal story as being of any particular interest or importance. Michael, however, saw the historical value of his father's recollections and the need to organize and preserve them. As Jim warmed to the project, he too began to recognize the fact that he had some unique insights to share in the areas of politics, politicians, government, and the law. Jim approached the job of writing his memoir with the same work ethic and high intellectual standards that earned his reputation for legislative and legal excellence.

The task of recording, organizing, and analyzing one's own life work is a daunting undertaking. When the subject is a life as full and productive as Jim McNulty's has been, the chore is even more challenging. We spent one year gathering the information and assembling it into the memoir you hold in your hands today. It took Jim a lifetime, however, to acquire the experience and the wisdom contained in it. I think that there were times when it probably seemed to him that it was taking a lifetime to complete the book. But through it all his intrinsic good-natured approach to life prevailed.

Jim was extremely forthright during the interviews and no area of inquiry was off-limits. He is not a man given to secretiveness. His remarks and writings ranged from the purely humorous to the historically significant, but most of it focused on the themes of politics, politicians, and the process of legislation. In this memoir we have concentrated on these areas of Jim McNulty's life. Consequently we have not examined his activities in charitable and community work, which have been substantial, or his work on various boards, commissions, and committees since leaving the U.S. House of Representatives. That material could easily fill another book.

For me, as a student of the rich history of Arizona and the South-west, the opportunity to learn about the state's political history in the last half of the twentieth century from a man who helped make it was like water in the desert. Most of us know the basic events of Arizona's recent history, but we rarely get the first-person insights that allow us to understand why it happened and who made it happen. In his memoir, Jim McNulty is offering us all a glimpse through that window.

ALEX WITZEMAN
June 2002

ACKNOWLEDGMENTS

MOST BOOK-WRITING EXERCISES benefit from the contributions of many folk, and this one is no exception. Friends and relatives of the author provide both moral support and guidance, which are indispensable in any risky endeavor, including the writing of an honest memoir.

My list of acknowledgments must begin with my wife, Jacqueline McNulty, to whom I have been married for 54 years. She has been involved with the project constantly for the last ten months. The quarterback of the effort has been my son, Michael, whose idea it was initially and whose intelligence and encouragement have contributed immensely to my sense of well-being about this whole enterprise. Two old friends, Stewart Udall and Bill Bradley, provided sympathy and support, as well as offering some kind words about this book and its author.

Alex Witzeman was brought to the project by Michael and has been on the case since the beginning. In addition to doing research, fact checking, and interrogating me thoroughly in interviews, he has helped to assemble all the pieces that make up my saga. He will be the subject of kind words by me in the future.

Dianetta Thomas has dispensed a substantial amount of labor on this memoir. She prepared interview transcripts, typed passages, as well as maintaining all the electronic files and communications on the project as drafts were written and revised. I believe she may be able to recite some sections from memory.

This memoir has also benefited from scholarly advice and expert opinion. Dr. Robert Glennon, Ares Professor of Constitutional Law at the University of Arizona, contributed his expertise on the one-man, one-vote issue. Dr. Jimmie Hillman, chairman emeritus of the Department of Agricultural Economics at the UA, provided details on historical changes in the agricultural sector that were used in the section on the impact of rural electrification in Arizona.

John Murphy and his able staff at the UA Library, Special Collections, were unfailingly helpful in providing access to the McNulty Collection. This is not to mention the excellent work they did archiving and preserving the voluminous collection of documents that I entrusted to them. I also extend my gratitude to the staff of the UA Press for the time and effort they expended on this project.

I am also intensely mindful of the many friends and colleagues who made possible the political career which is a major subject of this book. Any politician grounded in realism knows his or her success was achieved only through the dedicated efforts of many folks. My list of key political supporters includes people such as George Steele, Carla Blackwell, Priscilla Kuhn, Jim Altenstadter, Art Chapa, Thomas Chandler, Bruce Wright, Ruben Ortega, Allison Hughes, and Jim Barry. Add to these names the many dedicated campaign workers I mention in the chapters that follow and you have a tiny fraction of the political allies to whom I am indebted.

My political career could not have proceeded without my law partners, Matt Borowiec and Steve Desens. They took up their own professional burdens, and then took up mine as well. I had other outstanding partners beginning with Jim Gentry and Martin Gentry. They hired me for my first job as an attorney because of the efforts of J. F. "Pop" McKale, the legendary Director of Athletics for the University of Arizona. His was an act of kindness I shall not forget.

A lifetime in law and government necessarily exposes an individual to a wide variety of lawyers, judges, elected officials, and human shrines. I cast my lot with the people of Arizona and their leaders long ago. I feel strong connections to my many colleagues and mentors today, though many of them have long since passed into the realm of Arizona myth and legend. Indeed, they are a big part of the story that follows. This group would include people such as Ernest McFarland, who is the only man I ever knew to hold ranking positions in the executive, judicial, and legislative branches of government during his career. The names of these men and women brighten the pages that follow so I shall mention only one more here. That name is Morris King Udall, who honored our state with thirty years of service in the U.S. House of Representatives and who was my friend and colleague.

This book, therefore, is dedicated to the many men and women who, like Mo Udall and Ernest McFarland, served Arizona well in public office and in the courtroom. Lawyers and politicians are two groups who are much abused and little appreciated. Arizona, however, has produced some great ones. I, for one, intend to give them their due.

Finally, throughout the days of pondering and, ultimately, assembling this work, I have been conscious of the spoken moral suasion gifted me by the society of the law, especially the firms of Brown and Bain and Lewis and Roca. I am enduringly grateful.

J.F.M.

RUNNING UPHILL

INTRODUCTION

I'M A LIBERAL DEMOCRAT from an old mining camp on the Mexican border, and proud of it. I'm also a Boston Irishman who cherishes his Irish heritage. I'm a lot of other things as well: a sports enthusiast, a lover of music, as well as a husband, a son, a father, and a grandfather. I have been an Arizona lawyer since 1951 and an Arizona politician for almost as long. I'm an American just as good in the eyes of the law as any other American now or hereafter.

When the United States was formed some 225 years ago, my ancestors were still down in the bogs of Ireland. My grandparents immigrated to this country not much more than a century ago in search of political and religious freedom, economic opportunity, and education for their children. In two generations the McNultys marched out of those Irish bogs and into the professions of mainstream America because the opportunities they sought did and still do exist in this great nation. I am James Francis Patrick McNulty, the hard-working grandson of those hard-working Irish immigrants, and I like to think that my life's journey has helped to confirm the wisdom of their decision to leave the green hills of County Sligo and County Leitrim to carve out a life in America. But you will be the judge of that.

My journey has led me from the streets of an Irish neighborhood in Boston to the deserts of southern Arizona. It has taken me from the oldest school in America to an upstart land grant college in Tucson, Arizona. I have served as a buck private in the local Democrat party stuffing envelopes and serving coffee to poll workers, and I have also served in the venerable halls of the United States Congress. Along the way I have been blessed to have known and worked with some of the great figures in the modern history of Arizona and the nation. My trip to the Soviet Union furnished a great knowledge of the facts of Soviet life, its shortcomings, and its successes. Their stories are inseparably intertwined with mine, so they too will be the subjects of this account of the McNulty who went to Congress.

Although many actors have played key roles in this drama, it is my life story, and I have told it from my perspective. In so doing, I hope to provide the reader with some insights into political and legislative events of which I have some direct knowledge. I further hope to give an honest and frank account of matters great and small without bruising anyone. Humor and good will are at the core of this effort. Politics is a serious, high-stakes business, but it is certainly not without humor and pathos. Sometimes the jokes (or lack of them) say more about the candidate than the speeches and have a greater impact on the voters.

Finally, I ask in all humility for the tolerance of all the folks who were involved in the events described herein, but who are not specifically named in the text. Please recognize that what I may lack in thoroughness, I also lack in malice.

CHAPTER ONE

The Boon of the
Immigrant Ancestors

IN THE VERY LONG VIEW, the McNulty family's journey to America had its genesis in the eleventh century when the English King Henry II invaded and occupied a large part of Ireland. The history of British domination and suppression of the Irish is well known. The infamous "Laws in Ireland for the Suppression of Popery" (commonly known as the Penal Laws) were the primary mechanism for the persecution of the Irish. The Penal Laws were a series of statutes specifically designed to suppress the Catholic religion. The people of Ireland were overwhelmingly Catholic and they had vigorously defended their faith during the Glorious Revolution. In 1691 the Treaty of Limerick consolidated English dominion over Ireland. The English Protestant landowners, who dominated the Irish Parliament, began passing laws to expand their own rights and properties while suppressing and impoverishing Irish Catholics.

Catholics were forbidden to teach their children or send them abroad. If they had any property it had to be inherited equally among the sons unless one was Protestant, in which case he got it all. Irish property soon was split into tiny parcels which were not economically viable. An Irish Catholic could not own a horse or arms worth more than £5. Anyone was entitled to pay the Irishman the £5 and take the horse, or gun. The hierarchy of the Catholic Church was banished or suppressed, as was the Gaelic language. Catholics were not allowed to hold seats in the Irish Parliament, nor could they vote, serve in the army, hold public office, practice law, or have the right to a trial by jury.

The Penal Laws were extended and made more odious in the eighteenth century and they became a major impetus to Irish emigration. The Irish developed a general hatred for English law and government as they struggled to evade the Penal Laws. Bounty money was paid to those who informed on Catholics. The saying of masses was forbidden, so surreptitious masses were held outdoors in remote, hidden places. The Penal Laws were rescinded by the mid-nineteenth century, partly because the English needed Irish soldiers to fight the colonial wars that built the British Empire. Then came an agricultural crisis created by Ireland's English overlords and known to the world as the Potato Famine. It was right about then, around 1850 or 1860, that my ancestor, William Gallogly, spent a year in Galway jail for insubordination.

William Gallogly was one of the tenants (near serfs, really) on the ancestral estate of one of the English landlords. The story goes that the great Lord was planning a visit to his estate and William was assigned to help prepare a fitting reception. He devised a plan which he said would make the Lord's arrival more festive. He put up small British flags which he illuminated with candles. William's great coup was that he "inadvertently" placed the candles too close to the flags, causing them to ignite, and the English aristocrat was greeted by the sight of a row of little burning Union Jacks. Within the lore of my family William was a hero. He proved his worthiness by pulling this stunt off, and by spending a year in a British "gaol" as a consequence.

My great-grandparents' ability to participate in the civic and economic affairs of their community was severely curtailed. They lived in a political environment charged with the continuing struggle for Irish freedom. They felt the sting of persecution personally every day and chafed under laws designed to keep them poor. Education for their children was obtainable only through the Catholic Church. By my great-grandparents' day the state was willing to let the Church fulfill this function, but the school system which resulted limited our access to education and reinforced the rigid class system. My ancestors were all devout Catholics, and British interference in the operation of the Holy Roman Church was a constant insult which my great-grandparents had to endure.

On my mother's side of the genealogical ledger, my grandmother Mary Gallogly was the first immigrant ancestor. She was born on Christmas day in 1876 and in the mid-1890s she arrived in America, where she began working as a maid. Mary was one of twelve or thirteen children and served as the "beachhead" for the entire Gallogly clan in

America. In her letters to the family back in County Leitrim she wrote glowing reports of the possibilities in America, of the jobs to be had, of the town of Providence, Rhode Island, where she had landed, of the free public schools, and of a society where freedom was unrestricted and people were not held in check by a class-bound social system. She invited them to join her. All of her brothers and sisters but one eventually followed her to these shores. They always spoke fondly of Ireland, but most of them had no desire to return to the place. Only one of the family moved back to the motherland after tasting life in America.

Grandmother Gallogly was a beautiful young woman. She was tall for her day, had long raven-black hair which she never cut, a pretty face, and a quick temper. She soon met an ambitious young countryman named Edward Cull, who was a bleacher in one of the mills in Providence. He was also from County Leitrim; he had grown up in the tiny village of Aughraine, which was only a few miles from Drumraine, the seat of the Gallogly clan. Like so many other immigrants, they never knew each other in their country of origin, but they both gravitated to the Irish community in Providence where they met and fell in love. They were married, and in 1898 my mother, Florence Cull, was born, soon to be followed by a little brother who was also named Edward. My grandfather Cull secured a good job with the gas company in Providence and, for a short while, his little family prospered.

After Mary's marriage to my grandfather, their home continued to serve as the headquarters of the Gallogly clan. The family was very close. Years later when I was a child I can remember my great-uncles showing up at my grandmother's house around noon to have a cup of tea and play a little cards before returning to work. She was the information center that dispensed news of the clan on both sides of the Atlantic, and she was the glue that held them together in a foreign land. This continued long after the accident that ended Edward Cull's life on January 28, 1904.

My grandfather was killed while working for the Providence Gas Company. He was down in a manhole which provided access to the pipes and apparently leaking gas somehow ignited. The resulting explosion left my grandmother a widow with two very young children after only six years of marriage. My mother was five and my Uncle Edward was three. There was no pension or workmen's compensation or assistance of any kind for women in her position in those days—nothing from the government and virtually nothing from the gas company. As a concession to civility, the Providence Gas Company did furnish seven carriages for the funeral. We Irish take great stock in funerals. After the funeral was over, however, grandmother Gallogly had only her brothers to help her. And help her they did.

The first McNulty to immigrate to America was my grandfather's brother, Frank. Like Mary Gallogly and millions of other immigrants, he also wrote enthusiastic reports to the family back in Ireland. Frank advised my grandfather, John Davies McNulty (who was born in County Sligo in 1866), that the Boston and Albany Railroad was hiring. On the strength of that, my grandfather bought a ticket on a steamer and joined his brother. He came to Longmeadow, just across the Connecticut River from Springfield, Massachusetts. He was soon employed by the Boston and Albany as a car knocker, inspecting the railroad cars and making minor repairs. Primarily, his job was to open the journal boxes on the axles and replenish the oil-soaked cotton waste that was used for lubrication prior to the adoption of roller bearings. These journal boxes frequently overheated and caught fire, and he would put these out. He might occasionally pound out a rough spot in an axle or identify a wheel that had a flat spot.

John Davies met my grandmother, Mary Motherway, soon after he came to America. Mary was born to Irish immigrants in 1874 in Springfield, Massachusetts, and was my only grandparent born here in America. She was, as I remember her, a large, serious, and rather dour woman of the Victorian era. The name "Motherway" is an English rendering of an unpronounceable Welsh name, and my grandmother was Celtic to the core. They lived on Worthington Street in Springfield, Massachusetts, and had two children: a daughter named Helen born in 1895, and my father, James Francis McNulty, who was born on December 12, 1896. My grandfather worked hard, did well, and rose through the ranks of the Boston and Albany Railroad. He eventually became a conductor on the run from Springfield to Albany, and I remember well the times when he took us for rides on the train as guests of the establishment.

Both of my parents took advantage of the educational opportunities available to them in America and they were the first generation from their respective families to attain a high school education. After the death of my grandfather in the gas explosion, my grandmother Gallogly remarried, but the stepfather this brought into my mother's life was a tyrant. My mother graduated from Providence Classical High School, which was an excellent school. She was encouraged by her teachers to continue her education by attending a technical school to learn secretarial skills, but the stepfather forbade it. It was his opinion that they could not afford the cost of additional training for a girl, so an elaborate scheme was hatched to circumvent his decree.

First of all, my step-grandfather was informed that my mother had found a job downtown. She left every morning, ostensibly for work, and came home every night with her earnings, which she placed on the kitchen table. The money was apportioned out to my grandmother for household expenses and to my step-grandfather as room and board. The step-grandfather was pleased with the arrangement.

The truth was that my mother was only working a few hours, spending the rest of her days attending secretarial school. A bit of additional money was kicked in each day from the Gallogly uncles. The share which went to my grandmother was not spent on household needs. It actually was used to pay the tuition at the secretarial school while my grandmother covered the cost of running the household for practically nothing by dint of her own frugality and hard work. My mother did her homework secretly in the attic of the modest house which they occupied. She quickly learned Gregg Shorthand and got a job as a secretary for a lawyer by the name of Brownell. He was a very prosperous attorney and once gave my mother a leopard overcoat which he bought for her while on a trip to China. This was a very snazzy garment indeed for a woman from the Irish community in Providence.

My father attended high school at Springfield Technical where he was trained as a draftsman. He probably would have been an engineer if he had been able to attend college. He served in the Coast Guard during World War I as part of the Coast Artillery, manning the cannons on a flyspeck of an island out in Boston Harbor to fend off any invasion by the Hun. He then found employment as a draftsman with the Chapman Valve Mfg. Company, a large industrial concern which manufactured gargantuan plumbing for municipal water systems. My dad had a photo of an auto being driven through a valve manufactured by Chapman Valve.

Another old photo showed my parents when they were courting. The couple in the photo are young, smiling, and if it weren't for the cut of the clothing they wore, could have been a young couple of today. They were going to the beach. He had a car and she was secretary to a prominent lawyer and they appeared quite well off. They met when he was in Providence on business for Chapman Valve and courted for about three years. My parents were married at Providence on September 6, 1924, and soon after, they moved to Boston when Chapman Valve sent my dad to work there. My mother gave up her secretarial job and in short order, on October 18, 1925, I made my appearance. We moved around a bit, but my earliest memories are of our house on Woodlawn Street in Dedham, Massachusetts, on the fringes of Boston. We lived in the upstairs and I can see the house clearly in my mind's eye still today. I was soon joined by my younger sister Nancy who was born in 1926. My baby sister Ann was born in 1931 and our little family was complete. My earliest recollections include Nancy and the games we played together.

I had the most contact with my mother's side of the family and I think of them as the Galloglys despite the fact that my mother's maiden name was Cull. Grandmother Gallogly was a go-getter. The death of her first husband in a gas explosion was only one of the many blows she took in life, but she never stopped smiling. The church was central to her hopes, and life rotated around the rituals surrounding births, baptisms, confirmations, weddings, and funerals. She knew everyone in the community and called them by name. She was also, of course, the bell cow for the Gallogly clan. Her energy was spent keeping her brothers happy and catering to the entire extended family. There was always plenty of banter and laughter around her house.

Her second marriage produced a son named Tom who was quite a rascal. He was very active in the Seafarers' Union, where he worked for a fellow named Joe Curran. He was a real roughneck and those were the days when people regularly got black eyes in the resolution of relatively minor labor issues. My Uncle Tom was good at that work. He was also a funny, generous, shouting, cussing, drinking man who once told me that in one election he had voted for Dennis Roberts for Mayor of Providence seven times. He said if he'd been a little more diligent, it would have been ten. He was in the Coast Guard during the war. During the D-Day invasion he was assigned to pilot an old freighter into position and then scuttle it to help form a breakwater. He did as ordered, but before he abandoned the sinking ship, he stole the ship's clock.

My Uncle Edward—he pronounced it "Edwud"—was another "hale fellow, well met" type of guy. He was a customers' man for the Narragansett Brewery and he always wore spats. As a customers' man, his job was to be in the taverns all day treating the customers to free samples of the product. When he left one establishment for the next a chorus of Irish voices would call out, "Hey, God Bless you Edwud! And thank you!" Both of these uncles were colorful enough, but they did exasperate my Victorian mother with their unconventional behavior. I often felt they were unkind to her. She called them "fresh," an epithet that to her mainly conveyed unruly, undignified behavior.

We spent every Thanksgiving and Christmas with the Gallogly clan in Providence or Boston and my grandmother would cook a turkey. My Uncle Edward would take me to see the Brown-Colgate football game, and it was exciting and fun and we were glad to go. Visiting my other grandmother, Mary (Motherway) McNulty, in Springfield was not nearly as much fun. My grandfather, John Davies McNulty, died in 1931 so he was not in the picture during most of my childhood. In addition to being a dour Celt and a large, heavy woman, my grandmother McNulty was also ill much of the time. It seems like every time I did see her, she was lying down or sitting down. There was not much gaiety in her presence. When the kids were voting on where we'd go on these holidays, Providence was always first choice.

When I was six we moved to 12 Oriole Street in West Roxbury, another Irish enclave of Boston. Oriole Street was four blocks long. Each block had twelve two-story houses about thirty feet apart, and each house held two families, one upstairs and one down. The Sullivans lived above us on the top floor and we lived on the bottom floor. The Burns and the Hulls lived next door. Across the street were the Kenneys, relations of John Hynes, who became mayor. Everyone on Oriole Street was Irish (except Mr. Coggio, who was Italian) and everyone was Catholic. I knew only one Protestant lad, and he was treated pretty unkindly. It was a working-class Irish neighborhood and we thought of it as our district. Unlike the situation back in Ireland, here WE were the proprietors. Growing up in this homogenous neighborhood, I was somewhat sheltered from anti-Irish prejudice. I never saw one of those signs that read, "Irish need not apply."

Within this self-contained community, everything reinforced our connections with and dependence on one another. If Mrs. McCoy's kid showed real promise, strings were pulled and countrymen made sure that the boy went to a school where he was challenged. Mike O'Toole was the judge and our man Hynes was the mayor. The Irish have always been pretty good politicians, and I guess I fall into that heritage. Back in the bogs of Ireland, we had to at least coexist with our English enemies, and we grew pretty adept at making a contentious political system work. Over here in America we quickly began to take jobs in the police and fire departments in our communities. Once we established a beachhead, everybody who was recruited was a Murphy or an O'Brien. In time they became bosses, and they made similar choices when they promoted men from the ranks. Soon, we were running the joint.

My mother took a keen interest in local politics. If you were Irish Catholic as we were, you were a Democrat. Franklin Roosevelt was our hero. If you were a Protestant, we naturally assumed that you were a Republican. I don't think I got to know my first Republican until I was a teenager. Since the Democrats were virtually the only political party in the community, the contests were always within the clan: Irish Democrats fighting other Irish Democrats for office.

One of my clearest memories from childhood took place on a cold and rainy Election Day in Boston. My mother was a supporter of Hynes for Mayor and she wasn't bashful about saying so. On Election Day, however, you couldn't campaign or even talk politics at the polls. On Election Day, you kept quiet. My mother went down to the polling place with a big old purse. On the purse she put a sign which read, "Hynes" and placed it firmly over her right arm. She stood at the entrance in the rain all day and into the night greeting every voter. "Hello Mrs. Flynn." and, "Good evening Mr. O'Malley." She didn't need to say, "Do you see this sign Mr. O'Malley? I expect you to vote that way!" but the message was clear.

Years later I was pressed into duty for my ward on Election Day. My assignment was to drive the Hynes Coffee Wagon. This was just a car loaded with a whole bunch of pots of coffee and a selection of pastries. I knew who our poll workers were and my job was to drive from one polling spot to the next and hand out free coffee and pastries to the Hynes poll workers.

My mother was a loyal Democrat, but like many others in that era she was suspicious of the labor movement and a little scared of strikes and the violence they could bring. My father, on the other hand, was a classic union sympathizer, which was an inconvenient position for a man who was a manufacturer's representative for a big company. He wore a white collar, my dad, and was considered by the blue-collar workers at Chapman Valve to be on the management side of the labor equation. He had a company car which he washed every Saturday because he believed it had to look spiffy. But he always used to tell me that he was on the side of the guys in the plant, the workers. He certainly did not, however, express this opinion to his bosses. I suppose he was intimidated to some degree by the company hierarchy. My father also demonstrated some of the Irish skepticism regarding the clergy. He wasn't rebellious or even disrespectful about it, but he was a little caustic on occasion. Leaving a wedding once he said to me, "Well, that makes three people happy." "The bride and groom only make two," I answered, "who is the third?" My dad's response was, "You don't think the priest performed the ceremony for free, do you?"

In the Irish community of Boston we had our own priests and our own seminary to train them. President John Kennedy's father, Joe Kennedy, was the banker, and where would Mrs. Kelly deposit her five dollars every week? In Kennedy's Columbia Savings Bank, of course. The Kennedy clan is another that came over here with a pick in one hand and a hoe in the other and made good. Eventually we arrived at the forum and entered all levels of government, business, and the professions. We underwent the process of carving out a niche, as every immigrant group has done, and eventually it brought us to the table of the great American feast. I see many similarities in the progress being made today by recent Hispanic immigrants.

There was a row of shops on Center Street in West Roxbury which included a fish market and the First National Grocery, where I would later work as a stock boy. The Italian meat-cutters in the First National played the Metropolitan Opera on the radio and sang along in full voice as they did their work. There was an old movie house on Bellevue Street where we watched serials that always ended with the heroine dangling from a cliff or tied to railroad tracks with a train approaching. Just as the locomotive was about to crush the heroine, the words, "To be continued" appeared on the screen. We only attended the most innocent movies because my mother would always check the listings of the National League of Decency to determine the suitability of the films. Sometimes the review would say that a film was, "approved with modifications." My Victorian mother would grumble, "I'll modify it all right. There won't be any of us seeing it, that will be my modification."

The essence of a Victorian is dignity and my mother was of that mold. She had a clear sense of her own worth. We tend to laugh at Victorians today as being prudes and suppressed souls, but there was a lot more to them than that. Two of the greatest societies ever formed in the world, America and the United Kingdom, both emerged as the preeminent world powers under the influence of Victorian customs. The British obtained their Empire under Queen Victoria, and while they were not always gentle with the local populations as they built it, they certainly knew about order. My mother didn't care much for English persecution, but order was something that she was devoted to. She thought people should do what they ought to do and they definitely better not trespass on her. Her dignity alone precluded anything like that.

My mother ran her family by these same Victorian standards. We received very clear instruction on behavior and the difference between right and wrong. She was also a tolerant woman, to a certain degree. Talking to friends about her neighbor, Mrs. Ramsey, she'd say, "She's Protestant, but she's very nice." In my mother's day wives "gave" children to their husbands. I remember her seated in a funeral parlor bestowing the highest possible praise on the deceased woman with a slight Irish brogue, "And wasn't she after giving her husband four beautiful children?" Florence always wore a hat and gloves to church, doing so long after it was required by fashion. It was a matter of identification and dignity for her. It said to the world, "I know who I am and I am somebody." It wasn't an arrogant gesture, but it did show a certain pride.

My mother's attitude about men was shaped by Victorian standards and by her own experience with her brothers, uncles, and a stepfather who was not a gentle man. She knew instinctively that men were uncivilized and you just had to put up with them. God knows what else they might be up to! Boys, similarly, needed to be led with a firm hand. Within the family, her decisions were final. If she said we were going to do something, we did it and she had a clear idea of what should be done, when to do it, and exactly how to do it. My father was a man who liked to laugh and was very liberal with us kids. He always encouraged us and I don't remember either of my parents ever laying a hand on me. My father was not stern or domineering, but if he said "frog," we jumped.

He was a very frugal man for a variety of good reasons. We were always fed adequately and we ate every morsel of food on our plates. My father carried that trait with him his entire life. He had a particular thing about shoes. They were expensive and he felt that schoolboys and girls were not as careful as they should have been about them. My father had a fit if he saw anyone cramming his or her foot into a shoe without aid of a shoehorn. We had shoehorns all over the house. We wore our shoes until there were holes in the soles and then we purchased a repair kit from Woolworth's. The kits had a rubber sole and some glue and ostensibly would prolong the life of the shoe by several years. Of course, that didn't work because our shoes were wet half the time and the glue had a short life. My father was also very particular about his language and held to the Victorian standard that certain words were not fit for the ears of women. It was a minor shortcoming.

Some of the Gallogly uncles enjoyed a wee nip now and again and my dad also would imbibe occasionally. My dad, unlike other men of the family, could not tolerate alcohol very well and sometimes endured the consequences in the form of a hangover. He never missed any work and was not a problem drinker, but my mother hated alcohol and these events caused her concern. My father didn't drink much, but when he did it was a source of friction between him and my mother.

I attended the Randall G. Morris School, which was about 200 yards from our house, through the fifth grade. My mother knew every teacher there by name, and all of them were single Irish Catholic women. (It was not decent for a teacher in elementary school to be married.) These spinsters maintained strict order in the classroom. I never was spanked at home, but the teachers at Randall G. Morris employed corporal correction as necessary. The ultimate punishment, however, was if your parents were called to the school. That was something to be avoided at all costs.

We attended Mass every Sunday, of course, and also on every Holy Day of Obligation. Church rituals such as baptisms, confirmations, marriages, and funerals were frequent. Christmas and Easter were the most important religious holidays and we followed the Lenten practices. My sisters and I also attended catechism classes every Saturday when we were of the appropriate age. These classes were run by very tough Irish nuns, much tougher than the teachers at Randall G. Morris. Squirming or talking were not tolerated whatsoever. We used the Baltimore Catechism as a text and it gave us all the answers. Why am I here? Why did God make me? Where am I going? What is sin? How are we saved from it? We went through every chapter of the Baltimore Catechism in the course of the year. The nuns barked out questions straight from the text and we were expected to answer immediately when called upon.

This was before Vatican II and a great war raged within the church as to how to teach religion to kids. The old fossils stuck with the Baltimore Catechism while another more progressive and open-minded faction abandoned it. In my opinion, the progressives knew what Catechism really is about. However, our parish, St. Theresa's, was still using the Baltimore Catechism. Religion was very much alive in our community. I don't know how many of my old classmates still profess to Catholicism as I do, but in those days it was near 100 percent.

Life revolved around the Church and my elementary school in those days. I liked the Randall G. Morris School and was a very good student. I still have all of my report cards from those days, and almost every mark on them for five years is an A. Attached to one of them is a short note dated March 9, 1932 and signed by my first grade teacher, Miss Cassidy, who observed, "There is no place to record James' fine power of thinking and his interesting and interested attitude toward all his work. So I must mention those facts here."

But the report cards also reveal a less pleasant aspect of my young life. The column with the heading, "number of sessions absent" bears some rather large numbers. In second grade Miss Lenihan recorded 48 absences for me in March and April alone and an additional 14 during the balance of the year. I was absent 35 times in third grade and 62 times in fourth. I suspect the statistic would have been about the same for first grade, but Miss Cassidy left the column blank.

I had chronic asthma and assorted other related respiratory problems including crippling chest colds that would arrive annually with the cold and wet weather. I was sick in bed a great deal of the time and my mother was willing to do anything to make me well. Ephedrine was the standard treatment for asthma in those days, but my mother also called on God and the Saints. When I was perhaps ten or twelve I remember my mother had the priest from St. Theresa's Parish come by and visit me when I was sick. He would bless me and slap me on the back and console my mother. She asked herself at this time if there wasn't some personal pleasure that she could forego as an offering, a sacrifice and a prayer, for my health. She loved sweets and chocolates, they were one of her very few indulgences in life. She told herself that she was better off without them anyway, said a prayer for me, and gave them up.

During one of my periods of illness my father heard from an uncle in Providence that a Portuguese doctor who was famous for curing asthma and respiratory illnesses was slated to attend the upcoming wedding of a family friend there. My father drove up from Springfield, obtained an introduction to this doctor, and buttonholed him about treating me. The doctor told him that if I took his course of treatment he guaranteed that I would improve. This doctor lived in Providence and his course of treatment required me to visit his office every weekday night for five weeks. As a manufacturer's representative for Chapman Valve, my dad drove his company car every day to visit various accounts. For five weeks he would return home after driving all day and load me in the car for the drive to Providence and back.

Despite all the efforts of both my parents, my health did not improve. When I wasn't sick, I was quite capable of playing ball or other games with the rest of the kids. But I was on the runty side physically, and was very short on endurance. The worst part of it was that there were many days when I was simply too sick to play or go to school. Sometimes, when I was too sick to go to school but too well to stay in bed, I would go out on the street and find Mr. Hynes, the mayor's father. Mr. Hynes was a sick old man with an enormous red handlebar mustache who wore red suspenders. We would sit on a stoop together and keep each other company: two derelicts, an old man who would die soon and a sick boy. Both of my sisters enjoyed good health, I was the sickly one. I was also the first-born and the only boy in the family. I was treated as the favored son, everything yielded to what was good for me and my fragile health.

In between my bouts with respiratory disease there was a lot of fun to be had. We played all sorts of street ball games. One of these involved throwing a rubber ball against the steps of our house. The opposing team was positioned across the street and if they could catch the ball cleanly as it careened off the steps, that was an out. If you could manage to hurl the ball off the corner of a step it would arc high over the street and that would win a point. From the twelve double-decker houses on Oriole Street there were just enough kids to form a real baseball team. Our team was called the Orioles and we went out and sold tickets to our games with other neighborhood teams to pay for our jerseys.

We also played games where girls were allowed to join in, like "kick the can" and "relieve-O." We used the small playground at the Randall G. Morris School, but for the serious fun we went about three quarters of a mile to Billings Field. This was flooded about six inches deep in the winter and was used for ice-skating. In the spring the field was drained and used for playing football and baseball. We were daredevils on sleds and toboggans in the winter and formed into packs of little boys to play games in the warmer weather. There was a hill nearby we called "The Tower" where my sisters and I used to fly kites made by my dad. One Christmas my father gave me a splendid pair of woolly cowboy chaps. They were made of lambskin and when I donned them along with my six-shooter and hat, I made a pretty ferocious cowboy. I think I wore those things out.

My father also appreciated high culture and nice things although he wasn't exposed to them much during his boyhood days. He valued great writing highly and bought books when money for that purpose was scarce. His favorite muse, however, was music. He bought a Victrola for the family as well as records, many of which I still have. His taste ran to opera, but both he and my mother were also extremely fond of what passed for musical comedy in those days. On weekends he planned educational outings for us. We visited the Museum of Natural History and the Jack Gardiner Museum. I remember visiting the Great Glass Globe at the Christian Science Headquarters. We were regular patrons of the West Roxbury Library and for a number of years the family policy was to visit the library one night a week.

James F. McNulty Jr. and his father James F. McNulty Sr., about 1935. Growing up in Boston, a favorite outing was to the beach at Nantasket.

My father took us to the Commonwealth Pier, which was the largest in Boston. We also visited the pier at the Charlestown Navy Yard which offered a look at Old Ironsides. We often went to the Fish Pier, where I later worked as a Western Union messenger boy. I also remember my dad taking us to Plymouth to view what was ostensibly the first place in America touched by the Pilgrims. When I saw Plymouth Rock I thought either it had been moved or one of the Pilgrims was an Olympic quality broad jumper because of its distance from the shore.

A big weekend in the summertime for my family was to go to Nantasket Beach, about twenty miles from West Roxbury. This was a public beach and there were tiny wooden beach houses which could be rented for changing into bathing suits. That involved money, however, and my folks were not so inclined. Instead, they bought a newspaper on the way down to Nantasket and when we arrived, they opened up the pages and stuck them between the door frames and windows to achieve a sort of privacy. Each one of the family would then go into the car individually to don their swimming attire. Then it was out into the sun which rapidly turned our fish-white bodies a fiery red.

In later years my dad used to take great long walks around West Roxbury. We would walk for as much as two hours and cover a good part of the town. He was inordinately fond of baseball and often took me to the double-headers on Sundays. His ticket cost $1.10 and mine 55 cents, which made the outing fairly expensive for folks of our means. In later years when television came along he would watch any programs of classical music or opera, but that and some occasional news broadcasts constituted the extent of his viewing. We were poor, but we didn't act like it. There was none of the rowdy about my father, and his brothers-in-law may have found him a bit stuffy. But to me he was simply a good man who spent his life in and around his family.

Every summer as soon as school was out we were carted off to our little shack in Lyndeboro, New Hampshire, for some wholesome country living. Lyndeboro is about fifty miles from Boston and we stayed until Labor Day with no electricity, no gas, no running water, no telephone, and no indoor plumbing. We kids thought it was pretty much of a hardship, but in time we made friends with the local kids and learned to enjoy the simple pleasures the place offered. I can still remember my father's explanation for this annual New Hampshire trip, "I'm not going to have my kids growing up on the streets of Roxbury in the summertime." He wasn't so much interested in exposing us to rural life as he was concerned about making sure we avoided certain unhealthy trends prevalent in Boston. He didn't want us involved with kids who had too much time on their hands and filled the empty hours committing petty offenses.

My sisters and I had very little spare time during childhood. Between school, church, homework, family outings, and chores around the house, we nearly always had something we had to do. When my mother signed my report cards, she had to verify that I was spending three hours four days a week on homework. My mother was not the type to attest to anything but the truth. She did, however, consent to count our family library trips as homework time. By the time I was a teenager I was also working as a stock boy at the First National Grocery. In our tradition, work distinguished you, it gave you an aura of usefulness, and it was something to be treasured. Work generated money; it was to be respected. If you didn't have anything else to do, you ought to go find work and do it. And if you had a job you damn well held on to it. We also knew that the boss was the boss and you had to please him to keep that job. I believe that this attitude got so out of hand that it generated, at least in part, the enthusiasm for labor unions, better working conditions, and better wages.

The Lyndeboro place was way out in the country and we couldn't even see any of our neighbors' houses from our house. My father had to work through the summer so we were stuck out in the boondocks without transportation during the week. We were very happy to see the headlights of dad's Ford wheeling up the drive on Friday nights to join us for the weekend. (I'm not sure which we welcomed more, Dad or the car.) The place had two rooms with a small kitchen and an attic. As the years went by we made some improvements to it, but it was always pretty primitive. We once had to shovel out the outdoor toilet and lime it. My chores included walking across the road and down the hill to fill a pail of water and bring it back to the house every morning. I was also in charge of lanterns. Every Friday morning I had to wash the smoke-stained glass chimneys, trim the wicks, and fill the lanterns with kerosene. We had six or eight of those lamps.

We also had a garden in Lyndeboro where my mother cultivated flowers and, during the war, potatoes. My father had no knowledge of farming but he actually got a horse and plow, looked at pictures of farmers plowing, and figured out how to do it. Then I was assigned an additional duty: slayer of potato bugs. You get a good wide-mouth glass jar and put about three inches of kerosene in it. You then knock the bugs off the leaves into the solution and they will be soon gone. Their replacements, however, were never long in coming.

When Dad was there with the Ford we could go places, buy ice cream, go to the swimming pool, and attend the bean suppers that were the big social events of rural Lyndeboro, New Hampshire. Women would brag that the feast tonight was to include six or seven different kinds of beans for the entree, but no meat. All ages attended these events and there was softball as well as lavish desserts. During the long summer days we took hikes up Crotched Mountain (which Arizonans would call a hill) and in the evenings we fished in the local streams for horned pout (Arizonans call them catfish). These summers in rural New Hampshire began in 1935 and continued throughout my childhood. My parents continued the tradition until they moved to Arizona in 1962.

After completing five years at the Randall G. Morris School I was faced with a decision. Boston had many secondary schools from which to choose, and it was time to pick one. There were plenty of adequate to excellent public and parochial schools, and then there was Boston Latin School. Boston Latin was founded on April 13, 1635, and was the first public school in Colonial America. It was, and still is, a public school where all boys (it was an all-male school), rich or poor, are welcome if they have the academic talents and work habits necessary to succeed there. The alumni of Boston Latin include men such as Benjamin Franklin, Samuel Adams, and John Hancock. A sampling of more recent graduates would list author Theodore White and conductor/composer Leonard Bernstein.

Then, as today, students have to score highly on a day-long test to be admitted, and then they must study four years of Latin before graduating. The school's motto, *Sumus Primi*, means, literally, "We Are First," and it refers not only to the school's chronological primacy; the motto also reveals the academic and athletic standards which prevail at Boston Latin. It still boasts that 99-plus percent of its graduates go on to college or university. My dad used to say that Boston Latin was "all carry and no roll." This was a golfing expression which meant a difficult shot. It meant you better hit the ball out there high and far. You couldn't slap it in the general direction and expect it to bounce around and roll up to the hole. It was his way of saying that the place demanded precision, brains, concentration, and a whole lot of hard work.

I was adamant from the beginning that I would be going to Boston Latin, but all the forces were arrayed against me. Not only was it a very tough school to get into, it was also a one-hour trolley car ride each way from our home. And even if I was able to overcome those arguments, there was my health. Miss Cassidy, who was Head Teacher at Randall G. Morris by this time, may have written a very complimentary note

Boston Latin School, founded in 1635, is the oldest public school in the United States. Ninety-eight percent of its graduates attend college.

when I was in first grade, but she made a full court press to convince me that it wasn't a good idea to attempt Latin School. I was taken for a tour of Robert Gould Shaw High School in an effort to show me that I would like the place. (Robert Gould Shaw was the young patriot from one of the Brahmin families of Boston who led the first all-black American battalion in the Civil War. He lost his life in a desperate attack against Confederate forces at Ft. Anderson, in which nearly every man in the troop was killed or disabled.)

My father didn't want me to go to Latin School, my mother didn't want me to go, and Miss Cassidy didn't want me to go. In the face of contrary advice from nearly everyone, I stubbornly persisted in my plans to enroll there. I had the high grade point average that was required, and passed the admissions test ordeal. I entered Latin School in the fall of 1937 at the age of eleven years.

The curriculum emphasized classical languages, modern languages, science, and history. At one time my day consisted of classes in Latin,

German, French, English, and Science. Debating and declamation were required classes. In my third year I was allowed to choose either German or Greek if I had an adequate justification for my choice. If you wanted to go into medicine you took German, if you were headed for law school you damn well took Greek.

There was also a handful of African-American students when I was there. We all got along quite well and I am still in touch with a few of them. The term "elite" carries some negative baggage, but it is appropriate for describing the standards of the school itself and the academic credentials of the all-male teaching staff. They were referred to as "Masters" and they all wore suits. The students were called by their last names, and although most of us were poorer than church mice, we were required to wear jackets and ties. We used to joke that we could make a tie last for a year. It might have quite a bit of food on it by the end of the year, but we wore it anyway.

After I began attending Boston Latin my mother learned about Miss Widmer's School of the Dance. This was a place where the boys wore suits and the girls wore formal dresses and white gloves. (They also made us boys wear white gloves so that our grimy mitts would not soil the apparel of the girls we danced with.) This establishment aimed to turn us into little gentlemen and ladies and that fit nicely into my mother's Victorian view of the world. My sister Nancy and I were enrolled and I learned how to bow from the waist and how to request the pleasure of a dance. They had a piano player and we were instructed in the mysteries of ballroom dancing. We did learn some of the social graces at Miss Widmer's School of the Dance. I can't say we emerged with a full polish, but a few of our rougher corners were smoothed.

In a building with 2,500 boys, the only two females at Boston Latin School were the school nurse and the secretary to the headmaster. There was, however, a companion school for girls called Girl's Latin School, which was separated from us by a playground and Longwood Avenue. When my sister began attending Girl's Latin my dad used to drive us and two or three other neighborhood kids to school. Around this time I was crazy about a girl named Carol Peterson for a while. She was a friend of my sister's who also attended Girl's Latin.

There wasn't much dating during my Boston Latin years, but I would occasionally take a girl to the movie show. And of course, there was the prom which everyone attended. Most socializing with girls was done as part of a group, especially around Christmas. A little later the big attraction was a dance place called the Norumbega Park Totem Pole. It featured live big band music in a great big hall with overstuffed chairs and tables around the margins and a dance floor in the middle. The Totem Pole was not lighted very well so you could snuggle up a little bit, but they were very strict. No drinking (of course), no smoking, no uproarious conduct, and no admittance without a jacket and tie.

The biting damp and chill of Boston brought me down regularly and I was still missing way too much school during the first years at Boston Latin. My Masters from Latin School used to visit me at home during these periods, mostly just to talk and buck me up. I read voraciously when I was sick, consuming histories of Ireland and America, western adventure novels, and biographies. I tried hard to keep up with my studies, but I missed so much school in the fourth class at Boston Latin School (equivalent to freshman year in high school) that I had to repeat it.

There was a terrible stigma on being held back a grade in school then, as there is now. I was not bothered about being labeled as slow; I knew I was not held back because of academics. It was because of the damned asthma, and that did bother me a lot. I had grown to despise the time I spent sick in bed and the limitations I had to endure. I longed for a set of lungs that would allow me to do everything the other kids did. I guess it is not surprising that I had developed into a fierce competitor in the classrooms of Boston Latin; I wanted to win anything I did. But most of all, I didn't want to spend any more of my life practically bedridden.

Right about then I picked up an autobiography that was written by another sickly, asthmatic kid. He had found a way to transform himself into an icon of robust, vigorous manhood and he became my model.

CHAPTER TWO

Running

THEODORE ROOSEVELT DIED SIX YEARS before my birth, but he was remembered as a vigorous and bold leader who lived what he called "the strenuous life." In addition to leading his Rough Riders up San Juan Hill in 1898 during the Spanish American War, he took on America's business magnates by breaking up powerful trusts, settling strikes equitably, and imposing regulations on America's most powerful industries. After his presidency he hunted lions in Africa and explored the Amazon in Brazil. In October of 1912 he was shot by a would-be assassin just before he was to give a speech in Milwaukee. With a bullet in his chest that the audience knew nothing about, he gave the speech as scheduled.

I read his autobiography while I was laid up sick missing my freshman year at Boston Latin School. I was amazed to discover that in his childhood this tower of physical strength had suffered from a case of asthma even worse than mine. Asthma was a life-threatening disease (it still is), and young Roosevelt had several terrifying attacks that nearly killed him. His parents kept their sickly son closeted in their mansion. When he was sick he was sometimes forced to smoke a cigar to make him vomit, which gave some relief from the attacks. They took him for carriage rides at night, thinking the cold night air would help. Unlike me, he also suffered from unreasonable fears, but we both were good students who developed a keen competitive instinct.

When Theodore Roosevelt was twelve he was bullied by two boys during a trip to Maine. He realized that he didn't have the physical strength to fight his tormentors and was humiliated thoroughly. His father had already sat him down and discussed his physical limitations, challenging his son to build himself up with an exercise program. After the incident in Maine, Teddy accepted his father's challenge and undertook a regime of running and other exercises. His wealthy parents even built a gymnasium on their estate which Teddy used religiously. Roosevelt succeeded in increasing his strength through sheer willpower. For the remainder of his life he routinely went horseback riding, hiking, swimming, and hunting.

My parents certainly couldn't provide me with a gymnasium, but Boston Latin did have an excellent athletic program. When I returned to school in the fall after the period of illness that forced me to repeat the fourth class, I immediately went out for the track team. I was twelve years old and probably weighed 65 pounds, but I was determined to beat my asthma the same way that Teddy Roosevelt had beat his. I'm satisfied that initially, at least, I was the sorriest track prospect that Latin School had seen in over three hundred years of existence.

I trained with the team and pushed myself hard. The first two years I ran, I never placed in a race and never scored a point for the team. They didn't even give me a warm-up suit. I was more of a hanger-on than a member of the team. But races were held at the old West Newton Street Armory that were open to all comers and I entered them. The Armory where we raced was a great big empty building and to accommodate it to track they built enormous wooden ramps at the turns which they called corners. They made for an exceptionally sharp banked corner. The trick was to run into those things full tilt and just before you got to them, swing to the outside. Coming down off the corners we pulled back to the inside and this accelerated us into the straightaway by centrifugal force and gravity.

I gradually developed into a sprinter and eventually started placing and even winning. In those days we would run a preliminary qualifying race and ten minutes later run again. I remember one triangular meet at the Armory where I was running for Boston Latin. The first race was a preliminary and our coach had told me that I only needed to place among the first four to qualify our team for the final. He told me not to burn myself out by trying to come in first; he wanted me to save something for the final. When the starter's gun went off we tore off down the back stretch. Almost immediately a runner behind me stepped on my heel. I fell on the splintered wooden track and bruised my knees badly. Furious, I jumped up and ran for all I was worth to catch that son of a bitch. I passed him and everyone else on the track to win the race. My father was in the stands and witnessed my fall and my victory. He didn't say much, but his quiet pride was a fine reward indeed.

By my Junior year I had earned a warm-up suit and was on the relay team. That warm-up suit meant a lot to me, and I relished my little moments of glory with the team. I still got sick occasionally, but not with the depressing regularity of my previous confinements. I grew in size, strength, and confidence. I competed on the track and in the classroom, continuing to put in the required three hours of daily homework without any deviation. There wasn't a great deal of free time for me in those years, especially during track season. A lot was expected from kids at Boston Latin, and the school had a substantial failure rate.

Boston Latin School was a public school which *insisted* that one hundred percent of its graduates go on to college. They usually attained this goal, even through the depression. These were pretty lean times: kids worked incredibly hard to get good grades and to get the money to go back next semester and get more good grades. There was a level of commitment that we don't often see these days. We did look forward, however, to Jewish holidays because they sometimes provided a rare respite from the normal classroom work. As the Jewish high holidays approached we quietly counted heads in the classroom. If we got up to fifteen Jewish students who would be absent, we'd calculate whether there would be too few students to conduct class. If there were, the various Masters would advise us the day would be spent in study hall where little would be accomplished.

In the winter many Latin School boys, myself included, took the streetcars to school and back. The return trips were sometimes a bit unruly. This was especially true when there was a newly fallen snow in some quantity along South Huntington Avenue. The windows could be raised out of the slots into which they fit and allowed to fall outward which left the folks inside unprotected. These open windows seemed to stimulate the students from Jamaica Plains into throwing snowballs into the cars, which made splendid moving targets, packed as they were with boys from Latin School. The conductors viewed all of this with considerable disgust.

Our world was pretty small in those days. My childhood was spent within St. Theresa's Parish. In the Boston that I grew up in, you identified yourself by your parish. You were from Holy Name Parish, or Star of the Sea Parish, or from St. Theresa's. We didn't have a great deal of awareness of international affairs, or events outside of Boston for that matter. I grew up in the depression, and we certainly were aware of that. But my dad never missed a day of work during that period, or any other period for that matter. He earned about $60 a month, which wasn't bad for those years. I do remember Franklin Roosevelt coming to Boston and being received by enormous throngs of supporters. Roosevelt ran very strongly across the country in 1932 and even more so in 1936, but the big East Coast cities were the heartland of his support. The West didn't have the population or the political clout it does today. My only awareness of the West was through the cinema, and we all considered westerners to be either cowboys or Indians.

We were also aware of the emerging brute of Nazism. I remember seeing a play at the old Wilbur Theater which exposed the sinister nature of Hitler's government dramatically. I also recall some of the Masters at Boston Latin talking about Hitler in condemnatory tones. The Jewish kids at Boston Latin, including friends of mine on the track team, were far more sensitized to the true nature of the Third Reich than the rest of us. Conversations with them helped shape my distaste for the Nazis. There were Irish people in Boston, however, who reacted to British oppression with certain brutal tendencies of their own. To them, the prospect that Hitler would rise up and do enormous damage to Great Britain was a point in the guy's favor. None of my relatives were sympathetic to Hitler, and neither was I. But in the larger Irish society I heard congratulatory things said about Hitler and the German people. Some saw England's time of great peril as Ireland's moment of opportunity.

I was barely fifteen when the Japanese attacked Pearl Harbor. It was a Sunday, and we worshipped together in a state of shock and apprehension at a late Mass at Saint Theresa's. Instead of singing *Holy God We Praise Thy Name*, the standard recessional hymn we had heard all of our lives, the choir sang *America the Beautiful*. The congregation joined in and it was a stirring, unforgettable moment. Such a change in the ritual was unprecedented, and there was a palpable sense of foreboding. The death and destruction at Pearl Harbor was a total surprise, it was horrific, and I knew something terribly catastrophic was headed our way.

A great spirit of selfless dedication to the war effort swept the country, and St. Theresa's Parish was no exception. Many of the oldest boys at Boston Latin enlisted. We had a Junior ROTC program and we all wore uniforms and drilled with fake wooden rifles. It was a pretty poor substitute for military training, but it was something. We were very concerned by the destruction in England caused by German bombers and my dad became an air raid warden. We had air raid alerts when we attempted to shut off every light in Boston. This did bring the populace together, but otherwise had little effect. People used to save tinfoil for the war effort and I remember people rolling great balls of it to the defense headquarters. An enormous national effort to switch over to war production commenced and we felt that we owed it our best effort. We all knew it was time to get serious and do what we were here for. We all pulled together and were wholesomely, almost unquestionably patriotic. For the first year or two the news from the battlefields was not good and I knew that I would be joining up at age eighteen if it lasted that long.

In the spring of 1943 the track meet known as the Regimentals was held at the Boston Armory. The Regimentals was open to all the high schools in Boston and they sent their finest athletes to compete. We had set a record for the one-and-a-half-mile relay that year and we expected to win. I ran in three races and finished second to a student from Mechanics Arts in the last race. I came in fourth in the 440 and felt that I was able to run with the best. Boston Latin won that track meet, and I wanted to continue running at this level during my upcoming senior year. That year I was also a rarely used end on the legendary, undefeated Boston Latin School football team. Our bitter rival, Boston English, was also undefeated and unscored against that year. We played our annual game in front of 25,000 fans at Braves Field, the old professional baseball venue. That game ended in a scoreless tie due to the alert work of Assistant Coach Lambert. On a big play at the end of the game English School had an illegal receiver down field, which he pointed out to the referees. The play was called back, a substantial penalty imposed, and both teams maintained their undefeated records for the season.

I was eighteen on October 18, 1943, and in my final year at Boston Latin. Eighteen-year-olds were going into the army, and the Army Air Corps was the glamour outfit that we all wanted to join. I went down to the recruiting station to try to enlist in the Air Corps but failed the Ishihara color blindness test. They held up cards covered with colored dots of various shades. If you can differentiate the subtle differences in color, a number or pattern becomes visible. I couldn't even begin to see anything but little dots. I went to another recruiting station a little later where I flunked again. The Air Corps wouldn't have me.

At the front of my senior yearbook from Boston Latin is a memorial list of students who had been killed in the war. There are twenty-seven names on the list, and it was not complete. Following the memorial list is a message to the graduating class from the headmaster, Mr. Joseph Powers. He begins by noting that, "more than forty boys of the present Class are already in the armed forces." (By the time the book was published I was among that number.) "The defense of your country," he continues, "is your first and highest duty, and I know that each of you is ready to do his part with courage and devotion." He then advises, "Even though your country should require your services for a period of years, stick to your purpose to complete your college education."

Hundreds of ships, including troop ships, were being sunk by Nazi submarines and Powers had some very practical advice for us, "While you are waiting to be called, keep yourself in top physical condition. I have no misgivings about your mental preparedness. Eat plenty of plain, wholesome food. Get to bed early. Walk as much as you can, with well-fitting shoes. Take part in competitive outdoor sports. Learn to swim under water; and to float, whether the water be smooth or rough, without becoming panicky. Your life may depend on this kind of competence."

Right about this time the high schools and colleges in the Boston area got together and agreed to allow high school seniors who finished their first semester by Christmas with good grade point averages to matriculate at local colleges and universities. In December the headmaster of Boston Latin School told me and a couple of hundred other seniors that we could leave Latin School immediately and enroll in an accredited four-year college. He guaranteed our diplomas the following June. This got some warm bodies, and some funding, into colleges which had been depopulated by the war. Most of the kids that fit into this scheme were not yet eighteen. Since I had to repeat my freshman year, I was a year older than my classmates and it didn't look like I would be able to avail myself of this opportunity to finish high school at Boston College. Not to mention the chance to run on the BC track team.

The chairman of the Math Department at Boston Latin, Mr. Lucey, was also chairman of the West Roxbury draft board. I was friendly with his son who was in my class, and acquainted with Mr. Lucey as well. I approached him and said that I thought they would take me at Boston College. "You're going to have to go to the army, you were eighteen on October 18th" was the initial response. But in the end he decided to give me a short reprieve. I went straight over to Boston College, which was not very far away.

Boston College is a Jesuit school and it is probably where I would have gone to college if the war and the GI bill had not intervened. Most of the kids at Latin School who didn't get scholarships ended up at Boston College and most of the students there were from working-class Irish families. I ran down Jack Ryder, the track coach, and told him that the winter track season was coming and that I heard he needed a fourth quarter-miler. He verified it and I enrolled at Boston College. I was an instant member of the Boston College track team and got a fancy warm-up suit.

Jack Ryder was seventy years old and highly regarded as a track coach. He attracted some great athletes. Gil Dodds, who set an American record for the mile in 1943, trained with us even though he wasn't on the team. Dodds was a local hero to Boston runners and sports fans. In the summer of 1943 I had begged for permission to travel on the train from Lyndeboro to see him run against the Swedish champion, Gundar Haegg, at Harvard Stadium. At the time runners were competing to see who would be the first to run a mile in under four minutes, and there was some speculation that it might happen when Dodds ran against Haegg. I was in the stands when Dodds won the race. He didn't break four minutes; that wasn't accomplished until Roger Bannister did it at Oxford's Iffley Road track eleven years later on May 6, 1954. But it was a thrilling race and Dodds set a new American record of 4:06.5.

Ralph King was a state champion sprinter who was on the BC team. We had another runner named Herb McKinley who was from Jamaica and spoke with a very British accent. Jamaica had not declared war on anybody and wasn't about to, but McKinley was a hell of a runner who came to Boston College to be trained by Jack Ryder. I practiced with them for a few days at an outdoor facility where we had to shovel the snow off the wooden track. About a week later I was on the mile relay team that was to compete in the Boston Athletic Association games to be held in the famous Boston Garden.

To all of us in Boston, the legendary place was simply the "Gahd'n." I still have a vivid recollection of attending the Ringling Brothers Circus there as a kid and seeing a man being fired from a cannon. The human projectile lowered himself into the barrel of the artillery piece, then reemerged and did a vaudevillian double take. Then came a great explosion followed by a human figure flying through the air like Superman (who was not yet invented) and into a net. I also saw the rodeo there. My father had taken me down into the bowels of the place where we walked around among the horses and livestock. I had seen the Bruins play there. Now I was going to run the race of my life there in front of a cheering crowd that included my dad and lots of kids from Boston Latin.

We were running against Holy Cross in the mile relay and Ryder called us together to announce the order. He put Herb McKinley of Jamaica on the first leg, Ralph King, formerly of Rindge Tech, on the second, and Joe McDavitt from Watertown on the penultimate leg. Then he said McNulty would run the anchor leg.

Anchor! Anchor? You are supposed to put your fastest man on the anchor leg. Sickness had kept me out my entire freshman year. I hadn't placed in a race during my first two years. Now I found myself in some very fast company indeed. McKinley later would win a silver medal in the 1948 Olympics running the quarter in 46.4 seconds. He came back to the Olympics in 1952 and finished second again, this time in 45.9 seconds. When our race started he led off and defeated his opponent by over forty yards. King added twenty yards to that lead, and McDavitt maintained it. I was eighteen years old, very much alone, and about to carry the baton to the finish line in front of thirteen thousand spectators in the Boston Garden.

Seeing the lead we had built, the opposing anchorman from Holy Cross acknowledged that his case was hopeless, shook my hand, and wished me good luck. When the baton hit my outstretched hand I ran almost in a dream, trying to concentrate on not dropping the stick and not falling down. By the time we crossed the finish line the runner who shook my hand had cut the sixty-yard lead to twenty, and he wished he had tried harder. But he had not caught me. My three teammates were ecstatic, and so was I.

It was an heroic moment for me in the noise and bright lights of the Boston Garden. I remember noticing that the lofty roof was shrouded in concentrated cigarette smoke as I walked a victory lap amid the hub-bub. I was an instant varsity letterman. In those days any victory by the Boston College Eagles in any event, not excluding spitting contests, qualified one for such an honor. But these badges of athletic prowess had a special meaning for me.

There was a thick mantle of snow on the ground, and more on the way, so my father and I had taken the streetcar to the Boston Garden instead of driving the Ford. I knew my father was proud of me as we rode the streetcar home that night. As usual, however, his compliments were brief. We got off the trolley at Center Street and started walking home. I knew that no reasonable request would be declined at this moment and I asked to stop in at Fitzpatrick's Diner for two English muffins. Request granted. We then walked in the silent gathering snow up Center Street to Park Street and up Park to 12 Oriole Street. Inside our warm little home I recounted the race in detail to my beaming mother. Forty years later I would wear that letter on the floor of the U. S. House of Representatives to the delight and consternation of Boston College baseball letterman Tip O'Neill.

One week later we ran in the New York Athletic Club games in Madison Square Garden. This was another premier indoor track event where we were pitted against the University of Rochester, which had become a big naval training station. We lost that one, but the experience of running for a capacity crowd at Madison Square Garden was a major consolation. Gil Dodds, who traveled with us, went to the station early with our luggage and staked out some seats on the crowded train for us. Dodds was a fine man and an ordained Baptist minister who had studied at Boston Theological Seminary. In 1947 he would set the Madison Square Garden record for the mile, but on this trip he carried the luggage and held our seats. Right after that meet I received word from Mr. Lucey that my Uncle Sam would countenance no further delays. I had my taste of glory for a few weeks, but now it was time to get back to business. My cousin, Richard Mitchell, was also due to report for induction in a few days. His dad, my Uncle Joe Mitchell, decided that we ought to have a fling before we joined up.

In the 1920s Uncle Joe was a young dentist in Springfield and one of his patients was my dad's only sister, Helen. They married and had two sons, Richard and Joseph. Richard's nickname within the family was "Rìgh," which is Gaelic for "king." A few days prior to the date when Rìgh and I were to report for induction, my Uncle Joe handed us each $100 and told us to go to New York City and have some fun. I had never seen that much money before. Rìgh and I rode the train to New York and checked into an inexpensive hotel near Times Square. We went down to a store and bought two bottles of beer, one each. We drank them and then wandered around Times Square taking in the sights and sounds like two rubes. I could not, however, bring myself to squander the entire hundred dollars.

A few days later, on March 14, 1944, I was inducted into the army at Ft. Devens, Massachusetts, the same place where my dad entered the Coast Guard in World War I. After about a week there I was sent to Ft. McClellan at Anniston, Alabama, for seventeen weeks of basic training. During World War II the place expanded enormously, but the old part of Ft. McClellan was a lovely picturesque headquarters on top of a hill. Having grown up in a pretty disciplinarian culture, I had no problem adapting to military life. The Masters at Boston Latin and Irish nuns at St. Theresa's had accustomed us to doing what we were told, and to doing it the way we were told to do it. I was in excellent physical condition, so the drills were not a hardship. Following orders and physical training were things that I knew well.

Ft. McClellan was a training post for the Infantry Replacement Training Corps (I.R.T.C.) which provided replacements for combat units that had suffered casualties, sometimes very heavy casualties. Units which had been recruited from a few unfortunate towns or counties had suffered horrendous loses. These communities had paid a disproportionately high price. The I.R.T.C. was established to provide replacements that were from across the country, reducing the future probability that any one community would see a generation of their young men decimated. Most of the recruits in the I.R.T.C. were eighteen-and nineteen-year-olds, but we also had some draftees in their thirties. The invasion of Europe was under way and the need for manpower was at its peak.

The physical training was rigorous and it was particularly hard on these older soldiers. We marched, we ran for miles with packs, we crawled under barbed wire on our bellies as dummy mortar rounds whistled over our heads. We were separated into squads including Wireless, Motor Squad, and Intelligence Squad. The Intelligence Squad was trained to perform scouting missions at night. For no apparent reason, I was assigned to the Intelligence Squad. I was also named the guidon bearer for Company D of the 27th Training Battalion which meant I marched in front of our troop carrying a little triangular flag. We marched everywhere we went and the 200 men of the troop followed that little flag to the mess, to drills, and to the barracks.

Ft. McClellan lies in the middle of the Talladega Swamp and that is where the Intelligence Squad did its night training. We waded through the muck and brackish waters in the dark, always worried about the poisonous snakes that we had been advised to avoid. The real enemy, however, were the insidious and ubiquitous chiggers which tormented us constantly. One of the things I have always greatly appreciated about Arizona is that there are no chiggers.

After completion of the seventeen weeks of I.R.T.C. training most of the guys went into the 106th Infantry Division in Europe. I was held back as cadre, which meant I would be used to help train the new I.R.T.C. recruits flowing into Ft. McClellan. The 106th, where most of my buddies ended up, was composed mostly of young kids and middle-aged men and they were neither battle seasoned nor particularly prepared for what they encountered. The Germans found them in the Battle of the Bulge and advanced mightily in the space of two or three days. They broke through Allied lines and advanced about twenty-five miles into France and Belgium, isolating General McAuliffe and his paratroopers at Bastogne. By the time the Germans were driven back, 16,000 American soldiers had been killed and 60,000 wounded. It was heartbreaking news, but it was the last German offensive of the war. After they were pushed back, the American, British, and Russian armies marched to Berlin just about as fast as their feet would take them. It was not a walk in the park, but at least the war in Europe didn't have long to go.

I was assigned to help supervise the physical conditioning of the recruits. Part of this was a three-mile run with rifle and pack within a specified time. They had to do this repeatedly and I was the one who

The greatest generation? Fellow noncoms celebrate McNulty's promotion to Corporal at Ft. McClellan, Alabama, in 1944.

pushed them. I made no friends whatsoever on that assignment. We watched training films that showed horrendous battles on the Russian front while the soundtrack played inspiring Tchaikovsky concertos and symphonies. The narration explained the incredible sacrifices and bravery of the Russian people who were dying by the millions.

On the weekends we usually did nothing, but later I had the option of going into Anniston. I met a girl there and on Sunday nights her whole family would pick me up, take me out to dinner, and then return me to Ft. McClellan. The citizens of Anniston were very cordial to the soldiers and we had some happy times there amid the serious business of war. The town offered places with music and dancing, but with about fifteen soldiers for every available female, the odds weren't very good. Those lucky enough to find dance partners did the jitterbug. I wasn't much of a jitterbugger, but the big-band music was great and I loved hearing it.

I went to Birmingham for a couple of weekends, and once went to

Atlanta. Atlanta was very hospitable to soldiers. We all got a cot, a hot shower, and three square meals a day compliments of the City and local churches. I always went to mass on Sunday wherever I found myself, and without fail any unfamiliar man in uniform would be approached by some church member and invited home to dinner.

One day at Ft. McClellan the First Sergeant came up to me and said, "I've got to detail somebody to go to Boston, Massachusetts, to pick up an AWOL soldier and bring him back here. We're going to try him for desertion." He handed me a .45 and asked, "Do you know how to use this?" "No sir," I responded. "Well that's all right," he replied, "Don't shoot it." He handed me a paper with the name and location of the prisoner. I jumped on a swanky Pullman car with reclining seats and great big windows at the station in Anniston, and rode it all the way to Grand Central Station. I took another train up to Boston, and showed up unexpectedly at 12 Oriole Street. We went out to dinner at a restaurant and I had my only reunion with the family during my time in the army. The next day I reported to the guardhouse at Cambridge where I was to pick up the prisoner. The jailer pointed out that I was a day late, then handcuffed me to the prisoner. We rode the trains that way for two days all the way back to Ft. McClellan.

On August 6, 1945, a B-29 named the Enola Gay took off from Tinian Island and at 8:15 a.m. it dropped an atomic bomb on Hiroshima, killing 78,150 Japanese. Three days later a similar raid on Nagasaki resulted in about 40,000 deaths. Japan signed the formal surrender on the deck of the battleship Missouri in Tokyo Bay on September 2. I was honorably discharged almost immediately, having served eighteen months in the Army. I never heard a shot fired in anger during my service, and I never went overseas. My contribution was pretty insignificant compared to the sacrifices made by others of my generation. But I was a very small part of something much greater than myself, and I am proud of that. The true heroes of that conflict were pretty wholesome and the war brought out the best in us. We all knew what we had to do, and why we had to do it, and we gave it our best.

I headed back to 12 Oriole Street in Boston. My mother had accepted my diploma from Boston Latin School at the commencement the previous summer. I was a member of what we called the 52-20 Club. In order to smooth the transition to civilian life, the government paid unemployed vets the princely sum of $20 per week for up to fifty-two weeks. This allowed us to go to the fall baseball games at Fenway Park and contemplate our future. But the real opportunity that military service earned were the educational benefits now available to us through the GI Bill.

I always assumed I would go to college, and had been admitted to Boston College just before entering the service. The GI Bill now opened up the horizons. The question was simply where to go. By this time my proper Victorian mother had landed the prestigious job of secretary to the headmaster at Boston Latin. (I still have a letter from the Mayor of Boston recommending her for the job.) She asked one of the Boston Latin School Masters, a Mr. Cleary, about my options. Cleary told her that in January Harvard was going to make some rare mid-term admissions.

I began the process of applying for admission to Harvard, but an old nemesis reappeared and brought my plans into question. My health had held up during most of my eighteen months at Ft. McClellan. But eventually the damp Alabama air and time spent in the Talladega swamp had brought my respiratory problems back. I was not up to par when I returned to Boston, and the winter weather there didn't help. My parents summoned Dr. Barry, the physician who had cared for every member of my family since we had first moved to West Roxbury.

In those days doctors still drove out to your house to look you over. Dr. Barry was a big, jovial, outgoing guy with whom I had a long acquaintance. He had advised against my self-imposed running regimen and I enjoyed pointing out this mistake of his. Dr. Barry took guff from me that he wouldn't have taken from many. He was my friend, and despite our jousting, I knew he was in my corner. On this occasion I criticized him and medical science in general for their perceived failings in my particular case. Barry recognized my frustration, and he knew how to handle me.

"I know exactly what you need to do to get rid of this asthma," Barry replied. "If you followed these instructions you could do whatever you want to do. But you are too damn stubborn. You won't do what I say and there is no point in me making the recommendation." I leaped to the bait immediately and demanded he tell me, saying, "You think I won't do it? Tell me what it is and you'll find out!" He responded calmly, "Go to Colorado or New Mexico or Arizona or one of those God-forsaken places out West. That's your answer." Rising and reaching for his hat he added, "I expect I'll see you again soon."

"No you won't!" I shot back, "I'll send you a postcard from Colorado!" An enforced pilgrimage to one of the "lunger camps" of the Southwest had been a cure for tuberculosis and asthma patients since the turn of the century. I had not even considered such an unlikely possibility, but the next morning I was at the Boston Library researching southwestern universities and colleges. I considered Colorado schools first, but settled on a little known outfit called The University of Arizona. It had fewer students than Boston Latin School, and was in a place called Tucson of which I was only dimly aware. I fired off an application and packed a bag.

CHAPTER THREE

The University of Arizona

WHEN I STEPPED OFF the *Californian* from Chicago at the old Southern Pacific Railroad Station in downtown Tucson on January 4, 1946, I was riding the crest of a wave. Some 2.2 million World War II veterans obtained a college education through the GI Bill. By 1947 half of all college students were vets. Anxious to make up for lost time, we overwhelmed, and then transformed higher education in America.

The Servicemen's Readjustment Act of 1944, commonly known as the GI Bill, was one of the most profoundly successful laws ever passed in the history of our Republic. It broke the mold on the reward system for conquering armies. No slaves, no plundered works of art, no wholesale theft of private and public assets. Caesar would have been distressed and his legions even more so. But wise Americans swapped military service for education in an everlasting act of wisdom.

The legislators who drafted the bill were mindful of the shameful treatment of veterans in Washington, D.C., after World War I. The soldiers had returned home to a recession and were not paid the bonus money they had been promised. Angry homeless veterans had marched on Washington, only to have their camp attacked and burned by the U.S. Army. It was not one of our finer moments, and the country did not want to repeat it. Compared to World War I, twice as many soldiers were discharged after World War II. Their successful integration into the civilian work force was vital to the economy and the political stability of the country. The GI Bill became law just before D-Day, and it provided vets who enrolled in colleges and technical schools $500 a year for tuition and fees (more than adequate at the UA), as well as $50.00 a month for living expenses. It also offered mortgage subsidies that allowed vets to buy homes. In the twenty-year period following the war, 20 percent of all new single-family homes were built with funding from the GI Bill. Without it the postwar housing boom that impacted Arizona so dramatically probably wouldn't have occurred.

When Franklin Roosevelt signed the bill, critics worried that allowing all of this riffraff into colleges would have dire social and educational consequences. The halls of academe had mostly been reserved for the upper classes, but the GI Bill broke down barriers of race and class that had restricted access to college for many Americans. These new students were older, more disciplined, more diverse, and they weren't afraid to speak their minds. They had been to war, and when they got home they triggered big changes for higher education in America.

Colleges and universities which had seen their enrollments and revenues lag during the war now flourished and expanded. The vets were more politically active and the "left" became better represented on campus. The highly motivated new students pushed colleges to make course work more practical and degree programs in fields like business and engineering were added or expanded. Eventually, higher average levels of education among Americans inevitably led to higher average incomes and tax revenues increased. The middle class swelled and America prospered in general.

When I got off the *Californian* in Tucson back in 1946 it was already dark. I was still a little sick and was exhausted from the long ride. I had the name of a friend of a friend in Boston who might put me up. I had been told he lived near Armory Park, but I heard it as "Emery Park." So I walked around downtown Tucson for a while asking for directions to "Emery Park," and when this was unsuccessful, ended up back at the depot. I was still wearing army clothes, as were many of the other new students, and this may have helped me when I reported to the Traveler's Aide booth. I told the elderly woman who was on duty that I needed a room. The town was, of course, flooded with veterans but she told me there was exactly one room left in town. She said it was in a boarding house, "out near the University," adding that it wasn't very nice. I told her it would have to do and, since the hour was late, paid sixty cents for a cab ride to the address she gave me on East Third Street.

The Southern Inn at 207 E. Third was an old house that looked pretty shabby, but I climbed the steps onto the porch and knocked on the door. It was opened by an old slattern of a woman in a dirty housecoat who looked me up and down and did not utter any greeting. "I just called from Traveler's Aide about a room," I said by way of introduction. "It's five bucks," she replied. I said, "Okay." "NOW!" she added. She stripped the five-dollar bill out of my hand, then showed me to a small room with a large home-made bed constructed out of plywood and two-by-fours.

I took a shower, jumped into that bed, and probably slept better than I have slept since. When I woke up in the morning I found another guy sleeping next to me. The landlady had rented out half the bed to him in the middle of the night for another five bucks, and I never woke up. That was my introduction to Arizona hospitality. I had breakfast with the other boarders and headed off for the University to enroll.

Walking down Third Street (now University Boulevard) on that sunny January morning, I was absolutely stunned by the glorious weather. You didn't even need a jacket! The winter sun burned fiercely in a cobalt blue sky that stretched from one distant mountain range to the other. Compared to busy Boston, the place was quiet. The breeze carried a slight aroma of mesquite smoke. There were all sorts of strange plants that I had never seen before. Palm trees waved and exotic looking cacti bloomed with huge waxy flowers. Tucson was a small town of about 40,000 highly independent souls that petered out by the time you got to Tucson Boulevard. The University was out on the eastern periphery where the town began to yield to the desert. I fell in love with the place instantly, and never suffered another asthma attack.

The office of Registrar C. Zaner Lesher was in the Administration Building, right across the circle from Old Main. Professor Lesher, who was called "Zip," reviewed every student's application and summoned some of them for interviews. I stood on line with a group of other supplicants for a period of time, and was eventually ushered into his presence. I handed over my transcripts from Boston Latin and Zip was most cordial. He knew the school's reputation and made admiring noises as he perused the documents, "Oh fine. And look at this... Splendid!" He was very encouraging regarding my prospects at Arizona, and enrolled me in the College of Business. He also informed me there was no student housing available and I would have to find my own place to live.

Zip Lesher was a busy guy that year. Before and during the war most American universities had led a pretty sleepy existence. But the federal money available through the GI Bill enabled savvy administrators at state land grant schools like the UA to undertake building projects, expand their enrollments dramatically, hire more professors, and in general enlarge their fiefdoms. These expanded schools had the capacity to educate more students, so the percentage of high school grads who went on to college jumped after the war. The academic standards I found at the UA, however, were certainly not as high as at Boston Latin.

I headed over to the Student Union to register for classes and found the place jammed with students standing in lines. Another army vet was standing next to me and we struck up a conversation. His name was Thomas R. Johnson and he had been a prisoner of the Germans during the war. He was looking for a little peace and comfort after his wartime experience and, like me, he needed to find a room. One thing led to another, and we ended up rooming together at the Southern Inn that semester. We replaced the home-made bed with bunks and installed ourselves. I later learned that some of the boarders were tuberculosis patients, a fact that caused my mother a great deal of consternation. But the Arizona sun must have protected me, because I survived the place.

Within a week I had found a job as a waiter at the Varsity Inn. The Varsity Inn was a restaurant and student hang-out situated on University just west of Park. The proprietor at the time was Morris Kaplan, an old fellow who had fled Russia to escape czarist pogroms against Jews. Morris taught me a few Russian expressions and paid me 75 cents an hour and a free lunch. He treated me like family and many years later when his son, Manny, was married at a synagogue in Brookline, Massachusetts, Morris invited my parents and they attended. My mother pronounced the ceremony "beautiful," and my father wore his first yarmulke.

The Varsity Inn was a friendly, warm, enduring oasis of reasonably good character and wholesome ambitions. Many UA students who eventually made good were employed in the joint at one time or another. J. F. "Pop" McKale, who was director of athletics, owned a silent partnership interest in the place during the twenties and early thirties. In the mid-twenties the cashier was Jim Gentry, who would later become one of my law partners in Bisbee. Jim had sustained considerable damage to his right thumb in a farm accident in Arkansas during childhood. The accident left the right thumb and nail permanently mangled. McKale used to regale the gullible with a cautionary tale based on the injury.

He would inform people that Gentry had once worked as a cashier at the Varsity Inn and order Gentry to display the damaged digit. McKale would then explain that he had once caught Gentry with his hand in the cash drawer and that he, McKale, had promptly slammed it on Gentry's thumb. His exact words were, "I caught the son of a bitch stealing my money!" The performance would be completed by Gentry laying some heavy disparagement on McKale's silent, and presumably shameful, undisclosed interest in the restaurant.

Harry Bagnall was a "BMOC" and my boss at the Varsity Inn. He had already served his term as cashier there and later served as majority whip in the Arizona House of Representatives. Student Body President Doug Ward specialized in dishwashing at the Varsity Inn and Tobie Grose was another kitchen worker who would eventually become a professor at the UA. The restaurant served as the unofficial headquarters of the "Palm Road Gang," which included George "Buster" Grady (Varsity Inn soda jerk turned Tucson stockbroker), Jerry Budwig (once dishwasher now a Colorado engineer), and Mileana Drachman of the famous Tucson Drachmans. Jim Gentry's little brother, Martin Gentry, also worked there for a time. Gentry was allowed to sleep in the cellar for a while, a dubious privilege (due to rodent activity) that was also extended to me occasionally.

In addition to taking the job at the Varsity Inn, I signed up for the UA track team and was promptly provided with my own locker. Limey Gibbings was the track coach. He trained people to run the 400-meter race by bringing the contestants down to the finishing post and saying, "Keep to your left and get back here as quick as you can." Gibbings was a crony of legendary athletic director McKale and this is what made his job as track coach secure. We trained on the cinder track that circled the football field in Arizona Stadium, and in May I finished third in the 440 at the Border Conference track meet. I also ran a lap in the mile relay which we won. I weighed 153 pounds, the weight I maintained throughout college, and my respiratory problems were history.

Despite my middle-class origins, I also pledged at the Phi Delta Theta fraternity. This is something I probably wouldn't have done had I stayed in Boston, but the West was wonderfully lax about matters of caste. I could wait on a coed at the Varsity Inn at lunch time and date her that evening. I never lived at the Phi Delta Theta house, but I participated with them in the various tribal competitions and festivities that made university life so rich. For homecoming we built massive and elaborate floats, sometimes staying up for forty-eight hours to complete them in time for the parade. Freshmen were supposed to paint the "A" on "A" Mountain while wearing green beanies. And, of course, there were the obligatory panty raids, fraternity parties, and the whole gamut of college pranks and hijinks.

I took economics from Dr. Harvill that first semester. He later would be named dean of Liberal Arts and then president of the university. For English I had Dr. Tucker, one of the school's more interesting lecturers. He believed that students should wait on him, not the other way around. Consequently, he never arrived early for his classes and he habitually warned the class of his approach by singing the *Pater Noster* (in Latin) as he climbed the stairs. He would finish it just before reaching the door and this allowed us to assume a scholarly demeanor for his entrance. Dr. Tucker was Catholic and one of my classmates, Clint Fowler, was Anglican. (Today Fowler is an Anglican priest in Pennsylvania.) They enjoyed spirited theological debates and Tucker would frequently refer to Fowler as "the half-baked Catholic."

I became a member of Sts. Peter and Paul Catholic Church, which is still on Campbell north of Speedway. The Hispanic people of Tucson were very diligent about their relationship with the Church and this was a unifying force. Mexicans were not outsiders in Tucson. Tucson's long history as a Spanish frontier outpost, Mexican pueblo, and American town had always included Hispanics in all levels of business and government. The section of Arizona lying south of the Gila River, with Tucson at its center, was only acquired from Mexico by the Gadsden Purchase in 1853. It was the last piece of territory added to the continental United States. The Americans were the latecomers here; the majority of the population was Hispanic until around the turn of the century. In this way Tucson was very different from communities in central and northern Arizona. They were settled after the Civil War by Americans, many of whom had prejudices against Mexicans dating back to the Mexican-American War.

At the end of my first year of school I journeyed to Yuma to cash in on the summer "snow" season. When the moment of ripeness arrives in the cantaloupe fields the melons must be picked and packed immediately. Farmers and workers refer to this rush of melons and activity as the "snow." It was all over in about three or four weeks, but while the snow lasted you could earn a huge amount of money—as much as one hundred bucks a week! A small group of fraternity brothers including Dean Burch (later chairman of the Arizona Republican Party), and Larry Ollason (who became a federal judge), had told me about the money that could be made in the packing sheds around Yuma during the harvest. Another fellow I knew, Jack (John H.) Bryant, had an uncle who was once mayor of Yuma. He said he could help us get jobs in the cantaloupe sheds.

We drove to Yuma and went from shed to shed in nearby Somerton until we found jobs. We all arrived with empty pockets so we stayed at the Clymer Boarding House on Orange Avenue in Yuma. The place was run by Virginia Eastlick, who was the daughter of the owner, Mrs. Clymer. She would let us stay on the cuff until we were "in the snow," and could pay her. She was Yuma's equivalent of Tombstone's famous boarding house operator, Nellie Cashman. The place was an old style boarding house, not a hotel, so you had to be out of there with your sack lunch by 7:30 a.m. Folks of all walks of life lived there, from us melon boomers all the way up to the local judge of the Superior Court.

Cocopah Indians picked the cantaloupes and they didn't start until about 10:00 a.m., because even the tiniest amount of dew would be harmful to the melons. The cantaloupes were loaded into shallow trucks which hauled them to the packing sheds in Somerton where they were dumped into bins padded with a mattress of canvas. From there they rolled onto a belt and moved through the shed for sorting, spraying, and packing. I was a set-off man, meaning that I removed the sixty-pound crates from the conveyor, checked the melons for ripeness and size, and stacked the crates for removal to the waiting rail car. These were the old insulated boxcars that had bunkers for ice at either end and a crude fan system to circulate cool air over the load.

We moved the crates into the car with an Irish diesel (which the Arizona boys called a Mexican diesel), stacked them, and nailed the stacks to the wooden floor. Once both ends were loaded we had to load the "squeeze," the central space which had to be filled precisely to keep the load from shifting. When the snow hit, the rule was that every picked cantaloupe had to be sorted, crated, and loaded before the daily work was over. We often were still loading cantaloupes at two or three o'clock in the morning. When this happened there was no point in returning to the boarding house in Yuma for the night and we slept in the cushioned bins that had been emptied of cantaloupes. I made so much money in June of 1946 that I went and, for the first time in my life, got a shave from a barber. I would return to work the "snow" each June for the next two years.

By the beginning of July the cantaloupe season was over and I had no work and no place to live. My headquarters was my B-4 bag. I decided to go to the place where I knew they would feed me: 12 Oriole Street in West Roxbury. I started hitchhiking at about 5:00 in the afternoon on the corner of 7th Street and Grand Avenue in Phoenix. A few cars went by and then one stopped and the driver yelled, "Hey, Jim!" It was Roy Echeverria, a classmate of mine. His family was Basque and had come to Arizona to herd sheep. He told me he was headed to Williams and then to California and that he could take me up to Route 66 where I would head east. Roy was engaged to a girl whose parents owned a swanky guest ranch in Wickenburg. "Tonight you're going to have the best of all worlds, you're going to swim in the big swimming pool, have a big dinner, and sleep in a lovely room," Roy told me. "And in the morning we'll get in the truck and drive to Williams."

There were bunches of soldier hitchhikers at most of the highway intersections along Route 66 and rides were easy to get. Somewhere in Missouri an elderly couple stopped and asked me if I could help drive. They were going home to Indianapolis and had bitten off more driving than they could chew. I told them I was going to Boston, jumped in, and drove the car all the way to Indianapolis. They put me up in their guest bedroom that night and fed me a grand breakfast in the morning, then drove me back out to the highway. From there I got a ride to Philadelphia, and then another to Boston. In Boston I found a ride out to Lyndeboro, New Hampshire, where the family was spending the summer as always.

In the fall of 1947, I was enlisted as campaign manager for William Howard O'Brien, who was a candidate for UA student body president and who is still a friend. Besides being Irish, O'Brien was married to a girl from Boston, though I never knew her there. We threw a torch-light parade down Second Street, but to no avail. Our opponent was Morris

Udall and he beat us. I never again made the mistake of opposing Mo in a political contest. Udall, known around campus as "Big Shorty," was pretty hard to ignore. One year ahead of me in school, he was 6'4" tall, had one glass eye, and was blessed with a marvelous sense of humor as well as powerful persuasive abilities. His older brother, Stewart Udall, was also involved in student government before he graduated from the UA in 1948. Stewart Udall had leadership abilities that matched Mo's, he had that wonderful Udall sense of humor, he was smart, and he was ambitious.

The Udall boys were from a pioneer Mormon family in St. Johns, Arizona. Their father, Levi Stewart Udall, was a justice of the Arizona Supreme Court. Their grandfather, David King Udall, was an Arizona pioneer and a devout Mormon patriarch. He came from a culture that was almost Judaic in its reverence for law and respect for justice. In 1885 he was arrested on trumped-up charges of falsifying a document to prove up a neighbor's homestead claim. He had signed an affidavit at the court in Prescott affirming that Miles P. Romney, a polygamist, had proved up on a homestead claim. He initially said that Romney had not resided continuously on the property. The Court Clerk asked if Romney had abandoned the property. David Udall said that he had not abandoned it, he just had not lived there consistently. The clerk advised Udall that he could, therefore, answer affirmatively to the question of continuous residence. For accepting this advice, Udall was convicted of perjury and sentenced to three years in the Federal House of Corrections in Detroit, Michigan.

His real crime, of course, was a polygamous marriage in a Mormon-hating community. His second wife was Ida Hunt, whom he married in 1882 in a ceremony acquiesced in by his first wife, Eliza Ella Stewart Udall. An Apache County newspaper called for his hanging. It editorialized that other states got rid of the Mormons "by the use of the shotgun and the rope." The paper classified the LDS church (the Church of Jesus Christ of Latter-Day Saints) as a, "desperate disease" and demanded that only "outspoken, true-blue anti-Mormons should hold public office in Apache County." David King Udall subsequently received a full and deserved pardon from President Grover Cleveland, but even this vindication never wholly eradicated the wound of that incident. Mo, who was given his grandfather's middle name (Morris *King* Udall), once told me, "I kid Barry Goldwater because his family helped get bail for the old man. But there was nothing funny about it to David Udall. He worshipped the courts and the Constitution and to be found guilty was worse than anything."

Immediately after his election as student body president, Mo Udall appointed me as his assembly chairman and ordered me to advise the administration that the student body would have a general meeting once a week. I relayed the message to Bob Nugent, the vice president. He smiled and said very graciously that the University was filled to the gunwales: they simply had run out of classrooms and a request such as ours was out of the question. I reported this to Udall and we formed a committee to press the case. A half dozen of us went back to Dr. Nugent's office and Mo was the spokesman. He said the student body needed this weekly hour to conduct its business and to air complaints.

Dr. Nugent replied that the outrageous skits and other questionable entertainments that were planned had little to do with scholarship or student government. Mo argued that the nonsensical skits were the equivalent of comic strips in a newspaper. "We attract the students to the meeting with the silliness," he said, "and then we give them the serious messages." Dr. Nugent declined the request. At that point Mo said, "Can you please tell me the date of the next meeting of the Board of Regents? I would like to have our committee given a place on the agenda. We intend to pursue this matter."

Bob Nugent, vice president and a Rhodes Scholar, was too gentle for this crowd. He got up from his desk and said he was going to talk to the president immediately. He did so and in a few moments came out and announced that at 11:40 on Thursday mornings the auditorium would be available to the student body for such activities as it deemed appropriate. Appropriate activities were defined rather loosely in this setting. Over the next year there were political speeches, musical performances, and skits by various organizations on campus. I was Mo's assembly chairman and provided the fun and nonsense at the start of the hour. Then Mo came along and preached the word, usually insurrection.

These skits were known to stretch the limits of public decency and Dean George Herrick was appointed babysitter. Herrick and his wife lived in one of the dormitories and they were very popular with the students. Fraternities, sororities, and residence halls were all given the chance to present a skit at the assembly. Most western schools had a wide playboy streak, and Arizona's reputation for steely-eyed academics was non-existent. The Sigma Chi House was prominent and, predictably, had a great skit. Dean Herrick ordered me to review the first performance and to advise him whether decency standards were being bruised.

The auditorium (now Centennial Hall) was full for the much anticipated Sigma Chi skit. The program began when every light in the hall was switched off. Then someone shouted, "The British are coming, the British are coming!" The lights came on and thirty or forty young men with little to do jumped in the spotlight wearing red jackets and tri-cornered hats. All were equipped with female lingerie which they used to sling tennis balls indiscriminately about the auditorium. Havoc ensued.

The following day I was summoned to Professor Herrick's office and examined on my stewardship as the unofficial censor. I offered to let Herrick assume the responsibility of passing on the suitability of future skits. He declined. The skits continued. My personal favorite consisted of short musical acts with an ersatz woman claiming to be Margaret Truman who sang *Patrick McGinty's Goat*. The high point of this affair was bellowed contempt at me as Master of Ceremonies. Our shill in the audience addressed me by name and shouted that he was going to give me the bird. I challenged him to do so and he promptly opened a burlap sack out of which six pigeons flew in a great state of bird-like chaos.

Dale Chambers, now long gone, shouted from the wings that he would cure our society of these malicious birds. He owned an old muzzle-loading rifle which he loaded specially for the occasion. He ran toward the front of the stage vowing death to all pigeons and discharged his weapon. The gun had been loaded with hundreds of little shreds of Kleenex tissue which ignited in the firing. A tongue of fire ten feet long blasted out over the heads of the audience. Forces of the administration came forward to shut down the event and my fondest lingering memory is of the pigeon who landed in front of the stage, then walked over to the open exit door and strolled outside. A bird with great restraint.

To make ends meet, I had a wide variety of part-time student jobs while at the UA, and juggling them was sometimes a challenge. I was the so-called student manager of what is now Centennial Hall. To me it will always be "the auditorium." My job on performance nights was to get over to the hall very early, check out matters and then assign the various ushers to their stations. The student staff at the auditorium were all women from Pima Hall whose employment was an act of affirmative action. I got $5.00 for making out the payroll.

I also worked occasionally at the ticket office at Bear Down Gym. Once in a great while there was a basketball game the same night as an event at the auditorium. That taxed my imagination but I soon solved it. It was the habit of all ten-to-twelve-year-old boys in the neighborhood to ride their bikes to Bear Down Gym to see the basketball game. There was a place set aside where they laid their bikes down. Nothing was locked or chained and the bikes were quite safe until the game was over and the owners emerged from the gym and cycled away.

I worked out my time schedule and then picked through the bikes in the dirt patch in front of Bear Down Gym. Every forty minutes I took the lent bike and rode at high speed down the mall and around Old Main to the auditorium. After checking to insure that all was flowing smoothly there, I jumped back on the bike and raced back to the gym. I returned the bike to its original spot and jogged to the basketball ticket window where I would sell tickets for another fifteen minutes before repeating the process. It was the kind of job that kept your cardiovascular system functioning well.

The receipts from these events were delivered to Mr. Hubert De Wolfe at the cashier's window in the Administration Building. On Monday mornings I had to bring the deposit and endure a grilling from De Wolfe who was fussy beyond words. He demanded that all the paper money be faced the same direction and that it be unwrinkled. Otherwise he would not accept or count it. He also required a tape from an old hand-operated adding machine, accounting for the total amount deposited. This gave us the opportunity for sweet revenge.

One quiet afternoon we rolled the tape way ahead and entered one cent. We then rolled the tape back and ran the normal column of figures. It produced a total that was one cent off due to that one spurious penny. When quizzed by De Wolfe, I denied knowledge. He insisted that I leave the deposit with him so that he could work on it to determine how we had messed it up. After a sleepless night he called me the next day and said, "That machine of yours is on the blink. You better get it repaired right away."

We also sold football tickets at the Student Union building. Members of the faculty received a small discount and most were quite agreeable, but we had unpleasant experiences with one professor from the College of Engineering. Before every home game he showed up and demanded two tickets on the fifty-yard line in his heavy Russian accent. We would show him our plat which clearly marked seats sold and seats still available, showing nothing remaining on the fifty-yard line. He would invariably make a fuss and threaten to take it up with the administration. We decided some redress was appropriate.

In those days faculty members parked right outside the entrance of the building where they worked. The offending professor habitually parked in his reserved space about thirty feet from the southeast corner of the Engineering Building. Dickie Houston from Buildings and Grounds had welded together some old used pipe, cemented these make-shift parking bumpers in the ground at the faculty parking lot, and painted the name of the designated professor on each. We simply went out with a chain and chained the front bumper of the professor's car to the steel parking posts. We made sure there was not an inch of space between the bumper and the posts. We retreated to our office in the Student Union Building, which had an excellent view through some wooden blinds and awaited our moment.

The 2:40 class concluded and the professor came out as always at a high lope, never looking around and never speaking to anyone. He climbed into the car, turned on the engine, put it in reverse and stalled it. He did that again. He did it a third time with his engine revved up so high that the rear wheels spun in the dirt. After two or three minutes of rubber tires chewing at caliche, someone from Buildings and Grounds came by and freed the car. In later years Stub Ashcraft told me that Bumps Tribolet almost lost his job as Student Union Graduate Manager over this little incident. Apparently he was strongly reprimanded by Richard Harvill, whose many talents did not include a sense of humor. Tribolet walked around campus hunkered down for about a week.

In the spring of 1947 the A Club had its annual picnic. The A Club consisted strictly of athletes who had lettered in a varsity sport and were not women. The parties were generally held on Saturdays somewhere in the desert east of town and in 1947 we were at Sabino Canyon. At one point in the festivities our maximum leader, Morris "Big Shorty" Udall, announced that he had composed a special poem for the occasion. We had industrial strength chaperoning from Dean Carlson who had very clear ideas about what was and wasn't appropriate. Several of us were a little uneasy about having Dean Carlson hear a Udall literary effort, and the poem justified our concerns. Udall began, "When the day is sultry, that's the time to commit adultery." He didn't get any further than that before being silenced by Dean Carlson.

The fraternities and sororities were housed in large, graceful two and three story homes that surrounded the University. Since evaporative cooling was a new phenomenon and refrigerated air conditioning wouldn't be common for a decade, most of them had screened sleeping porches for sweltering summer nights. The University benefited from the additional housing provided by fraternities and sororities when the student glut arrived. It had always been the Greeks versus the barbarians on American campuses, but even this distinction was blurred by the tidal wave of vets who hit after World War II.

I was not a full-time participant in the fraternity lifestyle. I was just a hasher who didn't even live in the fraternity house because it was too costly. By this time I was rooming with Harry Bagnall on the second floor of a house at Third Street and Tyndall which was owned by Mrs. Hattie Solomon. Readers may remember it as the later location of Franklin's Men's store. I did, however, become good friends with most of my Phi Delta Theta brothers, some of whom I have known ever since. I was good buddies with a tennis player by the name of Herb Benham. Doug Ward was another friend from Phi Delta Theta. Bob Buchanan was a fraternity brother who went on to serve as a Pima County Superior Court judge for fifteen or twenty years. Paul La Prade was a rake and another fraternity brother. His father was one of three justices of the Arizona Supreme Court after many years on the Superior Court bench. Raiding women's dormitories for lingerie had suddenly become a national pastime sanctioned by large numbers of campus rule-breakers across the country. It was a regular phenomenon and we were not above it. On one particular weekend Paul La Prade announced that he would lead us on a raid of Cochise Hall.

Cochise was a big structure and one not easily surmounted. Paul led the charge up the fire escape stairs to a window which he worked on for some time. All the coeds inside the dorm were visibly excited, shouting encouragement to the raiders and cheering them on. Ultimately, our friend Paul succeeded and half a dozen men found themselves in the main corridor on the second floor. The panic was delicious. So was the response of the Forces of the Administration. The trespassers, however, ran far more swiftly, in many different directions, and left the campus officers scratching their heads. But the rules triumphed. Paul had left his watch at the window during the opening effort. The watch was engraved with his name. Trial and punishment soon followed.

The debating team was a more serious campus activity in which I participated along with guys like Ollie Niebel, Hank Kiker, Clint Fowler, and Marvin Cohen. We went to New Orleans and participated in a national debating competition at Tulane University known as the Glendy Burke. Students from the southeastern schools were over-represented at this event, and they were excellent speakers. Southerners really do come to this public speaking business with something special going for them. The topic was, "This House Pities Its Grandchildren," which required the affirmer to appraise the future and list the reasons why our grandchildren's life would be bleak. The opposing side would elucidate all the social and technological improvements that would make tomorrow so much better.

I took the affirmative position and wound up my speech by saying, "If you do not believe we should pity our grandchildren, and mine in particular, then you should know that I am black." We didn't win the debate, but my speech appeared in the annual review that was published that year. Our faculty adviser, Dr. Arthur Cable, was so uneasy about my remark and so straight-laced that he placed a clarification in the review. There is an asterisk next to my remark and down at the bottom of the page it says, "purely demonstrative, this speaker is not black." Despite the egalitarian influence of the GI Bill, there were precious few minority students at the University of Arizona. Arizona's culture and politics had a distinctly Southern flavor in those days. Many elementary and high schools in Arizona were segregated and, although things were beginning to change, the University of Arizona reflected those same attitudes.

Dr. Cable was an old-fashioned professor, but I learned a great deal about public speaking from him. I entered a contest sponsored by Earlham College which debated the general subject of peace. You had to write a speech on how peace could best be achieved, and then deliver it to judges. Dr. Cable had me come to his office every afternoon for a month to practice my speech. He would coach and criticize me, and my delivery improved tremendously. I think I won $25 and was quite pleased about that.

I was also involved in student government which was led first by Stewart and then by Mo Udall. They were real activists and were constantly pushing the limits. Mo had exposed a cushy deal made during the war which resulted in the bookstore manager receiving a higher annual wage than the president of the University. In 1948 with Mo Udall as student body president we found several issues to contest with the University administration. We fought for and got the right to help choose the performing artists who were booked at the University. But we expended real passion on our proposal to send student recruiting teams to high schools across Arizona. We were primarily motivated in this by the ancient rivalry between the University of Arizona and the upstart little rival school in Tempe. Intelligence had reached us that Arizona State Teachers College, the humble institution that would eventually grow to become Arizona State University, was aggressively recruiting top-notch athletes and scholars in a clear effort to challenge our primacy in the state and our sacred Wildcat honor.

We had to lean on Dr. Nugent again, but we eventually won the right to send recruiting teams all over the southern part of the state. We even got the recruiters excused from their classes in order to do it. We tried to send students from a particular town to recruit in that town's high school. I think we had three or four teams of four people each, two men and two women. Each team was assigned some southern Arizona towns to visit and we hit the road. In the high schools we made presentations extolling the many advantages of a University of Arizona education to anyone who would listen. The school principal would announce over the public address system that "the touring group from the University of Arizona would be in room 101 at 11:00 a.m. Anyone who wants to listen to their presentation may attend."

The recruiters were outgoing, made friends easily, and some of them were only a couple of years older than the high school seniors they were talking to. Our goal was to make sure that all of these kids would attend the University of Arizona. The rural Arizona towns we visited (Clifton, Morenci, Safford, Bisbee, Globe, and Miami) were mostly mining centers and this was my first exposure to the copper camps. When metal prices were good, they boomed. Three shifts of miners earning good wages meant lots of money flowing through the community. Conversely, tough times for the copper mining industry meant unemployment and general decline in these little towns.

In addition to the Mexican and American population, successive waves of immigrants from Cornwall, Wales, Ireland, Poland, Italy, Serbia, and a variety of smaller eastern European nations mined Arizona copper and made their homes in the copper camps. Until 1946 the Mexican miners had been paid under a separate, lower wage structure and were denied access to high-skilled jobs. In 1946, my first year in Arizona, the International Union of Mine, Mill, and Smelter Workers (I.U.M.M.S.W.) had gone on a long and bitter strike against Phelps Dodge that resulted in the elimination of the dual pay structure and equal employment rights for Mexicans in the Arizona copper mines. The I.U.M.M.S.W. was a very liberal union and very powerful in the copper camps.

In about 1948 Jack Bryant decided that a student literary publication was needed. He persuaded the student council to sponsor a quarterly magazine devoted to serious works of fiction and poetry by students. It was called the *Lit* and we were quite proud of it. It only survived as long as Bryant and I were there to publish it, and I still have a few issues. I also worked on the campus humor magazine which was called the *Kitty Cat*. Lots of other students were involved in student publications and one immediately attracted my attention: a stunning coed named Jacqueline Boevers. Jacquie had arrived at the University of Arizona in the fall of 1947. I think I first noticed her at the beginning of 1948 and we dated until we were married in September of 1950. She was a member of the Pi Beta Phi sorority, was academically ambitious, bright (she was valedictorian of her high school class), and extremely attractive. I knew then, and know even better now, that she is the best thing that ever happened to me.

As a girl, Jacquie had lived in the farming center of Duncan which is on the Gila River east of Safford and very near the New Mexico line. Her father, Kenneth, was the County Agricultural Extension Agent. He

In the 1950s, Jacquie always wore a hat and gloves to teas and bridge parties in Bisbee. The social scene had many "dress-up" events. She saved the prettier hats for many years, thinking the fashion would return.

was a bright guy with a college degree and knowledge beyond farming. In addition to his responsibilities for Greenlee County he was a pecan farmer, rancher, and a founding director of the Mojave Rural Electric Co-op. In the 1930s he bought a ranch on the Big Sandy River near Wikieup. Wikieup, as you all know, is a wide spot in the road in the middle of nowhere between Wickenburg and Kingman. For a while, Kenneth tried to run the new ranch by commuting across the state from the family home in Duncan, but he only succeeded in wearing himself out.

Mojave County is extremely rough, dry, and is no promised land for cattle. Kenneth made it work by growing hay along the river which he cut and fed to the cattle in the winter. He also raised pecans as a cash crop. All this required a great deal of work so it was decided that the family would move from their satisfactory home in Duncan to a remote and primitive ranch headquarters miles from anywhere in Mojave County. There were no high schools nearby, needless to say, so Jacquie boarded with a family in Kingman, sixty miles from home, to finish high school. It wasn't until the 1960s that Kenneth, who was very frugal, was persuaded by his wife, Sylvia, to build a proper home. Reluctantly, he borrowed the money necessary and hired local laborers to build the house that still stands about a quarter of a mile from the Wikieup post office.

While Jacquie and I were dating I drove up to the ranch many times to visit. I had a pre-war Ford coupe and the road from Wickenburg to Kingman was dirt. There were four streams to be crossed which actually carried water, although they don't now. One of the highest bridges in the state is over Burro Creek north of Wickenburg. You'd wind down the switchbacks to the bottom of the canyons, cross the bridge, and climb back up out the other side. It took hours. Despite Kenneth's hard work, the water he needed to make his cattle operation profitable always evaded him. One year he spent $17,000 drilling water wells that all came up dry. On one visit I helped develop a little seep into a well using shovels and picks.

Jacquie had all the best traits of the western culture she grew up in. She had a wonderful sense of humor and she truly never met a stranger. But neither of us wanted to spend the rest of our lives on a ranch. By the end of 1948 I had realized that a career in business was not what I wanted either. I had settled on a different path, so I transferred out of the College of Business.

CHAPTER FOUR

Learning the Law
in Arizona

BY 1948 I KNEW THAT the College of Law was where I wanted to be. To enter the LL.B. program all I needed was eighty hours of credit with an anemic C average. It was not necessary to complete an undergraduate degree first, so at the end of 1948 I transferred to the College of Law and entered the LL.B. degree program. The old LL.B., or Bachelor of Laws degree, dates from before the days when lawyers were first required to have college degrees in order to practice. It was dropped from the degree offerings of the University of Arizona soon after my entry, and I was one of the last to take this route.

To be an attorney today one must finish a four-year degree, then enter law school to earn a J.D. degree, a Doctor of Law. We old-timers with LL.B. degrees were grandfathered in when the J.D. became the new standard. I am told that I can mail my LL.B. degree to the University of Arizona along with a check for $25 and they will award me a Doctor of Law degree. But I don't believe in retrofitting people. And, one of my current ambitions is to live so long that I am the last living lawyer in Arizona with an LL.B. degree. (There is, however, a fellow named Thomas Chandler who intends to contest that honor with me very vigorously.)

The Dean of the Law School in my time was John D. Lyons from New York. He had been a Superior Court judge and was the image of a noble patrician. Exceptionally fair and gentle, he was a thoughtful man and an outstanding teacher. I feel competent to make those judgments because Boston Latin School had some of the finest teachers on the East Coast. Chester H. Smith may have been the best educator in the Law School. He had a passion for teaching and wanted you to learn. He also gave the bar review every year. Every warm body in the law school was in deadly fear of Prof. Claude H. Brown. He had a very slow, dry delivery and used the Socratic method, so if you did not tremble walking into his classroom you were a candidate for *rigor mortis*. Arthur Henderson, who was a partner in a law firm I was later a member of, taught corporate law. He was remembered there as one of the most brilliant people who went through a firm loaded with legal talent.

There weren't any African-American students in the law school and hardly any Hispanics. Women were also lacking, the notable exception being my classmate Mary Anne Reiman. She later became Mary Anne Richey and also became a Federal District Court judge. She was a bit older than I and had flown planes as a ferry pilot for the Air Force. It was a civilian job but it entailed more risk than many veterans ever faced. She was the only woman in the Law School at that time, and she bore this with grace and good spirits.

I had continued my grassroots involvement in the Democratic Party since arriving in Arizona and was getting more serious about it by 1948. I was painting signs and going to the committee meetings. Sidney Osborn, ("When I am in the house of labor, I am in the house of friends.") was governor, and I supported candidates like Richard Harless and Carl Muecke, who is now a federal judge. I backed incumbent Democrats like Ernest McFarland and Carl Hayden, who was first elected to the U. S. House of Representatives at the dawn of statehood in 1912 and had represented Arizona in the Senate since 1927. In 1948 I made a wager with Jack Lauver on the outcome of the presidential race between Truman and Dewey. The loser had to give the winner a ride around Old Main in a wheelbarrow. When Truman surprised everybody and beat his slick Republican opponent, I demanded payment. Lauver rolled me about half-way around the circle before proclaiming the debt paid. There were too many people watching for him to complete the circuit.

I was also on the periphery of an organization called the American Veterans Committee which was a very liberal group involved in veterans' affairs and politics. George Miller, longtime mayor of Tucson, was big in the AVC, as was Harry Bagnall, and both Stew and Mo Udall. The motto of the organization was "Citizens first, veterans second." It was often in opposition to conservative veterans' organizations like the VFW and the American Legion. The group didn't last long as its members moved into careers in law and education, but it helped to introduce a new breed of Democrats to Arizona. These "Young Turks" were college educated (thanks to the emancipating GI Bill) and they were liberal: they were not cut from the old "Confederate Democrat" cloth.

When I arrived in Arizona virtually everybody was a Democrat, although most were of the conservative, Southern variety like Carl Hayden. Democrats outnumbered Republicans by an eight-to-one margin in 1940. In 1945 an Indiana legislator wrote a letter addressed to "The Republican leader of the Arizona State Senate," which was the cause of great mirth when received at the Capitol building. The senators had the secretary of their body return the letter with the question, "What is a Republican?" In Washington, Arizona's senators and congressman (we only had one) usually lined up with the Southern Democrats. Hayden himself was not a bigot, but like most Arizonans, he was comfortable with folks knowing their place and staying in it.

Many of the people who settled Arizona, particularly the ranching and farming folk, had their roots in Dixie. Arizona had an especially large contingent of Texans who had moved here and set up ranches after the Civil War. They were forced to leave Texas by the hard economic conditions during reconstruction, and they were not favorable to the party of Abraham Lincoln. The Southern slant can be seen in the way that Arizona formed its government, organized its labor force, and managed its society. The legislature gave towns the option of setting up segregated schools in 1919. Phoenix had segregated elementary and secondary schools until after World War II. Tucson segregated elementary students but all races attended high school together at Tucson High. The African-American graduates, however, marched at the end of the graduation procession.

Prior to World War II, if you wanted to run for office in Arizona you registered as a Democrat. The unions, which were very powerful in the copper camps, constituted the liberal side of the Democratic Party. They maintained an uneasy partnership with the dominant conservatives who represented the mines, railroads, banks, and large farmers and ranchers. As in Boston, the real contest was within the clan, in the primary where the winner of the Democratic Party contest was the automatic victor in the general election. All that began to change when the first Right-to-Work initiative passed in November 1946.

Right-to-Work was the big issue in Arizona during my college years and it quickly developed into a nasty fight. The movement to outlaw the closed union shop in Arizona was spearheaded by the Veterans Committee for the Right-to-Work which organized in 1945 in Phoenix. Theoretically, it represented veterans who were denied jobs because of union rules. In his book, *Arizona: A History*, Thomas E. Sheridan points out that the Right-to-Work movement fit perfectly into the efforts of Phoenix Republicans to make Arizona more attractive to industry.

To me, Right-to-Work is a euphemism for the right to benefit from union wages and contract negotiations without paying for them. After efforts to pass a Right-to-Work law were stymied in the Democrat-controlled state legislature, it was placed on the ballot by initiative as a constitutional amendment in 1946. Strikes swept the nation that year and the public mood turned against unions. The popular, pro-union governor was Democrat Sidney Osborn and he won reelection handily. But despite his opposition to it, the Right-to-Work initiative passed narrowly. The issue was revisited in the election of 1948 when a referendum measure sought to strengthen Right-to-Work by outlawing jurisdictional strikes and the closed union shop, and by allowing judges to stop strikes with injunctions.

The Veterans Committee for the Right-to-Work included Republican up-and-comers like Barry Goldwater and John Rhodes, and their cause was pushed aggressively by Eugene Pulliam in the pages of the *Arizona Republic*. This was all occurring at the dawn of the cold war, and the *Republic* wasn't shy about printing stories with a heavy anti-union slant. Union supporters were accused of being communist sympathizers by pro–Right-to-Work groups. The anti–Right-to-Work forces, for their part, compared Right-to-Work advocates to Nazis.

The *Arizona Daily Star* in Tucson editorialized that folks who see an industrial future for Arizona should take a look at the great industrial states, none of which had a Right-to-Work law and none of which wanted one. It wasn't pretty, but when Eugene Pulliam and the Republicans won the second round in 1948, "Right-to-Work" became a permanent fixture in Arizona. Union membership and influence began a long decline and, according to Thomas Sheridan, average wages in Arizona eventually trailed the rest of the nation by ten to twenty-five percent. But Arizona did attract new industry and it grew exponentially. At least

Phoenix did, and to a lesser extent Tucson. Thousands of new folks were moving to Arizona and a good number of them were Republicans. Arizona's old conservative Democrats soon demonstrated they had no problem voting for Republican conservatives like Goldwater.

Rhodes and Goldwater both parlayed their anti-union stance into successful candidacies for federal office in the 1952 election. Rhodes was the first Republican Arizona ever elected to Congress. He was a pretty moderate Republican and at one time the labor unions considered backing him. His endorsement of the Right-to-Work law ended that. Goldwater went to the Senate where he was placed on the labor committee and made a national name for himself thundering against the unions.

In 1950 Sen. Joseph McCarthy, Wisconsin's famous demagogue, began purging communists, both real and imagined, while working with the House Committee on Un-American Activities. Hostility toward communists was everywhere. People for whom anti-communism was a faith were ever on the march looking for these wicked people. Efforts were made, even on the University of Arizona campus, to ferret them out. There were maybe a half-dozen very liberal folk on campus who were ardent friends of the Soviet Union. In 1950 we heard that the FBI thought they'd fingered a communist. UA student Alex Rojas, who later became the Secretary of Education for the Philippine Islands, was the target. Rojas was thought to be too friendly with the left wing. He was not arrested, but people kept coming to him and reporting, "Somebody came by and asked me about you." The pursuit of communists in the unions resulted in two Arizona leaders of the I.U.M.M.S.W. being jailed during this period.

I was never part of the ultra-liberal group that included Rojas, but I was pretty sympathetic to their views. Joseph Stalin was clearly one of the most disgraceful dictators and mass murderers that ever lived. But liberals felt that it was a mistake to isolate the Soviet Union. I was and am a political liberal and I always believed that somehow our two warring societies could just cut it out. Russia was once an extraordinary European society: it has produced marvelous composers, painters, writers, and musicians. For the purposes of World War II, Russia became our ally and bore a great burden of suffering and dying. Their military contribution on the eastern front was critical in the war's outcome.

I always found it fairly easy to find my ideological way through a society that preserved all these constitutional rights that we worked so hard to achieve, and still bear complete loyalty to the United States. I thought Joe McCarthy and his committee trampled all over people's civil rights. In their short four years in power they managed to sow discord from one end of this country to the other. By 1954 McCarthy had been censured by Congress and disgraced by his own sweaty antics. Now he is just an ugly postscript to history, but Rojas had a long and honorable career in education.

In the summer of 1950 North Korea invaded the South and the Korean War commenced. I felt that I had not contributed very much to World War II and that I'd make up for it by joining a so-called Ready Reserve army unit based in Tucson. There were a couple of hundred of us in the 413th Reconnaissance Battalion, and we were a very congenial bunch. The 413th consisted of lots of faculty, employees, and students from the University including a few bigshots like Dr. Bartley J. Cardon, Dean of the College of Agriculture, who was the unit's ranking officer in Tucson. On a hot Sunday morning at the end of July 1950, we assembled at the depot in downtown Tucson for two weeks of basic training at Camp Cook near Lompoc, California. We were loaded on old Pullman coaches with no air conditioning and set off for Phoenix where the balance of the unit joined us. The overall commander was Burton Barr of later state legislative fame. In my coach were several Tucson guys including Milt Whitley, Ferrell Copeland, Evito DeConcini, Merrill Windsor, and Dean Burch.

When we reached Yuma we were told there would be a thirty-minute delay. As veterans of the Yuma cantaloupe harvest, Burch and I led the charge from the depot down to the old Hotel El Sol, which had a saloon that was known to us. The bar only accommodated about twenty-five standing customers and the sleepy bartender barely spoke English. We almost overwhelmed him, but he did a week's business in the next thirty minutes. The heat was so great, the beer was so cold, and the saloon so comfortable that only upon our arrival at Camp Cook did we discover that we had left two Bisbee soldiers behind in Yuma. The two Bisbee guys showed up in camp the next day to tumultuous applause. Burton Barr had an extraordinary record in World War II, but years later when I was in the Arizona Senate and he was Speaker, I had some fun reminding him that in 1950 he wasn't able to get his unit across the Colorado River intact.

Our train pulled into the huge rail yard in Los Angeles just as night was falling. We ate a forgettable evening meal and sat around on the stuffy, stalled train complaining until Dean Burch reached into his duffel and brought forth a fifth of recognizable American whiskey. There was no question about the propriety of consuming the contents, but the whiskey was as hot as everything else on that sultry July evening. Larry Ollason, another experienced melon tramp, was with us and he spotted some ice cars with the bunker hatches open. "Surely," he opined, "we can have ice for this whiskey."

A volunteer was sought without success. Burch settled the matter by observing that we were a military unit and that there was an established pecking order. He noted that I was the lowest ranking of the eight would-be imbibers and delegated me to retrieve some ice. The old Pacific Fruit Express ice cars were several tracks away, it was dark, and there were trains moving all over the yard. I crossed the rails, trying to ignore the sound of large machines moving through the darkness around me. I found my objective and climbed the ladder up to the top of the reefer where I wrestled two melting blocks of ice out of the bunker. Somehow I juggled them down the ladder and across several live tracks. I had a bad moment when I couldn't find our train, but eventually located it and climbed in with the ice as ordered. Inside the lighted coach it became apparent that I had procured third-rate, brown, bunker ice. It was pretty unappetizing, but Burch made a determination that the alcohol would kill any active microbes. We broke up the ice and toasted good fellows all around.

I didn't have enough time in the army for my GI Bill benefits to last for the entire six years I was at the University of Arizona, so I had to hustle for work more than ever during my last two years. Harry Bagnall had finished law school by then and become City Attorney in Coolidge. In 1950 he talked to Coolidge's mayor, Ben Arnold (who was later the chairman of the Arizona State Senate Appropriations Committee), and Arnold hired me to run a summer recreation program. The City of Coolidge and the Coolidge High School both kicked in $50 a week for my salary, so I made $100.00 per week and spent practically nothing. With that sock, Jacquie and I got married at the end of the summer.

Our wedding was on September 9, 1950, at St. James Catholic Church in Coolidge. It was a mid-morning event and there was a breakfast immediately after the Nuptial Mass. My best man was William Kimble, a law school classmate who would later become a law partner in Bisbee. His wife, Jean, was Jacquie's bridesmaid. I had served in the same role for Bill at the Kimbles' wedding, so there was a certain symmetry to it. Guests included Jacquie's parents and about a dozen friends. We moved into a little stucco house on Third Avenue across from the Tucson High football field. Later we were able to rent a nicer house on East Blacklidge which was on the edge of town in those days. It was a guest house owned by Mrs. MacTavish, who ran the Buildings and Grounds Department at the UA. Housing was still tight, so when she offered to rent it to us we jumped at the opportunity. As this book goes to press, Jacquie and I are fifty-four years married and gaining.

At the beginning of my last year of law school, I was called in for a meeting with Dr. Larson. He was a very righteous (not self-righteous, just righteous) man who was Commissioner of the old Border Conference. He said that since I had participated in a track meet in 1949 against Western New Mexico, I had used up my eligibility to run for Arizona. My GI Bill benefits had run out by this time so I sought a meeting with McKale and track coach Limey Gibbings. They called me in and informed me that they had a scholarship which was not going to be used. "We've never had a freshman track coach," McKale told me, "but you can have the job if you want it." I think Gibbings talked him into it, but regardless of the authorship of the plan, I was relieved and grateful for the opportunity. The job pulled Jacquie and me through my last year at the University of Arizona. If you look at the 1951 *Desert* you will see one James McNulty, with a cap on his head and a whistle around his neck, described as the freshman track coach.

I was still a weekend warrior with the National Guard and we used the old Consolidated Vultee facility near the airport for our in-town training. I was attending one such session on the afternoon of April 29, 1951, when Col. Cardon's voice came crackling over the intercom, "I would like Corporal McNulty to report to the headquarters office immediately." When I entered his office Cardon said, "They just called from the hospital and your attendance is desired." Jacquie was in labor at St. Mary's Hospital and the arrival of our first child was imminent.

Cardon graciously released me from my duty (the day's training would end in twenty minutes anyway) and allowed me to drive to the hospital. He seemed quite pleased with his own magnanimity. Jacquie and our new son, Michael Francis, were both hale and healthy and our little family now numbered three.

In the spring of 1951, with graduation looming and a new little McNulty to think about, I approached McKale a second time for help. "I appreciate the coaching job very much, but no good turn goes unpunished," I told him. "Now I need a lawyer job."

"How would you like to live in Bisbee, Arizona?" McKale replied. "Martin Gentry, the captain of my 1928 football team, is an attorney down there," he explained. "Martin and his brother, Jim, have a nice law practice in Bisbee."

Martin Gentry had remained a close friend of McKale since his football days and was an active Arizona alumnus. "Sure, I'll move to Bisbee," I replied. McKale picked up the telephone and dialed. He got Jim Gentry on the line and wasted no time getting to the heart of the matter. "Do you need any lawyers down there? I've got a good one here." McKale paused to listen to the response. He covered the mouthpiece with his hand and said, "Jim Gentry wants to have lunch with you in two hours at the Copper Queen Hotel in Bisbee. Can you make it?"

I jumped into my old Ford and drove straight to Bisbee. I parked at the Grassy Park right in front of the Copper Queen and climbed two flights of stairs to the third floor of the annex adjoining the hotel where the firm had its offices. Jim Gentry was most congenial and led me to the restaurant of the hotel where we had an excellent lunch. The Copper Queen, built in 1902, has been painted and spruced up over the years but it is still essentially the same today as it was a hundred years ago. The ornate main lobby is on the second floor and guests would be taken up by the help in an old elevator. The stately old mission-revival style hotel was a bastion of Bisbee's ruling class. We had a pleasant conversation and by the end of the meal I had been offered a job to begin as soon as I had passed the Arizona bar exam.

Professor Chester Smith conducted a six-week preparation for the bar exam on the porch in his back yard. We attended two sessions each day six days a week, from 7:00 a.m. to 9:30 a.m. and again from 7:00 to 9:30 p.m. It was pretty intense. The actual bar exam was conducted at the University over two and a half days. It was all essay questions which we answered in long-hand. When it was done I was quite relieved to have finished the ordeal, but had no idea whether I had passed or not. It was anticipated that several weeks would be needed to grade the exams and I was in limbo until the results were announced. As soon as the exams were over, Jacquie took Michael to West Roxbury while I went to Camp Cook to do two weeks of active duty. After that I drove out to Boston and joined the family to await my scores on the test.

September came and went without any word on the outcome. My chances for employment as an attorney in Massachusetts were slim since a law degree from the University of Arizona was not very impressive on the East Coast. Then I got a phone call from Walter Roche, chairman of the Admissions Committee of the Arizona Bar, who said he had been trying to track me down. He informed me that my name had been called in front of the Arizona Supreme Court for admission to the bar. Nobody had showed up and he pointed out that the Court doesn't look favorably on that sort of thing. I protested that I had not received any word that I had even passed the bar exam. "Well take my word for it," he said, "you passed," and I told him, "I'm starting the car now."

So in October 1951, it was back to Tucson. The notice of my results on the bar exam had been sent to the Phi Delta Theta house, which was shut down for the summer, and had sat unopened for weeks. I called Martin Gentry in Bisbee and told him I was ready to go to work if the offer was still good. "Where the hell have you been?" he asked. "We were beginning to wonder if you wanted the job or not." My father sprang for airplane tickets to Arizona for Jacquie and Michael and they both took their first airplane ride to join me. I was paid $300 a month to start and offered rental of an apartment in the old Calumet and Arizona Mining Co. hospital building. (The Calumet and Arizona was bought out by Phelps Dodge in the 1930s.) The Gentrys had bought the building and renovated it into apartments. Our first home in Bisbee had a Murphy bed that pulled down from the wall for use. The place was so small you had to go outside to change your mind.

Bisbee, Arizona, is tucked into a couple of folds of the Mule Mountains in extreme southeastern Arizona, about six miles north of the Mexican border. Since it is located at an elevation of 5,300 feet, it is cooler and wetter than the desert towns of Arizona. The steep and windy streets of Bisbee usually get a light coat of snow a few times each winter. Copper was first discovered there in 1877 by soldiers from nearby Fort Bowie. Originally called Mule Gulch, the town was renamed in 1880 for the attorney of the Copper Queen Mine's owners: DeWitt Bisbee. (Bisbee apparently never visited the town named for him.)

In the early days of Bisbee a prospector would locate a claim and record it, perhaps giving some ownership to the man who had provided him with his grubstake. The ores were rich enough to allow for these small operations and at one time there were at least forty separate mining companies with headquarters in Bisbee. Gradually these disparate mining interests were bought up and consolidated. In 1881 the mercantile firm of Phelps Dodge went into the mining business. On the recommendation of mining engineer Dr. James Douglas, they began buying Arizona copper claims. They acquired the Atlanta Mine in Bisbee in 1882, and merged it with the Copper Queen when both companies tapped into the same rich ore body. Initially at least, other companies had the best claims, but Phelps Dodge had the money that was needed to fully develop them. The Copper Queen Consolidated Mining Co. soon became the second largest copper producer in the world, exceeded only by the Anaconda mines in Butte, Montana.

At the turn of the century Bisbee was a bustling community of 25,000 souls. The Douglas and Dodge families, along with the Brophys, Shattucks, and a few others, constituted the ruling class and royalty of Bisbee. One of Dr. Douglas' sons, also named James but known as "Rawhide Jimmy" Douglas, ran the mines along with his brother Walter. Rawhide Jimmy was a tough, hard-driving guy and there are many anecdotes about him. One of my favorites is of the newspaper reporter from Phoenix who came to do a story on the booming mining community and to sample opinion about the controversial Rawhide Jimmy Douglas. To get the reactions of the man on the street, the newspaperman interviewed men standing in the Phelps Dodge payroll line which, on paydays, used to weave through downtown Bisbee. Every miner expressed a negative opinion of Rawhide Jimmy Douglas except for one who said he was "impartial" on the question. The reporter asked for the reason behind this neutral position and the miner said, "I am impartial on Rawhide Jimmy because I just don't give a damn what happens to the son of a bitch."

In 1951 when we moved to Bisbee Phelps Dodge had just announced that they were going to turn a hill into a hole by developing the Lavender Pit. They were also building a new mill and other facilities so Bisbee was red-hot. The new open pit mine would promote 1,500 jobs in Bisbee, a town of about 10,000 people. The mine was working three shifts seven days a week and the miners' wages washed through the town's economy. Guys were buying fancy hunting rifles, pickups, and boats. The town really bustled, except during deer season when the mines almost shut down and the town emptied out. Bisbee was still a very important town in this state and Cochise County still sent two members to the Arizona State Senate while other rural counties had only one. Bisbee even had a daily Associated Press newspaper, *The Bisbee Daily Review*.

With miners constantly going to or coming from work, Bisbee never seemed to sleep. We had three twenty-four-hour-a-day restaurants, three motion picture houses, and numerous churches. I think we had about ten little league baseball teams. There was even a Class A professional baseball team called the Bisbee/Douglas Copper Kings that competed with teams from Phoenix, Tucson, and El Paso. Phelps Dodge always had a strong Puritan streak in the boardroom, and they helped with the development of schools and churches in Bisbee. The company officials sent their own kids to these schools and they wanted them to get an education equal to any in the state. The Dodge family came to town every winter and initiated the Bisbee social season with cocktail parties and formal dinners. They were Presbyterians and they built a jewel of a church in Bisbee with architects imported from the Netherlands. (We used to joke that the Presbyterian Church was the official state church of Bisbee.) The Catholic Church was almost as impressive with spectacular stained glass windows.

For a mining camp, Bisbee was pretty civilized, and the women of Bisbee deserve much of the credit. Any time help was needed to bring in performing artists, raise funds for a worthy cause, or support culture, the Women's Club got involved. It was a powerful institution in the town and this was never demonstrated more clearly than when the County Supervisors decided they were going to tear down the Women's Club building to make more room at the Courthouse. At the next meeting the Supervisors looked up to see forty women ready to scratch their eyes out filling the hearing room. The Board decided they didn't need the space after all.

The firm of Sutter, Roche, and Gentry had a history in Bisbee that stretched back to territorial days. It was founded by Frederick A. Sutter, who began practicing law in Bisbee in 1903, and it may have been the oldest law firm in the state. In 1912 Arizona became a state and Sutter became the first Cochise County Superior Court judge. Saying the job paid nothing, he quit a year later and reestablished his law practice in downtown Bisbee. Sutter hired Jim Gentry around 1920 and later invited Walter Roche to join the firm. Sutter died in 1941, having practiced law in Bisbee for about forty years. Martin Gentry came back from his stint in the Navy during World War II (he saw action at Guadalcanal) and was practicing law in Willcox before he joined the firm in 1946. Jim Gentry died in 1952, shortly after I was hired. Bill Kimble joined the firm about the same time I did, and it became known as Gentry, McNulty, and Kimble. In 1960 Kimble left the firm when he was appointed to fill a vacancy on the Cochise County Superior Court by Governor Paul Fannin.

There is an old saying that a judge is just a lawyer who knows the governor. The law practice Sutter founded produced an inordinate number of judges and public officials. Like me, Bob Pickrell was hired by Sutter, Rocher, and Gentry upon the urging of J. F. McKale, but he was assigned to the Willcox branch office. His wife, Nancy, didn't like living in Willcox and I filled the vacancy his resignation created. Like Bill Kimble, Pickrell also became a Superior Court judge. Matthew Borowiec was with the firm before he was elected to the Superior Court in Cochise County in 1979. Richard Riley was with us briefly before winning the race for County Attorney. He also went on to serve on the Superior Court.

Phil Toci was hired upon the recommendation of Tom Hall. He moved to Prescott where he was practicing when he was appointed to the appellate court. Bill Sherrill worked with us for two years before moving to Tucson and serving on the Pima County Superior Court until he retired. We hired Steve Desens, to our great satisfaction, and he is now serving on the Cochise County Superior Court where he runs a good ship. Tom Thode was with us for several years and was offered a partnership, but his wife didn't care for Bisbee, so off they went to Yuma. In short order Tom got a new wife and Yuma County got a new Superior Court judge.

Jim and senior law partner Martin Gentry (seated) were joined by Bill Kimble in 1952. Bill had been in law school with Jim and they were best men at each other's weddings.

Cochise County produced many other fine judges and Alfred C. Lockwood may be the best example. He was a self-taught attorney who farmed and taught school before being admitted to the Arizona Bar in 1902. Lockwood was an extremely erudite fellow and a jurist of great probity. He succeeded Fred Sutter on the Cochise County Superior Court bench in 1913. In 1925 he became a justice of Arizona's Supreme Court and was soon one of the most well respected supreme court judges in the country. His daughter, Lorna Lockwood, also became a Supreme Court justice in Phoenix. She was the first woman in Arizona to sit on that court and the first in the nation to become a Supreme Court chief justice.

Judge Lorna Lockwood presided over a few cases at the old courthouse in Tombstone as a visiting judge when I first began the practice of law. An oft repeated story among Cochise County lawyers, which occurred long before I arrived in Bisbee, involved a case which was argued before her by one of the more eccentric legal minds in Bisbee: a scrofulous old bachelor known as Star Williams. Williams lived and had his law office in dilapidated quarters in Brewery Gulch, once the red-light district of Bisbee. His sole companion was a ragged little dog which accompanied him everywhere. Williams promoted himself as the "Star of Brewery Gulch" and, for unexplained reasons, was held in some regard by a few of the Brahmins of Bisbee. Because of his great age, dubious health, and good connections, certain allowances were granted to him in the courtroom. The ratty little dog that was his constant companion was allowed into the courtroom with him and he was not required to stand while making his arguments.

The story goes that Star Williams had a hearing scheduled at the courthouse in Tombstone. He loaded his dirty little dog into his dirty old car and drove there, but when he arrived he had a fit. He was to be subjected to the indignity of arguing before a visiting judge who was a woman: Justice Lorna Lockwood. The hearing began with Williams seated at his table and the dog sprawled on the floor under it. As Williams made his arguments he quoted from three or four law books. He read the pertinent statutes and dropped the books in a pile under the table as he finished with each of them. As he concluded his statement, Justice Lockwood looked up to see the dog in an act of micturition on the stack of law books. I can not attest to this personally, but the story goes that she looked down on the Star of Brewery Gulch very calmly and said, "I see, Mr. Williams, that your dog shares my opinion of your arguments."

Martin Gentry, who would be my law partner until I went to Washington in 1983, didn't have a whole lot going for him in the beginning. He was on his own by the time he was sixteen and attended seven different high schools in Missouri, Oklahoma, Arkansas, and then all over southeast Arizona. His family consisted principally of his adoring older brother, Jim Gentry. Despite his small size, Martin Gentry played football for coach J. F. McKale in the late 1920s and was captain of the 1928 UA team. He was a McKale loyalist for life. He also played high school football in the mining camps of southeastern Arizona. His football exploits were legendary, and they reveal much about him and about life in the towns of southeastern Arizona in those days.

The traditional rivalries between these towns are still expressed annually on the high school football fields. Bisbee versus Douglas was one ancient rivalry, Globe versus Miami and Benson versus Willcox were others. Winning the bragging rights that were at stake in these annual rivalry games was critical to the emotional health of the community. The high school football coach was often the most important man in these towns. He held the power of life or death over the boys on the team: he decided if they played or sat on the bench.

Gentry told me that in the mid-1920s he played for the Tucson High Badgers during a season that saw the Tombstone Yellow Jackets win most of their games. The Yellow Jackets had a senior who weighed well over 200 pounds and had knocked down a lot of people. He was the son of Italian immigrants and we will call him Luigi. Tucson went to Tombstone for the game and coach Jake Meyer had Gentry line up across from Luigi. When the ball was snapped Gentry leaped across the line and knocked Luigi backwards for a loss. On the second play Gentry made a move to his right and then came back to his left and flattened Luigi a second time.

By now the hometown crowd was in a furor. Like so many fields in these little towns, in Tombstone spectators stood within ten feet of the sideline. Gentry knocked the much larger Luigi sprawling for the third time and was standing over him when he felt himself suddenly assaulted from the rear. He fell to the ground amid a hail of blows, and looked up to see Luigi's mother, who outweighed her son, with a parasol that she was employing in an attempt to beat Gentry to death. The woman was pulled off, Luigi did not come out for the second half, and the Tucson High Badgers won the day.

Gentry was renowned as a smashing force on defense or offense. (He was the same in the courtroom.) He came from the pre-helmet days of football. When he was at the UA, Coach McKale tried to make Gentry wear the new protective head gear. Gentry went along, but for one play only, and then tore the helmet off and threw it aside, saying that it annoyed him. McKale said that Gentry looked like a cat with his head stuck in a tuna can as he pawed the old leather helmet off his head. The only way McKale could discipline him was to take him out of the game in an era of mighty little substitution. Gentry didn't want to pay that price.

In 1928, or perhaps 1929, Barry Goldwater enrolled at the University of Arizona and went to advise McKale of his desire to play football. McKale was even then a robust Republican and it was felt he would take good care of the promising young Goldwater. McKale took care of him by putting him across the line from Gentry in his first scrimmage. In later years Goldwater would say that Gentry "simply killed him," and that his rosy ambitions to play Arizona football were knocked right out of him. Goldwater regularly told this story on his campaign swings through Cochise County in later years.

For Martin Gentry the University of Arizona was the family he lost and the child he never had. When he died he left more than a million dollars to the University of Arizona Foundation to be used as scholarship money for deserving athletes. There have been many beneficiaries.

Like everything else in Bisbee, the firm of Gentry and Gentry operated on a miner's schedule. We opened the office at 7:00 a.m. and closed it at 4:00 p.m. Soon after my arrival I was appointed by Judge Frank E. Thomas to represent a young man who had been jailed for livestock theft. He was a soldier at Ft. Huachuca who lived in Tombstone. A friend had told him there were some wild hogs in the hills and asked if he would like to go hunting. My client was agreeable, so they went out and found a hog which they shot, butchered, and placed in my client's refrigerator. The hog, however, had an owner. The Sheriff's office was informed, it investigated, and my client was arrested.

Cochise County is, of course, the real West. Fooling around with another man's livestock is considered very serious stuff indeed. In Texas they say you sentence a murderer to thirty days in jail but a horse thief gets the gas chamber. (This is explained by another well worn Texas saying: "I've known a lot of men who needed killing, but I never knew a horse that needed stealing.") Although in this case the object was a hog, not a horse, the principle was the same. At the trial it seemed like half the cowboys in Cochise County were in the courtroom waiting to see justice done.

The complainant was a tough old bird named John Sala who claimed that my client had shot one of his domestic hogs. His neighbors had told me that Sala's hogs had once been domestic, but he was too frugal to feed them and they had turned into feral hogs which ran wild. I subpoenaed Sala's records from the feed store in Tombstone to verify his purchases of feed in the last year to take care of these hogs. Of course, there were none and the jury acquitted my client. *The Arizona Cattlelog*, the journal of Arizona cattle producers, carried an article about the trial which branded it a terrible miscarriage of justice and named the culprits who had contributed to it. I won my first case but there were a lot of unhappy cowboys in Cochise County.

CHAPTER FIVE

Young Turks and
the Old Guard

BEFORE MARTIN GENTRY'S LEGAL CAREER was interrupted by his service in the South Pacific, he had been instrumental in the formation of the Sulphur Springs Valley Electrical Cooperative. One of my earliest assignments at the Gentry and Gentry law firm was to help close a loan that the U.S. Department of Agriculture was going to make to the cooperative. It was still an organization that existed mostly on paper, but it had enormous appeal in the rural agricultural areas of Cochise County. My involvement with Arizona's rural electrical co-ops would continue for the next thirty years.

It is difficult to understand today how desperate people in rural America were to hook up to electricity. Again, the women played a big part, desirous as they were of the latest labor-saving appliances like washing machines and refrigerators. The sign-up teams for the first electrical cooperatives soon learned to direct their pitch to the farm wife, who frequently signed the papers and paid the five-dollar fee while the husband was still worrying about going into debt to the government. Water had always been the key to agriculture in the West and for the farmer in Arizona; electricity meant he could pump more water. Farmers were the core membership of the Sulphur Springs Valley Electrical Cooperative.

At the beginning of the twentieth century over fifty percent of Americans were farmers. The simple business of growing and processing agricultural commodities consumed the bulk of our talent and energy. Today less than five percent of our population is engaged in the production of food and fiber and we help feed the world with our exports. In 1951 when I came to Bisbee, there were about 5,000 acres of irrigated farmland within the Sulphur Springs Valley Co-op service area. By 1970 that figure had grown to about 130,000 acres. I believe that the bounty and efficiency of our modern agricultural sector is due in no small part to two visionary acts of our government.

The first was the Morrill Act of 1862, when we decided to embrace and support agricultural science by establishing land grant colleges all across the country. One of their first endeavors was the study of the use of water in the West. Application of the scientific farming techniques developed at the land grant colleges was limited by the fact that most of rural America did not have access to electrical power. Farmers still constituted a significant chunk of the population, and they were clamoring for electricity. Congressman Sam Rayburn of Texas and Senator George Norris of Nebraska were two vigorous voices on behalf of the agricultural sector who took up this cause during the depression. Norris had fought for rural electrification for years and, in 1933, authored the legislation that created the Tennessee Valley Authority.

In 1935 Rayburn and Norris successfully pressured newly elected President Franklin Roosevelt to bypass Congress and create the Rural Electrification Administration by executive order. In 1936 they sponsored legislation in Congress which authorized the program. The REA brought rural America into the twentieth century and helped boost agricultural production to the levels we enjoy today. I have been a student of the legislative process for most of my life, and I believe that the creation of the Rural Electrification Administration ranks right up there with the Morrill Act and the GI Bill as examples of profound governmental wisdom. Today more than twenty million Americans buy power from the electrical cooperatives set up under the aegis of the REA.

America's first big national water reclamation project was the construction of Roosevelt Dam which, when completed in 1911, tamed the Salt River and turned the deserts of Central Arizona into green fields of cotton and produce. The development of rural electricity and the construction of large irrigation projects were the twin keys that unlocked the West's agricultural potential. They also made life a lot more civilized and comfortable for country folk. Windmills were replaced with electrical pumps and those smoky old kerosene lamps were retired forever along with washboards and hand-cranked phonographs.

To get the loan for the Co-op we had to do a feasibility study and in those days this was quite an obstacle. But we put it together and received the low-interest funding we needed from the Department of Agriculture. After the war the pace of rural electrification accelerated and was reaching into remote and sparsely populated areas that had not yet been connected. The Sulphur Springs Valley Co-op was the first of seven rural electrical co-ops in Arizona and it consumed a great deal of my time. We ran the most frugal operation imaginable. Initially, we stored all of our equipment and office furniture in an old dry goods store on Maley Street in Willcox. We were right downtown, one block from Willcox's only stop light.

In the beginning our main problem was getting folks hooked up fast enough. The directors received all kinds of pressure to appropriate the money needed to get power to certain farmers. Our general manager was an eternal optimist who tended to promise folks more than we could deliver. Summer thunderstorms wreaked havoc on the system in the early days and service was unreliable. The big investor-owned utilities saw us as a threat and much of my time was spent fighting off lawsuits. Their animosity towards the cooperatives was boundless. I once read a letter from one of the big utilities' lawyers which said, in part, "The writing of this letter by me is not to be construed as an acquiescence that your company exists."

But we finally got organized, became fiscally sound, and built better facilities. Eventually we were turning a profit and since it was a non-profit co-op, participants received a capital credit with their share of the profits at the end of the year. Our success stimulated the formation of electrical co-ops in other areas around the state. My father-in-law, Kenneth Boevers, was instrumental in setting up the Mojave Electrical Co-op in western Arizona. Trico Electrical Cooperative was created to serve the rural folks around Tucson, but it found itself in constant litigation with Tucson Gas and Electric. The folks in Safford decided they wanted their own company, so the Graham Electrical Cooperative was split off from the Sulphur Springs Valley Co-op. Little Greenlee County, not to be outdone, also wanted a separate company so the Duncan Valley Electrical Cooperative was split out of the Graham Co-op.

In those days farmers who were lucky enough to have power used small five or ten horsepower pumps to irrigate their fields. The normal approach was to build a dirt tank near the well with ditches connecting it to the field. As soon as the sun went down the farmer flipped the switch and the little pump began to fill the dirt tank. In the morning when the tank was full the farmer would open the head gate and allow it to flow into the head ditch. The water was lifted out of the ditch and down into the rows by fat siphon hoses. Once a furrow was completely soaked, the irrigator moved his siphon hose to the next row and so the work progressed through the day until all the water in the tank was used. At sunset the pump was turned on again and the process was repeated.

This system may sound primitive when compared to the high-volume pumps and center-pivot sprinkler systems that automatically meter out precise amounts of water today. But it opened up thousands of acres of new farm land in southeastern Arizona. Our operation expanded along with the general growth in irrigated acreage. Initially we bought our power from the big utilities, but they overcharged us and made life difficult in general. The only solution was to build a plant and generate the electricity ourselves. So in 1959 we formed Arizona Electric Power Co-op which was a power generation and transmission co-op. We built a generating plant at the little village of Cochise and all but one of Arizona's rural electrical co-ops joined. All the co-ops I was associated with are still operating. Today the Sulphur Springs Co-op has become part of Touchstone Energy.

Most of the farmers who made up the co-ops were principally interested only in generating the power they needed for their agricultural operations. Expansion was also limited by federal laws pushed through Congress by the big utilities which prevented rural co-ops from serving towns with populations above 2,500 people. Initially the 2-percent federal loans for rural electrification were also available to small municipal utilities. Stonewall, the predecessor of Tucson Power and Gas, once received some of this money. In later years the 2-percent federal loans which financed the rural electrical cooperatives were branded as dirty money, a sort of socialist plot, by the big utilities. Tucson Power was embarrassed by their predecessor's acceptance of this "tainted" money and repaid the loan with contrition. Rural electrical co-ops were restricted from competing with private utilities. Their role was simply to provide power in adequate quantities at fair rates to rural residents on a non-profit, cooperative basis.

While I was busy representing the Sulphur Springs Valley Co-op and other clients, Jacquie was working hard on the domestic front creating a home for our little family. After a few months in the tiny apartment in the old Calumet and Arizona Hospital we began looking for larger accommodations. The old hospital building was on top of a hill, it was winter, and we had ice and cold winds to contend with. It wasn't very comfortable and Jacquie and I both wanted out. War was still raging up and down the Korean Peninsula and the rent control rules were in effect. I put the word out that we were looking for a place to rent.

A Serbian woman named Olga Yuncevich located a house that had been converted into a duplex in a section known as Quality Hill. The Quality Hill development was constructed by Phelps Dodge during the early 1900s as housing for company officers and managers. It was situated in one of the few level, open spots around Bisbee. The house was owned by Pete De Gomez, who was the butcher for Phelps Dodge Mercantile. He lived in one unit and rented the other. It looked pretty good, especially for a family of three who were currently living in a place not much bigger than a walk-in closet. And it had a washing machine and dryer. We both wanted it badly.

I went down to the rent control office to make the deal but the bureaucrats there said the rent exceeded the limit by fifty bucks. We thrashed about over it for a while, and finally, in good lawyer fashion, I advised the rent control people that the amount was justified by the fact that the place had a washing machine and dryer and that I was going to write a letter formally appealing their decision on those grounds. They capitulated and we got the place. It was a wooden house and probably about fifty years old. We had a bedroom, kitchen, and dining room as well as a little yard for Michael to play in.

Less than a year later we bought an old house on the corner of Congdon and Shattuck Streets in Warren, another subdivision built by Phelps Dodge as company housing. This house had two bedrooms and even had an extra room which could be used for guests. Warren had a nice ballpark and was built on the English style with a long mall down the middle. At one time they had two water systems, one potable and one with water pumped out of the mines which was used strictly for irrigation. It gave lawns a bit of an acid fix, but it also made Warren a green oasis shaded by rows of enormous cottonwood trees.

In addition to representing the Co-op, I did a lot of estate work and handled personal liability cases. Many of the clients were ranchers, notwithstanding my defense of the soldier in the hog rustling case. As farming acreage spread, so did litigation over contested water rights. People would sue their neighbors, claiming that the neighbor's well was pulling water from underneath their property. The economy in Cochise County was pretty strong in the early 1950s between the farming and mining. The mines were expanding and the wages they paid were relatively high.

Our clientele at Gentry, McNulty, and Kimble (the firm's name change and my partnership status came around the time of Jim Gentry's passing in 1952) reflected the make-up of the community. In addition to the ranchers and farmers, we worked for a lot of second- and third-generation immigrants. Around the turn of the century Bisbee received a wave of foreign miners from Italy and the north Balkans: Bosnians, Serbs, Croatians, and Montenegrins. They joined the earlier arrivals who were Welsh, Cornish, Irish, and Finnish. The biggest group, of course, was the Mexicans.

Since there was no mail delivery in Bisbee, everybody used to come to the post office in the morning to pick up their mail. The ritual of starting the day by sauntering down to the post office was an essential element of life in Bisbee. People would stop to chat with their friends and catch up on the latest gossip. At the post office little clusters of people were usually scattered around the parking lot and the front porch was crowded. You could see most of the folks in town in about an hour and a half so it was a great place to politic. When the post office announced that it was going to begin delivering mail in central Bisbee the citizenry denounced the idea roundly.

On one particular morning the laughter and gossip in front of the post office was interrupted by Police Chief Clarence Malley. He drove his squad car into the parking lot, screeched to a halt, and yelled for everyone to clear the area. He said George Henshaw was coming down Tombstone Canyon in his car, he had already nearly side-swiped a couple of parked vehicles, and was headed for the post office to pick up his mail. Everyone, including Malley, sprinted around to the back of the building.

Bisbee was very protective of its respected elders. George Henshaw had once been Sheriff of Cochise County. Now in very poor sight, he was a routine problem for Malley and a real hazard for the pedestrians and motorists of Bisbee. People would really jump off the sidewalks when they saw George coming, careening from one side of the road to the other. Efforts had been made to convince him to stop driving, but to no avail. Malley didn't want to cite his old colleague, but he didn't want anyone to be killed either. Parked at the bottom of the hill, he had just watched Henshaw weave down Tombstone Canyon, and Malley feared for the safety of the folks in front of the post office. After this incident Henshaw's car and his license were finally taken out of service and his driving days were over.

In addition to my legal work I rapidly became increasingly involved in the local Democratic Party and local government. The Bisbee City Council appointed me to the part-time job of City Attorney in 1952. Soon I fulfilled the same role for Tombstone and Huachuca City. In addition to prosecuting cases for these towns, I was occasionally called upon to do other miscellaneous official tasks. Once, when the county coroner was unavailable, I was asked to visit a remote ranch where a body had been found to determine the cause of death. The fee for the work was fifty dollars, and I accepted.

I drove out to an isolated ranch headquarters and knocked on the door. It was answered by a leathery old cowboy who invited me in. I asked him where the corpse was and he took me into a back bedroom. In the bed was the body of a young cowboy with a fatal gunshot wound to the head. A large revolver was lying on the floor next to the bed. I quizzed the old fellow who told me he had found the body that morning. "Did he leave a note of any kind?" I asked. "Yes sir." he responded in his Texas drawl, "I reckon he did." He handed over a scrap of paper. It was addressed to a female and said, "I hope you're satisfied now, you dirty bitch. (signed) Slim." Case closed. I drove back into town, filed my report, and collected my fifty bucks for acting as ex-officio coroner.

Our family was also growing in these years. Our second child, Cynthia, was born on September 10, 1953. A certain Dr. Newcomb was the choice of the child-bearing women of Tucson and Jacquie wanted him to deliver the baby. All the arrangements had been made at Tucson Medical Center and when Jacquie announced that the time had arrived, we grabbed Michael, jumped in the car, and roared off to Tucson. The doctors at Tucson Medical Center looked her over and determined that she wouldn't be ready to deliver for another week or so. Somewhat disappointed, we headed back to Bisbee.

It was a pretty interesting drive. By the time we got there, about two hours later, Jacquie was having strong contractions and grumbling about Tucson doctors. We went straight to the Copper Queen Hospital where Cynthia Deirdre McNulty was delivered within two hours of our arrival by Dr. Joseph Saba, Chief Surgeon of the Phelps Dodge company hospital. Cynthia is our only child who was born in Bisbee, and that is only due to the fallibility of medical science.

Another exciting event occurred on a Saturday night in March 1953. Jacquie and I were at a square dance out at Riggs Settlement when a Forest Service Ranger informed me that a suspect wanted for burglarizing several homes in the area had been cornered by citizens in Bonito Canyon. There were no phones at Riggs Settlement so Jacquie and I volunteered to go find a deputy. About five miles north of Elfrida on Highway 666 we came upon Deputy Clyde Shields, who had just captured the husky young suspect with the assistance of a citizen.

Shields was an oldtimer and probably weighed about 140 pounds. He tried to radio for back-up to help him transport back to the jail in Bisbee the prisoner, the prisoner's pregnant sixteen-year-old Indian girlfriend, and his pickup truck piled high with stolen property. But we were in a dead spot where the radio didn't work, so I offered to drive the pickup with the badly frightened girlfriend while Shields transported the handcuffed prisoner in his police cruiser. Jacquie went ahead in our car.

The suspect was an Anglo kid but he exchanged a few words with the girl in an Indian language before we loaded them into the respective vehicles. I went ahead in the pickup with Shields following close behind. The girl began talking, and it was obvious that she was uneasy about something. Shields was apparently nervous too, because he soon passed me in an apparent attempt to speed up the trip. A mile or two further I saw the prisoner lunge across the car and grapple with the old lawman. The cruiser swerved off the road in a cloud of dust that obscured everything.

I got the truck stopped and ran up to the cruiser where I found Shields and his prisoner locked in a bloody struggle in the front seat. Despite the fact that he was handcuffed, the prisoner had managed to pull a big knife out of his sleeve and attack the old deputy with it. They were tangled over the steering wheel in a knot of arms, legs, and handcuffs struggling for control of the knife. "Get him off of me!" Shields screamed, "He's trying to kill me."

Shields had grabbed the blade with his bare hands to fend off the attack. His hands were bleeding badly, but he didn't let go of the blade. I pulled the door open, leaned in and started punching the prisoner in the head as hard as I could. I was half in and half out of the front seat and the suspect was using his boots to try to fend me off. In the midst of the fray I was suddenly aware of the girl standing right behind me screaming. I shouted something at her and she moved back. It was an awkward position for throwing punches, but I hit the prisoner as hard as I could ten or twelve times. Finally, he relented and Shields got control of the knife. He was cut badly on both hands.

Ed Walker, the citizen who helped Shields arrest the young suspect, came up about then. He drove the cruiser into Bisbee while Shields, hands wrapped in bloody rags, held a gun on the prisoner in the back seat. I followed in the pickup with the pregnant girl. When we got to the Cochise County Jail Jacquie was there waiting for us. Searching the suspect's truck we found three loaded hunting rifles, over 1,500 rounds of ammunition, and more knives amongst the swag. That girl could have easily shot us while we were fighting with her boyfriend, but she didn't. She had nowhere else to go, and no money, so the deputies let her sleep in a cell at the Cochise County Jail that night. Her boyfriend was arraigned on a charge of assault with a deadly weapon and bound over to the juvenile court. I had deep bruises on both legs where he had kicked me while I was hitting him, but otherwise was unscathed. So ended a night of square dancing in Cochise County.

In 1954 there was a different kind of fight when I made my first run for elected office. I declared my candidacy for the humble position of Democratic Party Precinct Committeeman in Bisbee. There were about fifty precincts in Cochise County and each could elect a party committeeman, and the larger precincts could elect two. Their primary job was to get out the vote in their precinct on Election Day. Precinct committeemen were often approached for help by candidates who were circulating petitions of candidacy. They were thought to be very savvy in matters political in their little fiefdom. After the primary election the precinct committeemen gathered to form the County Democratic Committee and select a chairman and representatives to the State Executive Committee. This system perpetuated an old-boy type of politics, but it was honest and direct. It was a real grassroots political job and it was filled in the regular election.

I got the usual nomination papers and petitions, performed the required rituals with them, and filed as a candidate. The Confederate heritage still hung on so there was effectively only one party in Cochise County: the Democratic Party. The unions had the votes, but Phelps Dodge would sometimes encourage people sympathetic to them to run for office. Phelps Dodge interests owned the *Bisbee Daily Review*, and they wielded enormous influence in the little company town. Politicians in Cochise County had to walk the tender trail between pro-company and pro-union positions. Some found it best not to be pro-anything. In those days we used the old paper ballots that were as big as a pillowcase. For the general election the ballot had a big square at the top which could be marked to vote a straight ticket.

There were six or eight contested committee elections in Cochise County that year, which was highly unusual. They were contested because we ran a bunch of young, liberal Democrats and Stew Udall was right at the heart of it. I had remained close to both of the Udall brothers and they were beginning to have a big impact statewide within the Democratic Party. In Cochise County we were clearly a challenge to the oldtimers who had long controlled Democratic Party politics. Jim Brophy, scion of a very prominent family in Bisbee and Arizona, had a fit when he found out that I and others like me were trying to get elected to the precinct committee. The Democratic Party in Cochise County had long been dominated by people like him and other members of the old guard such as Austin Jay, the Chevron oil distributor, and Spencer Shattuck, president of the local bank. Brophy said that I was "ruining the Democratic Party." The race for precinct committeeman turned out to be a hot political contest. It really started to get interesting when it was learned that my opponent had not filed his declaration of candidacy by the deadline.

The man went down to the Board of Supervisors' office and talked to the county clerk, a very powerful figure in those days. He handed her the post-dated application, mumbling, "these are a little late, but we've done that before." But she refused to accept it. I don't know if she had been threatened or not, but I do know that the old guard was quite unhappy over her adherence to the letter of the election laws. My opponent was reduced to running as a write-in candidate. We printed up campaign literature, we pounded the streets, we talked to the unions, all for a very minor office. There were maybe two hundred votes cast in my precinct and I got most of them. All of the Young Turks of the Cochise County Democratic Party won their contests and the old guard was appalled.

In that same election of 1954, Stewart Udall made his first run for Congress. I worked hard for him in Cochise County while I was running my own little campaign, and also campaigned with him in Tucson. Arizona's growth in population merited it a second seat in the House of Representatives in 1950 when Congressional District 2 had been established. District 1 was composed of Maricopa County; the other thirteen counties made up the new district. Republican John Rhodes held District 1, but most of the voters in District 2 were still Democrats and the incumbent there was a character by the name of Harold "Porky" Patten. As the 1954 elections approached, Patten was Udall's anticipated opponent in the primary.

"Porky" was a "hale fellow, well met" type and was known to take a drink. He had a distinguished war record, was active in his church, and was one of the good old boys who had come up through the ranks of Arizona's Confederate Democratic Party. Prior to the campaign of 1954 he attended a University of Arizona basketball game in Madison Square Garden where he had made a number of racist remarks about the presence of black players on the opposing team. (Arizona, of course, had none.) The newspapers got hold of it and it was more than most Arizonans could stomach. "Porky" withdrew from the race and Stew ran against Henry Zipf of Cochise County.

A few days before the election the *Bisbee Daily Review* published a story that said Stewart Udall had voted for Henry Wallace and the Progressive Ticket in 1948. Originally a Republican, Wallace switched sides and helped Roosevelt win Iowa in 1932. He was an ardent supporter of the New Deal and served as Roosevelt's Secretary of Agriculture during his first two terms and as vice president during his third term. Appointed Secretary of Commerce by Truman, he was subsequently fired for publicly attacking Truman's policy of containing the Soviet Union. He ran for president in 1948 as a very liberal third-party candidate and was smeared as a socialist or worse. Wallace later recanted his pro-Soviet position and donated millions of dollars to a foundation to build up our agricultural capacity.

The cold war was in full flower and the story was a nasty, last-minute attack on Udall. What made it worse was that there was some truth to it. Stew and I had both signed nominating petitions for Wallace, and the signatures did not lie. Wallace had some interesting ideas and he deserved a place on the ballot.

Stewart Udall won the election with 68,085 votes to Zipf's 41,587. He got a big majority in the mining communities where Right-to-Work was still an issue. Union leaders still hoped to repeal Arizona's Right-to-Work laws and judged candidates by their position on it. The majority of Arizonans, however, (particularly those in Maricopa County) supported Right-to-Work. Advocating the repeal of the Right-to-Work law was poison to candidates for statewide offices. In 1954 the unions in Arizona still had enough political clout to help balance out the growing influence of conservative Republicans. They could still raise money, they fielded their own candidates, and they could turn out a lot of voters in the copper camps. The Mine/Mill union was probably the most powerful. They went out on strike every three years, regular as clockwork, when it was time to negotiate a new contract. They won regular wage increases for their shrinking membership.

Strikes were a normal part of life in the copper camps and Bisbee had a particularly violent and contentious labor history. The best example, of course, is the infamous Bisbee Deportation of 1917 when 1,186 union men were rounded up in the middle of the night at gunpoint. They were forced into cattle cars and taken to Hermanas, New Mexico, where they were released in the middle of the desert without food or water. This, along with similar actions at Jerome, broke the power of the miners' unions in Arizona until World War II.

By the 1950s copper strikes in Bisbee had become ritualized into a game that both sides knew would eventually end with everybody working together again. Phelps Dodge led the way in settling strikes through negotiations at that time, and they were pretty casual about work stoppages and picket lines. The company used to run electrical extension cords to the strikers' shacks on the picket line so they could have hotplates and radios. Bosses would wave at the strikers as they drove past the picket lines and the strikers would wave back. Drinking water was provided for the strikers and there was a certain civility to it. The strikes during the 1950s sometimes lasted for months and occasionally there would be some ugliness, but nothing comparable to the violent strikes of an earlier day. And nothing like the bitter, violent strike which devastated Clifton while I was in the U.S. House of Representatives.

Some of the copper companies grumbled about Phelps Dodge and their penchant for settling strikes peacefully during this period. I remember the attorney for Kennecott saying, "We'd have had this thing (labor trouble) over long ago if Phelps Dodge hadn't caved in at every turn of the road." Union membership, however, continued to decline despite their victories on the picket line and at the negotiating table. According to Thomas Sheridan, by 1958 Arizona had 450,000 workers and only about 33,000 were union members.

Today unions play an almost insignificant role in Arizona elections. They still endorse candidates, as they have often done for me. They work like the devil for their candidates but they just are not big enough players. They simply do not have the votes. Industry took away the unions' reason for existence by learning how to run a business profitably without fighting with their workers. Some of this was forced by laws which protected workers, some of it was forced by the marketplace, but the fact remains that eventually the unions simply became irrelevant in Arizona politics.

The unions, however, still carried a lot of weight in Bisbee and the other copper mining communities in the 1950s. When I first moved to Bisbee the International Union of Mine, Mill, and Smelter Workers still led the labor movement in the copper camps. Soon after that, the United Steelworkers assumed that role. The old Mine/Mill Union was not a bashful bunch. They filed grievances over any perceived violation of their contract which tied up company and union resources. The grievance hearings were held in the Cochise County Courthouse in Bisbee. The firms of Evans-Kitchel and Ellinwood and Ross represented Phelps Dodge, and eventually these battles became too expensive for the unions. Gentry, McNulty, and Kimble did not represent either labor or management.

I ran for precinct committeeman again, and was elected again in 1956. I was also selected for the Cochise County Executive Committee around that time. The county committees each selected their own chairman, and I won that post for Cochise County in 1958. In that year I was also appointed by Gov. Ernest McFarland to a five-year term on the Board of Directors of the Arizona State Hospital. During my term the de-institutionalization of mental patients was the big issue.

Dr. Sam Wick of the hospital medical staff was a real pioneer in this area. He felt strongly that mental hospitals should not be used as storehouses for the mentally ill. Some of the patients were not mentally ill, they were developmentally disabled ("retarded" was the term we used then), and they clearly were not receiving the treatment they needed. It was the dawn of a more progressive, humane approach to treating mental illness, and our board went along with Dr. Wick's recommendations. We implemented programs that put patients to work out in the community and taught them how to live outside the institution.

The number of patients at the State Hospital declined from about 1,800 to between 500 and 600 during my five years on the Board. In 1962, my last year on the Board, Jacquie, the kids, and I spent the Christmas holidays in the guest cottage on the campus of the State Hospital at 24th Street and Van Buren. The kids tried to be upbeat about it, but it certainly wasn't the way they would have chosen to spend the holidays.

The new regime of de-institutionalization also made it easier for people to escape from the hospital. Earlier in 1962 the notorious Arizona murderess Winnie Ruth Judd walked away and the press was able to revive Arizona's biggest murder story one more time. Arizona oldtimers will need no prompting to remember the sensational murders Judd committed in Phoenix in 1931 when she was the attractive twenty-seven-year-old wife of a physician. While he was working in Los Angeles she murdered two of her girlfriends and, with the assistance of her lover, dismembered them and packed them in trunks which she had shipped to her hubby in Los Angeles.

She traveled to Los Angeles on the same train, carrying a valise containing more parts. The odor and the blood dripping from the trunks led to their opening at the depot in Los Angeles and her arrest. The case had sex, booze, and mayhem, so the newspapers had a major story that soon became a national sensation. When she was brought back to Phoenix from California in a convoy of law enforcement vehicles, newspapers reported that 30,000 people lined the streets of Phoenix to catch a glimpse of her.

She was convicted and sentenced to death, but the warden of the State Prison in Florence ordered a psychiatric evaluation. She was judged incompetent and transferred to the Arizona State Hospital where she was a considered a model patient despite the fact that she escaped in 1939 (twice), 1947, 1951, 1952, and 1961. The reason native Arizonans over the age of fifty know her story is because the lurid details of the crime were revisited in the press each time she escaped. I remember her as the manager of the beauty shop in the hospital where patients were trained as beauticians and also got their hair done. She was very satisfied with this role, always dressed well, and advised the Board about the beauty shop and the supplies she needed to run it. In 1962 she used her key to unlock the front door and walk away again. She was gone for six years before being recaptured. Released at Christmas time in 1971, she died in Phoenix in 1998 at the age of ninety-three. Needless to say, we took a lot of heat from the press when she made her last escape in 1962.

Back in the late 1950s Tucson's glittering social season began after Labor Day with the first University of Arizona home football game. People (especially wives and kids) still spent the sweltering summers in the White Mountains or San Diego, and things in Tucson were dormant until fall arrived. The first Arizona home football game was always the occasion for cocktail parties at the homes of the notables in Tucson. It was also a time for the Arizona alumni from Bisbee, Willcox, and Benson to gather at the Panda Steakhouse out on North First Avenue for dinner before attending the game and then driving home. In 1958 Jacquie and I were at one of these cocktail parties where I had a conversation with Stew Udall. Stew asked me, "What do you think of your fellow Irishman, John Kennedy?" Kennedy was already well down the road toward declaring his candidacy, but he was only one of several Democratic contenders including Lyndon Johnson, Stuart Symington, Hubert Humphrey, and Adlai Stevenson. "I think a lot of him, but I don't know if he has a prayer of winning the nomination," I responded.

"Oh, he has a prayer all right," Stew said. "This is how serious they are." He pulled out his wallet, fished a fresh airline credit card from it, and showed it to me. He told me that Joe Kennedy gave him the card with instructions to use it for his traveling expenses during the campaign. "Use this anywhere you can do some good with it," the Kennedy patriarch told him, "no questions asked."

I was very aware of Jack Kennedy and his career. After all, he and I were of the same tribe: the Boston Irish. We were both liberal Democrats and Catholics. That night was the beginning of my work with Stew to help JFK win the Arizona delegation's votes at the Democratic National Convention coming up in 1960. In those days the county committees were very important within the party and my ascension to the chairmanship in Cochise County in 1958 allowed me to play a key role. We began laying the groundwork for our plan to elect a slate of Kennedy delegates to the Democratic National Convention. The county chairmen had almost unlimited power in those days and we worked hard to get them lined up. I headed up the effort in southeastern Arizona.

I have a copy of a letter, a campaign report really, which Stew Udall sent to Jack Kennedy on November 24, 1959. It is a detailed analysis of every Democratic Party County Committee in the state with information on their chairmen and key members. It assesses their degree of support for Kennedy and his opponents. Under the heading of Cochise County it reads: "Chairman is attorney James F. McNulty, Jr., of Bisbee. Jim is a native of Boston and perhaps for reasons of overweening local pride, is already a 100-percent JFK man. Expect to rely on him as the main leader and ramrod of the District #2 delegate group. Strong leader with a winning personality. Will meet you at Tucson or Phoenix." (A campaign trip to Arizona was being planned.) "A key man in our plans. Alternate will probably be the publisher of the Tombstone Epitaph, Clayton Smith, who will follow McNulty's lead."

A year and a half of laying the groundwork for the Arizona Kennedy campaign culminated at the Arizona Democratic Convention held at the Westward Ho Hotel in Phoenix on Saturday, April 30, 1960. Arizona was the only state west of the Mississippi, and perhaps west of the Hudson, where Kennedy had an organization in place and a chance to win the state delegation. Carl Hayden, the ancient patriarch of Arizona Democrats, had endorsed his crony and fellow Southern Democrat, Lyndon Johnson. Hayden was chairman of the Senate Appropriations Committee by this time and one of the three or four most powerful men

in Washington. Sen. Stuart Symington of Missouri was another contender who was backed by Joe Walton, chairman of the state Democratic Party. Walton had invited Symington to speak at a fund-raising
dinner at the hotel the night of the convention.

Joe Walton was a Phoenix attorney and had been a conservative
force in the Democratic Party for years. He played golf regularly with
Eugene Pulliam, publisher of the *Arizona Republic* and *Phoenix Gazette*, and had promised Symington to deliver the Arizona delegation.
The Democratic Party in Arizona was run by consensus agreement of
big hitters like Joe Walton and Francis Byrnes, chairman of the Maricopa
County Committee. They weren't happy about the challenge they faced
in 1960 from the liberal forces led by Congressman Stewart Udall. Charlie
Hardy and Bill Mahoney were two important Maricopa County allies
of Udall and supporters of Jack Kennedy who played important roles in
the outcome.

At the convention the question of the adoption of the unit rule by
the individual county delegations was a critical preliminary issue to be
decided. Approval of the unit rule would mean that the individual county
delegations would be bound to cast all their votes for the candidate with
a majority within the delegation. Another issue was the selection of a
chairman for the Arizona delegation to the national convention in Los
Angeles. Walton thought that as chairman of the State Democratic Party,
he should have this plum. Frank Minarik, chairman of the Pima County
Committee and a Kennedy supporter, also sought the chairmanship.
The exact composition of the Maricopa County delegation was another
disputed matter because their delegate list was two years old and several
folks on it had died or moved and been replaced. The county chairmen
met the night before the convention to thrash out an agreement on how
to proceed the next day. Among other things, we agreed that county
committees would caucus at 9:00 a.m. and the convention would convene at 10:00.

That Saturday morning the *Arizona Republic* ran a Reg Manning
cartoon lampooning Stewart Udall on the front page along with a story
about the fight shaping up between his liberals and Walton's conservatives. The cartoon showed Udall riding a donkey on a trail labeled "to
the chairmanship of the Arizona delegation." Udall's Democratic donkey was being whisked out from under him by a cloud of dust that said,

"Hayden's endorsement of Lyndon Johnson." The accompanying story reads in part:

> There is a deep ideological split in the party. One faction represents Sen. Carl Hayden (D-Ariz.) and his candidate, Sen. Lyndon Johnson of Texas. This faction stands for conservatism and the backing of a candidate familiar at first hand with Arizona's problems.
>
> The OTHER faction represents Rep. Stewart Udall (D-Ariz.) and his candidate, Jack Kennedy of Massachusetts. This is the liberal group.

That's all the *Republic* needed to say to make the Pulliam preference clear, in case the cartoon didn't get the message across.

Joe Walton gaveled the convention to order that morning and indicated he would accept the credential report submitted by the Maricopa County delegation. This triggered loud opposition on the floor as the Maricopa County delegate list was padded and out of date. Ancient antagonisms towards Maricopa County and their way of doing things surfaced, and the convention demanded an accurate list. The convention recessed so Maricopa County could caucus and come up with an accurate delegate list. Maricopa had almost 200 delegates, about half of the total number for the entire state, and subsequent votes were so close that the corrections to the list would be crucial in determining the eventual outcome. The convention was reconvened and Walton announced that he would now appoint various committees to determine the rules. By doing this he was ignoring the agreement we had made the night before when the county chairmen had met. He was proceeding to run the convention as he chose.

I grabbed a microphone and asked for the floor. When I was recognized I made a motion to reject Walton's nominations and to have a committee composed of the fourteen county chairmen set the rules. During discussion it was made clear that Walton's move was in violation of the agreement we had made the night before. It was another example of the old guard in Maricopa County trying to run over the will of the rest of the folks in the state, and it was not appreciated. My motion was approved overwhelmingly and we went back upstairs to set the rules while the Maricopa County delegation caucused yet again, this time to decide on the unit rule.

After vigorous debate and several votes, Byrnes announced that his

Maricopa County delegation had adopted the unit rule by a vote of
ninety-three to ninety-one. Others present came up with a different count
which had the caucus tied. The sixty Kennedy backers voted against the
unit rule and they were joined by another thirty or so who simply wanted
to register a protest against Walton's autocratic leadership. Meanwhile,
the county chairmen thrashed out the rules, the most important being
that the delegates to the national convention would be selected by a
nomination committee with a representative chosen from each county
by vote of that county's delegates. The convention then voted to approve our proposed rules. This meant Byrnes and Walton would not
choose the Maricopa County representative to the nomination committee, the Maricopa County delegates would.

In the critical Maricopa County vote for its delegate to the nomination committee Byrnes expected a victory similar to the one he achieved
on the unit rule. There were many ballots without any majority, but Bill
Mahoney and Harold Scoville hung tough and eventually led the
Kennedy forces to victory in yet another long Maricopa County caucus.
Walton's dictatorial handling of the Maricopa County Committee caught
up with him and several delegates who voted with him on the unit rule
switched and voted for Charlie Hardy for the nomination committee.
Hardy, a Kennedy man and later a federal judge, finally won by about
ninety-five to eighty-seven after what seemed like endless votes without
a majority. John P. Frank wrote an analysis of the event in a report to
Carl Hayden's assistant, Paul Eaton, which said, "His (Walton's) high-
handed tactics had utterly enraged those from the outside counties, men
who are well known to be temperate fellows, but who don't like to be
pushed around. In fact, I am told that the Rules Committee came within
one vote of deposing him as Convention Chairman."

The nomination committee went upstairs to select delegates to the
National Convention and I acted as chairman of that meeting. All of my
rural troops stayed hitched to Kennedy, of course. So with Hardy representing Maricopa, and Minarik with his Kennedy forces from Pima, we
had the majority and picked a pro-Kennedy slate of delegates which
also included a small number of representatives of the other major candidates. We seriously considered excluding Walton from the Arizona
delegation, but in the end it was decided that to deny the chairman of
the State Democratic Party a trip to the national convention would be a

bit much. Minarik then beat Walton soundly in an election for the post of National Committeeman. I was selected as one of two Arizona representatives to the Democratic National Platform Committee.

Senator Symington went ahead with his speech in the Thunderbird Room that night, but it was poorly attended and completely overshadowed by the events of the convention. It was all over by nine that night. I had driven up to Phoenix with Clayton Smith and we drove the 240 miles back to Bisbee that night pumped up naturally from the thrill of the victory. Walton, Byrnes, and the conservatives had been out-maneuvered, out-thought, and out-voted. A bunch of farmers, cowboys, miners, and union members from the rural areas of Arizona pulled off a coup that was truly a shocking and unprecedented event in Arizona politics.

The Sunday *Arizona Republic* which came out the next day led with a story headlined, "Udall Wins Control of Democratic Party." The report begins:

> Representative Stewart Udall yesterday seized control of the Arizona Democratic Party with the help of Joe Kennedy, father of Sen. Jack Kennedy. The Kennedy forces won an estimated 25 of the 34 Arizona delegates to the national convention in Los Angeles in a day-long battle that left bitter, conservative delegates vowing vengeance.

It went on to intimate that Joe Kennedy bought the delegation and said,

> There have been reports of proxies being bought, of delegates being offered bribes.

On the selection of Minarik as National Committeeman it snarled that this "made Pima County the official center of Democratic power in the state." The 47 percent of the state's Democrats who lived in Maricopa were "practically disenfranchised," it fumed. This was an astounding outcome for the old guard of Confederate Democrats who always believed that Maricopa's primacy in the state was the natural order of things established by God himself during the creation. The Arizona Democratic Party had always been run by the consensus of heavy hitters like Walton and Byrnes. Those who disturbed the consensus were regarded with particular hostility.

John F. Kennedy came to Phoenix in 1960 to campaign for delegates to the August nominating convention to be held in Los Angeles. Jim and Jacquie appear with state Democratic chairman Steve Langmede. Jim was the Platform Committee delegate from Arizona to that convention.

Kennedy made his tour through Arizona in May of that year, flying to Flagstaff, Yuma, Tucson, and Phoenix to attend meetings with local Democratic functionaries set up by Stew Udall. The day he flew to Phoenix I was in Chandler attending a meeting of the State Bar Board of Governors at the San Marcos Resort. That afternoon I drove up to Phoenix for a campaign planning meeting at the Westward Ho which included Kennedy, Stew Udall, Bill Mahoney, Harold Scoville, and maybe a few others. It was a small strategy group which discussed the Arizona Kennedy campaign for maybe an hour before Kennedy got on a plane and flew out.

Kennedy was charismatic, physically attractive, and he was smart. He was also a very urbane man with a well developed but dry sense of humor which he used to his advantage. His father, Joe, was a graduate of Boston Latin, but he himself had attended Choate. I could not resist the opportunity to question him on this. I pointed out that I had something in common with his dad, Joe. We were both Latin School boys. I then asked why he didn't attend Boston Latin. He laughed and admitted disarmingly, "Latin School was too tough for me." He took my little jibe with good grace. I also met Jack Kennedy briefly at the Arizona Inn in Tucson later on during that campaign. He was a charming man and his views matched mine.

That summer I went to Los Angeles one week prior to the convention to attend the Platform Committee meetings. I sat through speeches from some of the most famous people in the party including labor leaders like Walter Reuther, who was a great speaker. When the convention began, my Cochise County delegates were all set to go and Stew had the state as a whole in similar condition. I don't think it was ever in doubt that Kennedy was going to win, but there was enough drama, some created and some real, to boost the public's interest in the proceedings.

Some of the excitement came when I confronted Bernie Wynn in public about a story he wrote on the Democratic National Convention for the *Arizona Republic*. Essentially, he said that Arizona delegates, including myself, had cast their votes for Jack Kennedy because of pressure from Stew Udall. My support for Jack Kennedy was visceral, almost genetic, and I would have voted for him regardless of Udall's opinion. It was one more fabrication crafted by the *Arizona Republic* to discredit Kennedy, Udall, me, and all liberal Democrats. I confronted Wynn the next day at a state caucus meeting and told him so. I may have even offered to take stronger actions; at least he claimed in print that I did. I definitely told him in unambiguous terms what I thought of him, his story, and his newspaper, and he left the room immediately. Despite this incident Wynn would write laudatory columns about me later in my political career.

There were the usual shenanigans such as using official delegate tickets multiple times in order to pack the floor with sympathetic bodies. We went through the formalities of nominations and voting, which were exciting enough, but the outcome was foreordained. In the old days it was not uncommon for there to be ten or twenty ballots, truly spontaneous outbursts of enthusiasm from the floor, and unanticipated outcomes. But since World War II Democratic conventions have been managed and the drama is often manufactured. There was no way the prize could be taken away from Kennedy in 1960, although Lyndon Johnson would have done it without a moment's hesitation.

I did see some old friends from Latin School at the convention, including Jackie Farrell and Herbie Shulman, who were there as delegates from Massachusetts. Farrell was from Park Street in West Roxbury, about ten houses away from our house on Oriole Street. For guys from the Irish Catholic neighborhood of West Roxbury, the Kennedy triumph at that convention was a heady experience indeed. I will admit, however, that I never developed the same fondness for Robert Kennedy that I had for his brother Jack. Bobby was Jack's right hand man, totally loyal, and willing to undertake any difficult task for him. He was a bulldog in a fight and extremely tough minded, but I had a lot of second thoughts about the way he went after Jimmy Hoffa and the Teamsters. Hoffa was pretty ruthless, but Bobby Kennedy was equally so in prosecuting him.

Jacquie and I left Los Angeles a few hours before the convention ended, driving east across the desert to Arizona with Stew Udall and his wife, Erma Lee. When we got to Indio we stopped at a bar to watch Jack Kennedy's acceptance speech on television. It was late but we had to work the next day and we drove on to Phoenix, where we dropped off the Udalls at their home. Jacquie got into her car with the kids (she had left it parked at the Udalls' house) and drove up to Wikieup for a visit with the grandparents. I drove on to Bisbee that night because I had to be at work on Monday morning. But there was another reason I was anxious to get home.

In 1959, after about eight years of saving, Jacquie had announced that we had enough money put aside to build a proper, permanent home. We already owned a lot in San Jose which was an area of new homes a few miles southwest of town. San Jose is perched on a bluff overlooking Greenbush Draw, a major tributary of the San Pedro River. While we were in L.A. for the Platform Committee meetings and the convention, our new home had been finished. There was practically no furniture in it yet, but I spent the night there for the first time after driving all night from Los Angeles and the 1960 Democratic National Convention.

The job of getting Kennedy elected wasn't over yet. To get the Democratic vote out in Cochise County we set up a sub-headquarters for every three precincts and put a poll checker in each precinct. On Election Day the poll checker wrote down the names of every voter who voted. Periodically, a runner would come by to pick up the lists and take them to the sub-headquarters. There the names of those who had voted were checked off the roster of registered Democrats. People who had not voted were called to see if they planned to vote later, or needed any help getting to the polls. If they still hadn't voted by 5:30 we called again. My law office in the annex adjoining the Copper Queen Hotel was one of the sub-headquarters, so that is where I was on election night in 1960. From there I could easily move back and forth to the hotel where the victory party invariably was held.

When the results swung in Kennedy's favor and his victory against Nixon appeared likely, I walked across the street to a Bisbee landmark called Wallace's Smoke Shop and bought a little sissy cigar. Not a big politician's cigar, but a little thin one with a wooden mouthpiece. I lit up my celebratory cigar out on the sidewalk and Police Chief Clarence Malley walked up. We were both elated over the election. It was a close one both in the popular vote and in the electoral college, but the Kennedy/Johnson ticket won and this meant that Stew Udall and the Kennedy forces in Arizona won too. Malley was an oldtimer and Irish to the core. "When did you start smoking cigars?" he asked. "I just started," was my reply.

CHAPTER SIX

From Bisbee to Siberia
and Back

WHEN JOHN KENNEDY TOOK OFFICE in January 1961, and Stewart Udall took over at the Interior Department, a vacancy was created in Congressional District 2. Along with a half dozen other Democrats, Mo Udall announced his candidacy for his brother's old job.

By this point I was considering my own political future. The political victories won by Stew Udall and the liberal Young Turks of Arizona's Democratic Party in 1960 enhanced my ability to influence the political process, both inside and outside of Cochise County. Committed to a public life by this time, I was participating in the campaigns of Democratic candidates and watching for my own political opportunity. I believed that I could do some good things in political office and was working to get the opportunity to prove it. At the beginning of 1961, I chaired the Udall for Congress Committee in Cochise County and campaigned with Mo there, in Tucson, and in the hinterlands of Santa Cruz, Graham, and Greenlee Counties.

Mo loved the give and take and the good humor of small-town campaigning. His liberal political philosophy may not have been shared by many rural Arizona folks, but his personal and political styles were the ultimate for campaigning in the boondocks. His repertoire of funny stories was vast and legendary. He kept a catalogue of stories under subheadings of subjects or situations. He carried it around like a concealed but non-harming weapon.

For the candidate who is not going over well, he had the story about the young candidate (actually Udall himself) who addressed the Legion Post in Tombstone. Arriving at the finish of his statement, the candidate looked up and in a semi-pleading voice said, "And so ladies and gentle-

men, those are my positions and if you don't like 'em, I'll change 'em."
For candidates who were attorneys, as he was, he would put the candidate in the same venue facing a sullen, suspicious audience. When the candidate finished his talk, a gnarled old cowboy in the back of the room would jump up and say, "Sonny, I like the things you said just fine. But there is one thing I need to know. You're not one of them damned lawyers are you?" The candidate, who was indeed a lawyer and desperate to find a way out of the trap answered, "Yes sir, I am a lawyer, but I'm a damn poor one."

Since Mo Udall was running in an off-year special election, and because it came on the heels of the political orgy which had culminated in the Kennedy nomination and election of 1960, we had a devil of a time stirring up voter interest. The primary was scheduled for March 8, 1961. The electorate and the party troops had gotten their fill of political wrangling and didn't show much enthusiasm for yet another election. The voters who did turn out for the Democratic primary had six candidates to choose from, which fractured the minority who voted against Mo. Udall received 21,075 votes (58 percent of all votes cast) to win the Democratic primary against contenders including Harold "Porky" Patten, who garnered 10.5 percent, and William Hendrix who came in second with 11.2 percent.

Udall ran against Republican Mac Matheson in the special election which was held on May 2. Matheson was very active in the Mormon Church and it turned into a pretty mean campaign. He disparaged Udall for straying too far from the Mormon fold, and District 2 had a lot of Mormon voters. Mo's liberalism seemed to be his primary heresy. Mo was once asked if he had any obstacles to overcome in his political life. He responded that he was a one-eyed, liberal, Mormon, Democrat from St. John's and if that didn't add up to a handicap there weren't any. Udall won, but only barely. In Cochise County I think he only beat Matheson by a couple of thousand votes, not much of a margin for a Democrat in Cochise County. The final tally for the entire congressional district was 50,560 votes for Udall to Matheson's 48,599. Mo would serve in the Congress for the next thirty years, take a run at the presidency, and leave public life in 1991 as arguably the best known and most admired member of the House of Representatives.

In Washington, Secretary of the Interior Stewart Udall soon became one of Kennedy's most trusted advisors and a leading figure of the New Frontier. Jack Kennedy and his administration believed that they brought a new vision of international relations to the presidency. They wanted to interact as directly as possible with the leadership of the Soviet Union. The State Department viewed this with some skepticism, as it always did with any new administration. The sages at the Department of State felt they had the education, the long experience, and the special expertise to handle the nuances of the contentious relationship with the Soviets. There was a certain tension between these foreign service wonks and the young visionaries of the Kennedy administration.

Jack Kennedy assumed the presidency during one of the worst flare-ups of the Cold War. The Soviets beat us in the race to put a man in space in April 1960, when they launched Yuri Gagarin into orbit. An American U-2 spy plane was then shot down over Russia in May 1960, and Nikita Khrushchev made his infamous shoe-pounding, finger-wagging tirade at the U.N. in September. Kennedy was inaugurated in January 1961 and invaded Cuba in April. After the debacle of the Bay of Pigs, Kennedy met the Soviet leader in Vienna in June 1961, where they discussed Cuba, Berlin, and other hotspots but failed to reach any agreements.

Russia was, of course, perceived by the public as America's greatest military threat and most dangerous political and technological competitor. Americans were scared to death of the Soviets, and not without reason. We were still reeling from the fact that the Russians had put up the first satellite when they put Gagarin in orbit. We were trying desperately to catch up to their space program. The Korean War was fresh in our collective memory, Berlin was a continuing hotspot, and Vietnam was entering our vocabulary. Our two nations were crouched and circling one another, armed to the teeth with nuclear weapons, and our relations were governed by fear and mistrust.

Stew Udall had an international orientation and he was one of the voices in Kennedy's inner circle who were seeking ways to defuse the tense and dangerous relationship. Finding a way to step back from the brink was not just important, it was a survival issue for the human race. This overarching reality engendered the occasional thawing period between the two nations and conditions were ripe for one in 1962. The Russians began to call for increased "economic coexistence" and an

January in Bisbee can be very cold. Here three generations of McNultys are leaving for Mass at St. Patrick's Catholic Church. Jim's father came from Boston to oversee the construction of our new home in San Jose Estates.

opening of trade. Their primary motivation was to encourage the American side to lift an embargo imposed on trade with the Soviet Union.

All this was very far from little Cochise County, and although I followed it all closely and talked to Stew regularly, I didn't think it affected me any more than any other citizen. I was more concerned with my parents' move from Boston to Bisbee, another event that occurred in 1962. My dad had been retired prematurely from Chapman Valve years before, and it had wounded him greatly. At about the same time, my mother was appointed secretary to the headmaster at Boston Latin and, for many years, my father's primary chore was to drive her back and forth to work. When she retired this made him willing to leave New

Every two years for two decades Jim and his family drove to Boston for a month's vacation. This picture is the last one to include his grandmother, Mary Gallogly, an immigrant from Ireland who was followed by eleven brothers and sisters. Others in the photo at 12 Oriole St. include: James F. McNulty Sr., Jacquie, Nancy (center), Cynthia, Anne, Jim Jr., Florence, and Michael.

England to live out the rest of their lives in a warmer climate with grandchildren around.

As a child my father had worked as a caddie and had a great fondness for the game of golf. Golf, however, was for people who had money, so his golfing was very limited in Boston. Once in Bisbee, he quickly found that he could telephone the Bisbee Golf Course and be on the tee thirty minutes later without putting any strain on his budget. He played three or four, sometimes even five, times a week and the hot weather was no burden to him.

In addition to such family matters, at the dawn of the 1960s I was immersed in a whole host of political and legal projects. There was no way of knowing that my alliance with the Udalls and my involvement with the Sulphur Springs Co-op would soon allow me a firsthand glimpse at our dreaded Cold War opponent. I was busy with my law practice, my incipient political career, my family, and efforts to establish an electrical power generation facility in the little crossroads known as Cochise. Another current political issue that took some of my time was the establishment of a junior college in southeastern Arizona.

California had a very successful junior college program and I was a strong supporter of adopting the idea here in Arizona. We believed that it would increase the educational opportunities available in the rural areas and strengthen Arizona higher education in general. In 1960 the state legislature had passed a law allowing the creation of Junior College Districts in every county and establishing a State Board of Directors for Junior Colleges. The law stipulated that any county wanting a junior college had to pass a bond issue to fund construction and had to provide it with a dormitory. This meant getting a substantial bond issue on the ballot and getting it approved, and that is one of the things I was working on in 1961.

Phelps Dodge was strongly opposed to our efforts and internal political wrangling also made the job challenging. All the little burgs in the county wanted this plum to be located in their area, so settling on a site was tough. Finally, in 1962, Eastern Arizona College became the first school authorized under the new legislation. Eastern Arizona had been around for years as the Gila Academy, originally a Mormon school located in Thatcher. Getting it into the new state junior college system meant we didn't have to build a new school from the ground up. Passing the bond issue was an uphill battle and it all depended on garnering a substantial vote in Bisbee.

By summer of 1962 the Kennedy administration had decided to give the Russians an affirmative reply to their invitation for a delegation of technical experts to visit Russia. Stew Udall was one of the early voices advocating increased contacts with the Russians, but several federal agencies now jockeyed to send the first official visitors to the Soviet Union and to see what this fellow Khrushchev was like. The State Department viewed the whole affair with little enthusiasm, but participated in the internal debate about the purpose and composition of the delegation. In 1961 Stew Udall had arranged for Robert Frost to read his poetry at the White House, and it was his idea that the delegation should include Frost to provide a cultural component to the visit. For the Kennedy folks this gesture fit nicely with the image of the New

Frontier which they wanted to project. It conveyed the confidence, pride, and urbane sophistication that was the essence of Camelot. Frost's inclusion also made the idea more politically palatable.

Stew Udall, trusted ally of Jack Kennedy, was chosen to lead the delegation to Russia. There was a special reason for his selection. During his years in government, Stew Udall and his wife Lee became close friends of Anatoly Dobrynin, the Russian ambassador to the United States. That friendship extended over a period of twenty-five years. The purpose of the delegation would be to inspect some enormous Soviet hydroelectric facilities and learn about their innovative approach to long-distance electrical transmission. Robert Frost would travel separately and perform poetry readings in a few Russian cities. In the early summer of 1962 Stew told me that I would be on the delegation. I went through the process of obtaining a security clearance and was placed on the federal payroll as a temporary consultant so that I could be paid expenses.

There was considerable debate about who should go and what their qualifications should be. In addition to Secretary Udall, his assistant, Orren Beaty, and his undersecretary, James K. Carr, the group included high-power federal officials like Floyd Dominy, commissioner of the Bureau of Reclamation; Joseph Swidler, chairman of the Federal Power Commission; and Gen. R. G. MacDonnel of the Corps of Engineers. There were high officials of the Tennessee Valley Authority and the Bonneville Power Administration. The list included the inevitable State Department people, of course, and a few obscure souls such as Lee White who was an assistant special counsel to President Kennedy, Paul Shaad who was general manager of the Sacramento Municipal Utilities District, and, lastly, James F. McNulty who was described as the attorney for the Sulphur Springs Valley Rural Electrical Co-op in Willcox, Arizona.

I was clearly the youngest and least experienced in the party and somebody raised the issue of what McNulty was doing on this trip. Lee White's presence on the delegation also elicited some curiosity. I believe we were scrutinized by both sides—Russian and American—as to why we were being sent with the delegation. The Cold War was raging. No one doubted that there would be an intelligence aspect to the trip, they only wondered exactly who the spies were. I had enough experience working with the Rural Electrification Administration and setting up local electrical co-ops in Arizona to make me at least superficially acceptable. The real reason I went to Russia in 1962, of course, was that I was a no-holds-barred, at all times and under all circumstances, stalwart loyalist to Stewart Udall. I think he wanted to do something memorable for me, and he may have seen me as someone who would be useful to him on the trip.

I flew to Washington where the delegation was assembling. We were briefed by the Central Intelligence Agency, who had a few minor requests involving some innocent tourist snapshots of a few areas about which they had a strong interest. We were also briefed by the State Department regarding the various areas of contention with the Soviets. Vietnam was just beginning to receive American military advisers, so it was an issue, as were the trade embargo, the arms race, and the Berlin Wall. The State Department people didn't try to dictate how we would respond to questions on these topics and others. They did, however, inform us how they themselves answered these kinds of questions. On the topic of Vietnam, for example, they advised us, "We tell them that we are assisting the Vietnamese at the invitation of their legitimate government." The State Department presentation on American foreign policy was very solid and sensible, and it was not excessively partisan from the Russian viewpoint. I thought that our foreign service was presenting an honest and responsible case without any overt whipping on the dogs. My respect for them went up a notch.

The delegation left on the evening of August 28 and our dinner was cooked in a small galley on the plane as we flew through the night to London. We arrived early on the 29th to a beautiful, brisk English morning and were immediately loaded into cars for a whirlwind sightseeing trip around London arranged by Gordon Chase at the American Embassy. We viewed Trafalgar Square, Buckingham Palace, Westminster Abbey and then forged on to rip by Big Ben and the Houses of Parliament. After four hours of that we were driven back to the airport where we boarded a British European Airlines flight for Moscow. I found English first class service to be inferior to American first class, but this could be the Irish patriot in me speaking.

Moscow was cold under a dark overcast sky when we touched down at the rigorously controlled Scheremetievo Airport. Scheremetievo was strictly for flights from non-communist nations, and we were greeted in style by Russian officials and what passed for the Moscow press corps. The American Embassy had a bunch of old black Cadillac limousines lined up waiting, and they took us to the ornate but dowdy National Hotel. Most of the folks in our group were accustomed to staying at the best hotels of New York and Washington, so the National Hotel was somewhat of a shock. It was unbelievably archaic, unpainted, and shabby, with unreliable plumbing fixtures from the previous century, surly staff, and a musty smell that must have predated the revolution.

I'm not sure if it was the jet lag or all the spy movies I had watched over the years, but as the elevator operator closed the doors, leaving me on my floor in the sad old edifice, I felt a sudden flood of loneliness and an intense sense of isolation. I was in a land where I did not speak the language, in another century, and in an alien world. I felt acutely the distance between Moscow and Bisbee. I grabbed a badly needed shower using a hose arrangement in the antique bathtub, changed into some fresh duds, and joined some of the other pilgrims downstairs in the restaurant.

Before I left the room I stuck a few small threads across the door, my luggage, and my briefcase to see if anything was tampered with during my absence. I had seen this trick in some film somewhere, and if the Russians did surveil my room this probably demonstrated that I was a pretty amateur sleuth. We were fed a crude but adequate dinner on our first night in Russia, and immediately retired to our rooms for some much needed sleep. All of the threads were in their original positions. I continued to place and check threads throughout the trip and never found any changes in them.

Breakfast was served by an aggressive Slavic woman who suddenly turned polite after I used a few words of Russian acquired from a phrase book I had been studying. During the course of the trip I found ordinary Russian people to be uniformly gracious and hospitable if any friendliness was extended to them. After breakfast we had another State Department briefing at the American Embassy. Among other things they reviewed the paranoiac Soviet policies regarding photography, telling us we should always ask permission before taking any pictures. Then we were driven to the Ministry of Power Station Construction for their briefing on the trip. Pictures of Lenin were everywhere and of Marx somewhat less

The delegation to the Soviet Union in 1962 was led by Stewart Udall, John Kennedy's Secretary of the Interior. The schedule was arranged by Anatoly Dobrynin, the ambassador to the United States. Also included was a visit by poet Robert Frost to Khrushchev's home on the Black Sea.

frequently. Life here began with the Bolshevik Revolution and Lenin is father and prophet. Literally millions of signs, posters, billboards, plaques, medals, and paintings made Lenin's presence an influence felt daily. Stalin had been discredited by this time and his likeness was absent. With these stern visages looking down, we sat through a lecture from Ignaty Novakov of the Ministry of Power Station Construction, which

Stewart Udall, Jim McNulty, Robert Frost, and Jim's sister Nancy at a reception in 1962.

was our initial introduction to the autocratic nature of the Soviet bureaucracy.

The friendly ambiance that normally characterizes these international get-acquainted sessions was completely absent. My impression was that these Russian functionaries were keenly aware of their power and were accustomed to behaving as superiors. In his message to us, Novakov was humorless and unconcerned with trivialities like good manners. This autocratic, dictatorial tendency, which seemed common among the Russian leadership, may have been as much a Russian characteristic as a communist one. I think this is the same way that the Czars behaved for centuries.

Novakov's presentation was followed by a color movie with English narration showing the progress achieved by the Soviets in the area of power generation and transmission. The great hydroelectric plants at Bratsk, Irkutsk, and Kuibyshev were shown in all their immensity, and they were impressive indeed. The biggest of them were built on a massive scale that dwarfed any similar developments in the United States. The narration was unflattering to the United States and it freely predicted that Russia would produce more power than America by 1975.

We were constantly challenged during the trip by this kind of aggressive comparison, this boastful and hostile competitiveness that the Russians engaged in. At the same time, the Russians were very anxious that we should praise the technology and culture that they were showing off to us. The Russians may have feared us, but they also measured themselves by us, and disliked themselves for doing so. They rarely heard a positive word about us and they were regularly fed reasons to believe that we were the root of the world's problems. Yet they bent over backwards to impress us throughout the trip and blatantly solicited our praise of their accomplishments. It seemed to me that the Russians knew that America represented the gold standard in national achievement. If they were going to take what they considered to be their rightful place among the great powers, they had to meet or exceed America's accomplishments. They were constantly striving to do this in various fields and power generation was one area, like space exploration and weapons development, where they had made some real technological advances.

This effort to impress our delegation was exemplified by the official Soviet banquets for us that were scattered throughout the trip. The first of many followed the meeting at the Ministry of Power Station Construction and was held at the Prague, one of the best restaurants in Moscow. It consisted of caviar, mineral water, red and white wine, brandy, and the ever-present vodka all wound around a moderately tasty breast of chicken. The ice cream that followed was excellent, but then the toasting began. Toasting in Russia is obligatory and it is vodka. It is considered very bad form not to down the small shot after each little speech, but I soon found that such forbearance was absolutely necessary. At first I would simply raise the glass to my lips without drinking, but that caused the Russians to stare at me suspiciously. So I just put the glass down and left it there and said I didn't drink alcohol. They looked at me like I had lost my mind.

After lunch we were given a tour of the Kremlin which included a walk through the sacred precinct of Lenin's private quarters in the Hall of the Supreme Soviet. This was a holy place to the Soviets, and visitors were required to remove their shoes as a sign of respect. It was roughly equivalent in size to an American two-bedroom rental apartment and was furnished with very humble furniture including Lenin's desk, which the Russians treated with great reverence.

We walked through the Church of the Assumption and the Kremlin's Armory Museum. We saw amazing art and architecture, finely made armor and weapons, opulent and ornate carriages, Fabergé porcelain eggs, thrones, royal vestments, and the like. It appeared that every handsome relic of Czarist luxury had been saved, preserved, and restored to its ancient luster in appropriately impressive surroundings. Czars' boots and suits, Czarinas' gowns and jewels and coaches, and the Orthodox Church's chapels, bell towers, icons, and mitres: all were magnificently restored and displayed at enormous cost. The condition of these treasures was as good or better than when the Czars ruled Russia in a climate of pre-Revolutionary conspicuous consumption. The message conveyed during the tour by the Russians was, "We are a civilized people and were so long before you were around. Nobody has anything superior to Russian culture and art."

We were driven back to the National to prepare for our flight that night to Irkutsk. Before we left for the Vnukovo airport, I went out on the street to sample Russian attitudes and was quickly surrounded by a mob of ordinary Russians. I had brought lots of photos of Bisbee, our house, and Jacquie and the kids, and began showing them around to great interest. I gave nickels to two boys in the crowd, along with a short spiel on Thomas Jefferson and the Declaration of Independence which they did not understand. I then observed a man in the crowd take them aside and bawl them out.

Scolding, like singing and toasting, is a given in Russian society. It may even be that the Russians scold for entertainment. No one, Russian or foreigner, is immune from scolding and no scolder lacks a scoldee. In communist Russia improved worker performance and efficiency could not be stimulated with monetary incentives, so instead they hectored laziness, discourtesy, or non-performance with scolding. It is done vigorously and loudly. If the scoldee is a foreigner he may not even know the reason, which might be something like stepping off the curb or wearing a hat in the courtyard of the Hermitage Museum. No matter that the lesson is obscure, the scoldee knows he is being rebuked, as does everyone else within earshot.

On our way to the airport we drove past endless rows of highrise apartment buildings that housed hundreds of thousands of workers. But it was all shoddy and depressing. Maybe their space program furnished something that lightened the bleakness and dreariness that seemed so ubiquitous. Americans were highly anxious about Soviet competition, but I soon formed the opinion that as few as the categories are where the Russians have real superiority, we should not be so jealous of them.

Irkutsk is in far Siberia, 3,000 miles from Moscow. We took off on an Aeroflot TU-104 and were fed a very good meal of tenderloin and rice before an unscheduled landing at Omsk around midnight. The airport at Irkutsk was socked in by fog, so we were taken to an old-fashioned government guest house, given rooms, and told to sleep. The ubiquitous official guest houses were mostly quite comfortable, although they were often very old. Most of them had once been the dachas and estates of the Russian nobility which were confiscated by the state after the revolution. About ten minutes after I got into my room there was a knock at the door telling me to get up and prepare to get back on the plane. The fog had lifted in Irkutsk and we didn't even have time to clean up, let alone sleep. We arrived on Friday, August 31, and were received by the Minister of the Oblast (province) of Irkutsk. We were served a breakfast that included wine, vodka, and more rounds of toasting. This was a bit strenuous, as most of us had slept not a wink.

We were driven to a guest house through dusty streets teeming with children who were out registering for their first day of school. All the girls wore lacy middies and the boys all had those big, flat Russian caps. We had time to wash up at the stately old guest house where we were lodged before heading out for a three-hour tour of the Irkutsk Dam. There, among other odd sights, we saw crews of women painting and doing heavy repairs on the generators. Women in Russia were doing all sorts of work that Americans found shocking in 1962. They were plasterers, bus drivers, welders, and railroad workers. Some had jobs which appeared to be make-work, such as the old women who swept the streets with bundles of twigs, but everyone had a job and the streets were clean.

In terms of Russian hydroelectric facilities the Irkutsk station was medium sized. It was situated on the Angara River forty-four miles downstream of the sole outflow of Lake Baikal. In America it would rank as the seventh largest hydroelectric generating plant in terms of capacity. It was capable of producing 700,000 kilowatts of electricity. Compare this to the Sulphur Springs Valley Electrical Cooperative, which was the largest electrical co-op in Arizona at the time, with an annual average peak of 30,000 kilowatts. The power generation facility we were building at Cochise, which would feed four rural electrical co-ops in Arizona, was to have a capacity of 85,000 kilowatts.

The Irkutsk station was big, but some of the workmanship we saw was surprisingly poor. The main building was seven years old but already showing signs of age. The dam itself was full of stairways, no two stairs of which were the same length, width, height, or slope and all the conduit containing the wiring was simply nailed to the walls.

We were again treated with very special hospitality and fed lavishly. The meals in Russia began with buttered bread, cold cuts, cold fish, caviar, vodka, and mineral water. All this before the main course. Breakfast the next morning was boiled potatoes, soft-boiled eggs, cold fish, pancakes, preserves, coffee, milk, cold lamb (good) and beefsteak with onions (very good). The negative aspect to all this VIP treatment was that we didn't have much contact with ordinary Russians.

On Saturday, September 1, after this enormous breakfast which, thankfully, did not include vodka, we were flown to Bratsk for a look at the largest hydroelectric plant in the world from the standpoint of installed capacity. This facility was not quite completed but we saw installed six turbine units each with a capacity of 225,000 kilowatts. Twenty such units were planned which, when operational, would have an ultimate capacity of 4.5 million kilowatts. The Grand Coulee Dam on the Columbia River, America's biggest hydroelectric facility, has an installed capacity of 1.9 million kilowatts.

That night we were fed another belt-stretching dinner. By the time we finished it was nearly midnight but I felt restless so I took a long walk through Irkutsk with one of our Russian escorts, Denis Poliakoff. The streets were full of young people coming home from dances and parties. There were lots of well-behaved teenage girls strolling unescorted and equal numbers of boys in their school uniforms. Irkutsk is on the edge of Asia just north of Mongolia and I saw many people in the street with Asian features. The conduct of the young people was very orderly, especially when compared to American teens. The Russians had a policy of suppressing what they referred to as "hooliganism" and this is a partial explanation for the orderliness we saw. Drinking too much or simply being rude was considered hooliganism and was routinely punished with jail time. The Russian constabulary were ever-present and ever-vigilant for hooligans.

During our stroll I had a long ideological talk with Poliakoff, who was obviously with the delegation in the capacity of a spy. He was a very bright and able spy, however, and I learned much of Russian attitudes about America from him. He told me he had been a party member since 1942 and had traveled to America twice. In the journal I kept during the trip I recorded some of the comments he made during this conversation. Among other things, he said that Americans "fear God," and that our "factories are idle." I couldn't disagree when he said that he found New York to be "a dirty, nasty city." In those days it was. He went on to say that while in New York, "five detectives followed us all the time." He confidently predicted that "Russia will outstrip the U.S. in my lifetime."

The next day, September 2, we were driven by car to the picturesque Lake Baikal for some recreation and sightseeing. With us were many Russian officials including the Minister of the Irkutsk Oblast, whom we began to call "the Governor," which was soon shortened to "the Gov." Fishing was the activity listed on the itinerary as our entertainment, and fish we did. But we also organized some purely American activities including games of baseball and football. In my luggage I had brought a football in addition to a baseball, a bat, and a baseball glove for this very purpose. We divided up and formed mixed teams of Russians and Americans for a game of football. I held the ball for the kick-off. A burly Russian soccer player was our kicker, but he missed the ball and kicked me in the hand. After the game we were treated to a four-hour dinner which consisted of caviar, cheese, smoked fish, two varieties of cold pork, currants, steak with fried potatoes, and a wide variety of adult beverages.

Then the toasting began. There were seventeen toasts given and mine was a recitation of the inscription on the Statue of Liberty followed by an announcement that I was withdrawing my candidacy for the office of governor of Irkutsk. The whole affair had a hilarious finale with much singing, an area where the Russians were clearly superior. I coaxed the Americans to contribute by singing *God Bless America*. The Secretary of the Interior and the chairmen of the Federal Power Commission and the Bonneville Power Administration and fourteen other pathetic, American, male singing voices stumbled through the longest two and a half minutes of the decade and then mercifully ended the ill-fated gesture.

The "Gov," a great bear of a man, then led the Soviets in a wildly enthusiastic Russian song. He apparently decided that we ought to have Lake Baikal as a backdrop to the performance, so as he sang he went to a large picture window. With a grandiose, operatic gesture, he pulled back the curtain so forcefully that he tore down one end of the rod fixtures. Wholly unmoved by the blunder, and singing in full voice the whole while, he then moved to the other side of the window where he tore down the other curtain, rod fixtures and all, revealing a beautiful view of Lake Baikal.

We were taken back to Irkutsk where we exchanged gifts with our hosts and prepared for our midnight flight to Kuibyshev. I had brought a variety of gifts including coins, American cigarettes and whiskey, maps and photos of Arizona and Cochise County, and some polished sections of minerals. These were mostly malachite and cuprite with little silver plaques which said, "From the Copper Queen Mine, Bisbee Arizona." I had a large supply of these remaining at this point and was receiving as least as many gifts as I gave.

The flight to Kuibyshev was another long one across maybe eight or ten time zones, so we had to stop for refueling at Novosibirsk which was about midway. There I got out of the plane to stretch my legs. I took a short walk around the tarmac with a few Russians including a fellow named Boris Markovnikov who worked in the Russian entertainment industry. We sang as we walked and I discovered that Boris was familiar with Gershwin and knew all the songs from the musical *Oklahoma*. We strolled arm in arm and sang his favorite American song:

This is the Army, Mr. Jones
No private rooms or telephones
You had your breakfast in bed before
but you won't have it there anymore.

After about an hour of musical fellowship, it was announced that Kuibyshev was socked in and we were taken to an Intourist hotel in Novosibirsk where I shared a room with Paul Shaad and a journalist from the *New York Times* who was covering the trip. We got a solid five hours of sleep in a clean room but were awakened at 6:00 a.m. by a loudspeaker in the room which could not be turned off and was screeching something in Russian. We were all unshaven as our luggage remained on the plane, but we had a pleasant breakfast and then swapped lies to kill time while we waited to resume the flight to Kuibyshev. We finally arrived there in the afternoon of September 3 and were back in European Russia. We were taken to the Volga River hydroelectric station named for V. I. Lenin, which is larger than any such facility in America. It has a capacity of 2.3 million kilowatts from 20 turbines of 115,000 kilowatts each.

Unlike the Siberian plants, this one was quite clean and well constructed. They seemed to run a much tighter ship in European Russia compared to Siberia and we also observed a general firming-up in attitude. Guards armed with rifles were on patrol at this station and we were reminded again of the Soviets' prevailing vigilance. A conversation with Denis, who was wounded defending Stalingrad, helped me understand the fearfulness inherent in Russian behavior. The Tartars ran all over the Russians for 250 years. Sweden beat them up pretty well until Peter the Great finally did in King Charles. The Poles and the Turks both had a go at them and Turkey was still feared in Russia. They defeated Bonaparte, sort of, when the French army finally faltered at the frozen gates of Moscow. The Japanese defeated them in 1904. They were then overrun in two World Wars, most brutally in the relatively recent Nazi bloodbath.

There was a vast gap between the worldview of the people of the Soviet Union and those of the United States. The Russians had never known anything but the constant invasion of greedy and warlike forces, while the Americans had never taken territory outside of their hemisphere and were not interested in doing so. They could not understand an adversary which was not poised to invade, and we could not understand an adversary who momentarily expects invasion from a non-invader.

At the Lenin Hydro-Station we learned that the shafts of the turbines and generators are welded together of six-inch steel plate. General MacDonnel told us that this is something we hadn't been able to do in America where such parts were cast, not welded together. Another innovation used by the Russians, and one of the primary things we wanted to see, was a very high voltage power transmission system that used direct current, which allowed them to send the power much longer distances than our alternating-current transmission methods. The Russians had developed rectifiers which changed the electricity back to alternating current at the point of delivery.

The old Soviet Union was richly blessed with rivers: there were seven major river systems in the country with many ideal sites for hydroelectric installations. The nation also covered a vast amount of territory and, consequently, great distances had to be conquered to integrate a truly national power system. Long-distance power transmission by direct current made all this possible. It also allowed them to have a sort of rolling peak in power demand that moved across the enormous land with the sun and allowed them to use most of their capacity most of the time.

The dam on the Volga at Kuibyshev creates the enormous, inland Volga Sea and we were scheduled to travel across it by boat to visit a nuclear power station on a small island in the middle. This is a place where the CIA had suggested that we attempt to take innocent snapshots, and we were all braced for that when, at the last minute, the Russians announced that there had been a change in plans. They told us that the island was a closed area and we were taken instead to yet another guest house on the shores of the lake for a brief stop before returning to the dock at Kuibyshev. We never saw the nuclear facility, let alone took any pictures.

At a banquet that night Commissioner Dominy accepted the drinking challenge of a Russian chief engineer and matched him drink-for-drink. Dominy was a westerner and he liked to drink. He was the type who drank, wiped his nose, and went back and drank some more. But not even he could outlast a Russian in a drinking contest. He did, however, win the respect of at least one Russian. A few of the party didn't appear for breakfast the next morning after the carousing of the previous night, but Dominy did. When the large Russian woman who was the boss of the guest house saw him entering the lobby she gave him a huge embrace and kissed him repeatedly, Russian style, on both cheeks. A crowd gathered around the scene and applauded this display of affection for the hard-drinking Dominy.

Whenever we had the chance we were not reluctant to espouse American democracy and political values. The Russian officials seemed to resent our advocacy of the American political system and discouraged this as well as they could. Stew Udall, however, was adept at making our ideological case at social affairs and at doing it graciously. Denis Poliakoff told us that the Russian Constitution forbade religious discussion or arguments. In all of huge Moscow, there were only two places holding open church services, and one was a chapel at the American Embassy. It was also a crime to make war propaganda, thus no western newspapers or magazines were allowed with the exception of technical journals, which were consumed voraciously. The Russians were all how and no why. Many spoke English, which they considered the international language, and many English words had crept into their vocabulary.

I had given out coins and photos to some kids on the dock at Kuibyshev, which had ended with me being mobbed and all the photos torn from my hands. They took my last pictures of Jacquie and this left me a bit melancholy. I missed her badly. A couple of days later when we were back in Moscow, I was made the target of some pointed ribbing over the coins I had given out. At the inevitable banquet one of the Russians got up and made some remarks in Russian which elicited lots of laughter from the Soviets. He then presented me with a box of coins and said, "We knew a capitalist would never turn down a gift of bona fide currency." I thanked them as graciously as I could and said that I was very complimented by their gift, but would like to donate the money to the local home for orphans. They told me that they don't have orphan homes because they didn't need them. I asked if that meant there were no orphans in Russia and this touched off a socioeconomic debate that was good-natured enough, but which had a keen edge to it. Apparently the Russians disapproved of my choice of gifts.

We had been in Russia over a week by this point and the trip really had been grueling. We had finished our tour of immense hydroelectric stations at Volgograd, which was known as Stalingrad during World War II. It had been almost completely destroyed in what may have been the pivotal battle of the war on the eastern front. Subsequently the city was rebuilt, so it appeared relatively modern. The night we were there I was given a telegram which had been sent to me by Dr. George Spikes back in Arizona.

George was one of the community leaders I was working with to pass the bond issue that would create Eastern Arizona Junior College. They needed a candidate for the Arizona Junior College Board of Directors who could win the post and bring along a lot of Bisbee votes for the bond issue. I was amazed Spikes had been able to contact me along the Volga, but I groaned when I read the telegram. The Junior College Board was not the ideal platform for launching a career in public office, and an announcement of candidacy from the Soviet Union wouldn't be looked on favorably in Arizona, so I declined.

When we got back to the National Hotel in Moscow, Stew Udall received word that he was to be flown to Sochi on the Black Sea for a meeting with Nikita Khrushchev. He was accompanied only by Curtis Kamman, our State Department interpreter, who went along to translate. Stew had held up quite well on the arduous trip so far, but many of the others in the delegation were exhausted, as was their supply of clean clothing. I was considered somewhat of an oddball because I had been doing my own laundry by hand in the bathroom wherever we were put up for the night. The hotel in Moscow was the first place we stayed that offered laundry service. I just continued doing my own washing, however, and was subjected to some pretty stern disapproval from the hotel maids because of this strange behavior.

On September 5 and 6 we toured some power facilities in the Moscow area, laid a wreath at a memorial to Russian soldiers, went to a cocktail party packed with whiskey-fueled diplomats, and attended an opera at the Bolshoi. I went to a bookstore where the intensity of the propaganda effort was staggering, and enjoyed an unaccompanied early morning walk around Moscow. We also got a chance to experience Russian shopping.

The retail trade in Moscow was hopelessly inefficient, with dreary merchandise and little service or selection. To buy something people stood in lines to get a ticket showing the item and the price. Then they took the ticket to the cashier where they stood in another line to pay for the article. They next went back to the original line and stood in it again to pick up their purchase. There were lines to buy cabbages, longer ones for underwear, and ridiculous ones to buy meat. There were even lines of people waiting for buses. Muscovites seemed to carry their string shopping bags with them at all times, always prepared for unexpected opportunities to buy scarce goods. The merchandise had no color to it, prices were high to outrageous, and great crowds packed every store.

No one in the Soviet Union was supposed to profit from the labor of anyone else. In practical terms this translated into an incredibly inefficient retail system. Wages had no relation to service so the clerks were indifferent and the lines endless. There were limited amounts of goods to sell, and there was no hurry to sell it. There were much better stores reserved for foreigners which the natives frequently attempted to infiltrate, resulting in their unceremonious ejection. Using any currency other than rubles was a major transaction. The Russian clerk would look suspiciously at U.S. currency, then call up "the most recent quote" on the exchange rate. It would run about seventy kopecks to the dollar. Meanwhile, on the street, squads of money changers offered two, three, or even four rubles for an American dollar bill. The government warned that the harshest kind of punishment would be administered against such economic crimes. We were scared but the money traders weren't.

September 7 was our last full day in Moscow. Stew Udall and Curtis had returned from Sochi and the meeting with Khrushchev. He told me he had dinner with Khrushchev as well as his ministers Mikoyan and Novakov the previous evening. After the meal he had been challenged by Novakov to a cognac consumption contest. Udall was no innocent, but the Mormon from St. Johns, Arizona, was clearly out of his league in this competition, and Novakov was the clear "winner." That morning Udall was scheduled to give the first ever international press conference at the American Embassy in Moscow. The State Department people were extremely apprehensive about this event, but Stew had insisted that it be held. He called me up to his room prior to the press conference to help him prepare for the questioning. He was still feeling the effects of his dinner the night before with the alcoholics who governed the Soviet Union.

We reviewed answers to questions he was likely to get as he dressed and tried to fortify himself with some hot soup. We had to find a clean shirt for him at the last minute, but by the time we got to the Embassy he was ready. At the press conference Stew introduced everyone in the delegation, then opened it up for questions. He did a splendid job, partly because the Moscow press corps offered up only softball questions, and not many of them. Later Denis Poliakoff told me that they didn't ask any tough questions, and that the interrogation had been brief because they "wanted to be friendly." I guess it wasn't "friendly" to ask questions of political figures in Russia, especially tough questions.

We had a "dinner" of canapés, hors d'oeuvres, and drinks eaten while standing and shmoozing. It made me eager for the trip to end. Back at the National Hotel after our diplomat-style dinner, we went up to Stew's room and many folks drifted in to say goodbye. We exchanged presents with the Russians who had been with us on the trip. Stew was presented with some beautiful lacquered wooden boxes containing exquisite Georgian wines which were for him and his wife and also for Jack and Jackie Kennedy, gifts from Khrushchev. Stew had also been given a private letter from Khrushchev to Kennedy which he took back to Washington for delivery. After the Russians cleared out of the room, Stew shared some tidbits from his meeting with Khrushchev. Stew Udall had his share of rural Arizona machismo and I think he knew how to react to a shoe-pounding, finger-wagging bully like Khrushchev. In my journal I wrote that Udall said he told Khrushchev to "go ahead and shake your finger."

The next morning I boarded an early Aeroflot flight to London. The trip to the Soviet Union was officially finished and most of the delegation dispersed. I flew to London with a group that consisted of Orren Beaty, General MacDonnel, Joe Swidler, and Lee White. After a four-hour flight (we said goodbye to Russia with two kinds of caviar, three types of fish, chicken, and so on) we were in London on another beautiful, bright English morning. There was some difficulty over my reservation, but once that was solved we boarded a BEA flight for Paris. It only took fifty-five minutes to get there, but that was time enough to feed us another large meal.

After we breezed through customs at Le Bourget, we met Lee White's cousin, Al White, and then drove into Paris with him as our guide. The ride from Le Bourget to the George the Fifth Hotel made a dramatic contrast to our ride through the gray highrise apartment blocks of Moscow on the way to the Scheremetievo Airport several hours earlier. After checking in and washing up we plunged into Paris. We spent an afternoon touring all the usual tourist attractions and then went to a little hole-in-the-wall restaurant which was Al White's favorite. There we had a marvelous gourmet feast highlighted by kidney, sweetbreads, and rabbit that is better than anything we had in the Soviet Union. It definitely felt good to be back on our side of the iron curtain.

From there we were taken to the Folies Bergère where we saw a three-and-a-half-hour show that was definitely an eyebrow-raiser by American standards. After that we walked down to Montmartre through the raunchy sections of Paris. Again, the contrast between the two worlds that were separated by the iron curtain was, to say the least, striking. We paid four bucks each to enter the Folies Pigalle, where nothing was left to the imagination. The next morning we were up early after only five hours of sleep and had breakfast on the sidewalk of the Champs Elysées. After that I went to Mass at Notre Dame. They had a one-hundred-voice male choir and an enormous pipe organ which, in that awesome space, produced truly inspirational results. From there I rushed back to the George the Fifth to pack, check out, and join the remaining gang for the trip to the airport.

We hooked up with Stew Udall and Robert Frost at Orly Airport where we all boarded a Pan Am flight for Idlewild Airport in New York. I had a long and memorable conversation with Frost, who had also been granted an audience with Khrushchev. Robert Frost has a very warm and fuzzy reputation as a poet, but at his core he was a tough-minded, conservative Yankee and a very dubious New Frontiersman. He disagreed with Kennedy on many issues, but he loved being on the center of the stage and Kennedy had focused the spotlight squarely on him. Frost grumbled that he didn't want to be used "to spare the good-for-nothing (Kennedy) from embarrassment." Stew Udall told me that Frost had admonished him in particular and the Kennedy forces in general to "stop buying people."

Like Stew Udall, Frost apparently had to deal with Khrushchev's aggressive, confrontational style. Frost said he told Khrushchev that opening Russia to the outside world would inevitably "humanize" the Soviet regime. Khrushchev argued that it would, instead, "naturalize" the nation, meaning allow it to take its natural leading role in a world evolving towards communism. Frost said that Khrushchev had brought up the subject of our support for the people of West Berlin and made his normal blustering threats. Frost told me that his reply to Khrushchev was simply, "You're not afraid of us and we aren't afraid of you either."

According to Karl Marx, history is an ascending line going inevitably from a slave-owning society to feudalism to capitalism and finally, to communism. In the Soviet Union that I saw, concerns for the poor and the workers, which had inspired socialism, had been twisted into a strictly scientific theory of communism as a natural and necessary stage of development. But, the sun rose every day on an inescapable, living contradiction of all this: America. Did the Soviets, in their darkest moments, suspect that their scientific view of human societies was flawed? That their "first socialistic state" was fragile? That private property still beguiles humankind?

Some of the xenophobia that I saw may be purely a result of political realities. How do you keep a quarter billion folks, the world's largest non-homogeneous society, in one fold? You have citizens who speak over a hundred different languages, use eight different alphabets, and come in every size, shape, color, religion, and culture under the sun. In 1986, after a second trip to the Soviet Union, I wrote this prediction on the outcome of the cold war in a guest editorial for the *Arizona Daily Star*: "How does it all come out? Assuming no maniac's thumb on the nuclear button, we will win—but not in my lifetime—and not without change ourselves." I was wrong about the timing, but correct about the result. I am glad that I lived to see it.

I returned to Bisbee after a sojourn that had lasted, all together, about three weeks. It was certainly wonderful to be back in the arms of Jacquie and the family. One month later, on October 12, my assumption that we would out-compete the Soviets barring any "maniac's thumb on the nuclear button," was brought into question. It was learned that the Soviets had placed nuclear armed missiles in Cuba, ninety miles from our borders. During the next month, the world stood on the brink of nuclear annihilation and any good will resulting from our delegation was quickly forgotten.

CHAPTER SEVEN

Making the Law in Arizona

When I returned from the Soviet Union in mid-September 1962, it was election time once again. I was taking an active role in the campaigns of a variety of Democratic candidates for statewide office and was able to be very helpful to them in Cochise County and southeastern Arizona. In addition to running for reelection as Democratic precinct committeeman from the Don Luis precinct of Bisbee, I was co-chairman of Sam Goddard's Cochise County campaign committee. Goddard was the Democratic candidate for Governor and was running uphill against Paul Fannin, the well-respected Republican incumbent. Mo Udall was running for reelection to his second term in Congress in 1962 and I led his Cochise County campaign committee. Mo won his race with 59 percent of the vote, but Goddard lost, leaving the Republicans firmly in control of the Governorship. I was reelected to the precinct committeeman post and selected as vice chairman of the State Democratic Party Committee.

The daily minutiae of Democratic Party politics in Cochise County required everything from sending out thank-you letters for $10 donations to arranging a fund-raising dinner with Eugene McCarthy as featured speaker and Mo Udall as toastmaster. I worked with Mo on certain issues, such as the selection of postmasters for tiny Cochise County communities, and with Stew Udall on others, like minimizing the infighting within the Arizona Democratic Party Committee. I continued to act as attorney for two electrical cooperatives, and held up my end of the law practice. I was also on the Board of Governors of the Arizona State Bar during these years. Meetings, conferences, and conventions frequently took me to Phoenix.

On November 22, 1963, I was eating lunch in the Copper Queen Hotel when an ashen-faced Clarence Malley walked up to my table and asked me to step out into the lobby for a private word. There, in the formal upstairs lobby, Chief Malley informed me that Jack Kennedy had been shot in Dallas. I went home and, like most of America, watched the ominous developments of the next seventy-two hours on television. Those were some of the saddest days this nation has known, and they were particularly so for the Boston Irish tribe. Stew Udall remained in his post at Interior after Lyndon Johnson was sworn in as president. Johnson would have loved to jettison him, but Udall was too powerful by then and he was reappointed after Johnson won the Presidency on his own in 1964.

Arizona governors served a term of only two years in those days, so Goddard had another go at the governorship in 1964 and once again I headed his campaign in Cochise County. I was also the Cochise County Coordinator for the Renz Jennings for U.S. Senate Committee, and, as usual, led the Cochise County troops for Mo Udall. For a budding politician like myself, campaigning with Mo in the flyspeck communities of southeastern Arizona was always a lesson in the importance of humor and humility. As a native of tiny St. Johns, Arizona, he had a full repertoire of jokes that appealed to the rural audiences. He used to say that St. Johns isn't the end of the world, but you can see the end of the world from there. He frequently observed that St. Johns is the only town in Arizona where the "Welcome to St. Johns" and the "Now Leaving St. Johns" signs are mounted on the same post.

During the summer of 1964 Mo and I were motoring around southeastern Arizona on a campaign swing for his Congressional race. We arrived in Bowie which wasn't much then and is somewhat less now. The central point of community life in Bowie was Skeets' Tavern, which was run by the irascible Skeets Thomas. We went into the dingy bar for the scheduled campaign appearance with ten or fifteen Bowie voters. Before Mo could even get warmed up, Skeets got up and pointed his finger in Udall's face, saying, "When are you going to stop giving away all this money and start taking care of old bastards like me?" Udall had gotten legislation passed in the previous session of Congress which authorized the Post Office to include the illegitimate offspring of postal workers as beneficiaries of their death benefits and pensions. So, without missing a beat Mo said, "Funny you should ask, Skeets. Let me tell you exactly what I did for a lot of old bastards like you this past year."

He then explained the new law regarding death benefits for illegitimate survivors of postal employees.

Mo Udall was one of the first Democratic politicians to denounce the war in Vietnam. It was an enormously unpopular position at the time and put him in opposition to the Democratic president, Lyndon Johnson. He took this position while his brother, Stewart, was Johnson's Secretary of the Interior. Lyndon Johnson was a big man with an imposing physical presence. He had a favorite trick of coming up to a congressman who was wavering in the blocks, putting his great rough hand on the man's shoulder, and pinching the trapezius muscle very hard. He would squeeze until lesser individuals would cringe or even cry out. When he did this to poor little Hubert Humphrey it seemed that he squeezed Hubert right down into his shoes. Johnson thought of this as the process of "reasoning together." But Johnson's physical persuasiveness just didn't work on Mo Udall, who was 6'4" and weighed 220 pounds. Lyndon actually had to reach up to grab Mo's trapezius and he couldn't get the usual leverage. Lyndon Johnson couldn't even out-grin Mo Udall while he was doing the pinching.

I learned a great deal campaigning with Mo Udall. By the time I ran for the Arizona State Senate in 1968 I had a full decade of experience in Arizona politics and was completely familiar with the key people and the process. Campaigning in rural Arizona was back-slapping and making the voters laugh, and it was a great deal of personal contact. For starters, you touched base with every precinct committee person, trying to enlist them to endorse your candidate. There were seven little local newspapers in Cochise and Graham Counties and you talked to all of the publishers. It was counted as superior wisdom for the candidate to "do" the courthouse. That means you shake hands with every warm body in every courthouse in your district. And you had better know the names of each of them. The supervisors and chief officers you know, of course, but don't leave out the Chief Deputy Treasurer and the Deputy Assistant Recorder or any of the secretaries. If you didn't know all the names you took someone with you who did and who could whisper them discreetly in your ear.

In those days all the candidates for statewide office used to tour the hinterlands together, a kind of massed campaign road show that appeared at big rallies in one rural county after another. They would all agree on a schedule and then all went out shaking the electoral tree together. When they were due in Bisbee we would send a car with a loudspeaker on top through town urging everybody to come to the Grassy Park in front of the Copper Queen Hotel on Saturday and "meet your candidates." Aspirants to offices ranging from Mine Inspector (not an insignificant office in Bisbee) to Governor and Senator appeared on the makeshift stage, took turns speaking through an antique P.A. system, and then there was always some kind of modest banquet. Each candidate was trying to say something that caught people's attention or trying to get some local bigshot to say something kind about their candidacy. Newspaper people followed the candidates around and recorded every pearl of timeless wisdom that they uttered.

At these rallies candidates would always yield to questions from the audience at some point. Often, someone who was trying to raise some hell or have a bit of sport with a politician would ask a hostile question. If the crowd was especially lucky some local drunks would work their way in and express their political opinions. The crowd always loved this and the politician who handled it well, like Mo Udall, gained points. At one rally in Bisbee a well known local alcoholic, who viewed a recent crackdown on the illegal importation of mescal and tequila from Naco as a threat to his lifestyle, expressed his outrage to Senator Carl Hayden. "I don't give a damn what your position is on all this other stuff, Senator Hayden," he growled, "I just want to know what your position is on prohibition!"

Renz Jennings lost his Senate race in 1964, but Goddard won, which put the Democrats in the governor's mansion for the first time in over a decade. Barry Goldwater, the conservative phenomenon from Maricopa County, went down to ignominious defeat in his presidential campaign that year, and Mo Udall was, needless to say, reelected to Congress. I was again reelected as a precinct committeeman and continued to serve on the State Democratic Party Committee. In March 1965, Governor Goddard appointed me to complete the last year of what was normally a two-year term on the Arizona State Board of Education. I was reappointed to a full two-year term in January 1966.

The Board of Education had recently been restructured and it now included teachers, other education professionals, and the Superintendent of Public Instruction. In the summer of 1965 I was dispatched to conferences in Portland and Kansas City which discussed something called the Compact For Education. This was an honest attempt by the states to head off federal intervention in local education by solving educational problems at the state level. I reported back to Governor Goddard that Arizona would benefit from participation in the compact and he initiated legislation to join. Membership would cost the state a few thousand dollars and the legislature killed the bill on that basis. The conservatives who dominated the Arizona House and Senate were certainly not lavish in their spending on education. Goddard went ahead and made Arizona a member of the compact by executive order.

Squeezing the funding needed for operating schools out of the Arizona State Legislature was the biggest challenge we faced on the Board of Education. It remains the greatest roadblock to improving Arizona's schools today. We met with members of the education committees of the House and the Senate and lobbied vigorously, but the state school system remained inadequately funded. The old joke that Arizona should thank God for Mississippi because it always saves us from ranking dead last in per-capita spending on public education was told then and is still repeated today.

While I was on the Board of Education we addressed other issues that may sound familiar: dropout prevention, juvenile delinquency and violence, and how to improve reading skills. We had a wave of infatuation with vocational education, which did help to focus our training programs on high-demand occupations. The use of phonics as a technique to teach reading was an issue we heard a great deal about. There were some sensational crimes involving teens at that time, including a murder on the Mt. Lemmon Highway. This generated a lot of discussion about our juvenile justice system and resulted in some fundamental changes. The Gault case established that juveniles charged with a crime have the right to be represented by an attorney. Changes were also made that kept juveniles out of adult jails and provided other protections.

Arizona's State Senate District 2, which included Cochise County, still elected two senators to the Arizona State Senate in those days, a vestige of Bisbee's importance during the boom years of the copper camps in the first half of the twentieth century. Dan Kitchel was the incumbent in one of those slots. Kitchel had been the Cochise County Clerk for years and when he retired he was elected to the Senate. He was a bright, good-natured Norwegian who had come from the Dakotas to work in the mines of southeastern Arizona. He was pretty liberal by the standards of the day and he was definitely no friend of Phelps Dodge. In the summer of 1968 he approached me and said that he was retiring from the Senate and wanted me to succeed him. He was confident that I would not become a puppet for Phelps Dodge and offered his support.

After ten years of work in the party, I was ready. I entered the primary as one of three Democrats running for two Senate candidacies. Kitchel's help was largely behind the scenes since he did not wish to appear to impose a successor on the voters, but he did campaign with me in Santa Cruz County where he was very popular. Democrats have a tendency to destroy each other in the primary, leaving the field to the Republicans. This primary was fairly civilized, however, and there were no Republicans running for either Senate seat. The two winners of the Democratic primary would be unopposed in the general election. The Republicans may have taken control of Maricopa County, but we still had Cochise.

I think my total campaign budget in 1968 was about a thousand dollars. We gratefully accepted many donations of five or ten dollars, and to receive a check for fifty bucks was a major accomplishment. Television was not a factor in a Cochise County campaign in those days, but radio was. I did a few radio interviews in addition to appearing before groups ranging from the VFW to the Bisbee Women's Club. The Farm Bureau was influential so I courted it. The feed-lot operators and ranchers came around to talk to me. The teachers were well organized and gave me valuable support. I had been on the Board of Education for three years, was thoroughly familiar with the needs of Arizona's schools, and favorable to most of the teachers' positions. The unions were still a presence in Cochise County politics and I got the endorsement and support of the United Steel Workers and others.

We also ran a few ads in the little local papers of Willcox, Douglas, Benson, Tombstone, Nogales, and Bisbee. When I ran for reelection two years later I decided that I wasn't going to spend any money at all and the editor of the *Willcox Range News* called me on the phone. "Is it true that you're going to run a campaign and you're not going to spend any money?" he asked. I said yes. He sensed a dangerous trend for the local newspaper industry. "Do you know what you are going to do to me?" he fumed. "The revenue that I get from political advertisements is critical to me. I can't make it without that income." So I amended my decision and announced I would buy a few ads. I had the money, I just didn't think I particularly needed to spend it in that campaign.

In my two state senate campaigns I received donations from many individuals including friends and clients, and a few organizations such as the International Brotherhood of Electrical Workers and the Arizona Education Association. I had a strict rule that we never bought on the come: no invoices went out that weren't already covered in the checking account. This was easy enough in little state senate races, but much more difficult in my later congressional races. It was a pretty wise practice, however, and I stuck with it all the way through my political career. Many campaigns ended up deeply in debt, and even more do today. I am the only politician I know who refunded to my contributors all the campaign money that remained after an election. Money was then, and shall always be, an unavoidable reality of politics. All politicians start out saying they are going to try to keep their campaign spending within rational limits. But in fact you are out taking all the money you can legally take because without it you aren't competitive. By the time I ran for Congress I was spending $600,000 to run my campaign.

I did not have a campaign manager in the conventional sense for either of my two state senate races. My campaign staff consisted of a few smart senior kids at Bisbee High School who wanted to learn about politics. My campaigns were a kind of on-the-job-training program for kids interested in government and elections. I told them that some of the work would be interesting and challenging, and a lot of it would be sheer manual labor, but I promised to show them the election business. My son Michael was among this group, as were local Bisbee kids like Jim Gjurgevich, Arthur Gonzales, and Michael Foudy. They were my campaign managers and staff, and three of the four are practicing attorneys in Tucson today.

There wasn't a terribly profound level of debate in the Cochise County primary election of 1968; it was all pretty superficial. It was partly about one's record of accomplishment for the voters in the past and your plans to benefit them in the future. The basic question, however, was: *are you a good guy?* Indeed, this may be the crucial test of any politician. This is where the candidate's facility with a joke, a humorous story, or a one-liner was critical. Reporters began to note my "Boston Irish wit" and I was even compared to Mo Udall in the category of political humor. They also found my speaking style to be a bit on the intellectual side for an Arizona politician.

In rural areas like Cochise County, a politician could always win a lot of affection by complaining about the big urban areas' stranglehold on power and resources within the state. Decrying the selfishness of Phoenix was given wisdom in the rural areas of Arizona. It still works today. Providing an issue that the rural voter could really get his teeth into, the first "one-man, one-vote" decision had recently come out. In a series of decisions, the courts ruled that districts must be roughly equal in population in everything from congressional districts to the districts of members of the state legislatures. Because of the population explosion in Maricopa and Pima Counties, "one-man, one-vote" threatened to erode further the dwindling political clout of the rural areas, especially Cochise County which still clung to two seats in the State Senate.

In 1968 I ran for one of the two seats in District 2, which consisted of Cochise, Graham, and Santa Cruz Counties. By 1970 a reapportionment law passed by the Republican-dominated legislature put me in the new District 9, which consisted of most of Cochise, portions of Pima, and all of Santa Cruz. That district stretched from the Mexican border between Nogales and Douglas to Green Valley and up to the far west side of Tucson. Bisbee and the Arizona-Sonora Desert Museum were both in the same district. I would regularly fly into Tucson from Phoenix with various legislators including Senate President William Jacquin. I never failed to point out to him the northern boundary of my Senate district out the right window as we began our descent. Redistricting would shape the political terrain I operated on and control my options for the remainder of my political career.

James Elliott and I won the two District 2 Senate candidacies in the Democratic primary and our election was formalized in the general election on November 5, 1968. We entered a legislature dominated by Republicans in both houses. Thanks to a big Republican vote in Maricopa County, they had a seventeen to thirteen margin in the Senate and a thirty-three to twenty-seven majority in the House. The session started at the beginning of January 1969, and I found a small apartment near the Capitol. At various times while the legislature was in session over the next six years I would live in motels, apartments, and once in a small bungalow.

Over half the legislators lived within driving distance of the Capitol. The rural folk, however, would become transients, living out of a suitcase for four days a week and returning home on weekends to do laundry and get a brief glimpse at the family. Some members would stash their clothes and toiletries with friends over the weekends and there were some other pretty scruffy living arrangements. I stayed at the grand old Adams Hotel during one blisteringly hot summer special session, sleeping on the old second-floor screened outdoor sleeping veranda.

The Adams had once been known as the "third house" of the Arizona Legislature. In the early days many of Arizona's laws were hammered out in the smoky male bastions of the lobby, card room, and bar of the Adams Hotel. By the time I entered the legislature the Adams was still the residence of a few legislators, but it was not the power hub that it once was. In the old days when most legislators came from the rural areas they all stayed at the Adams and it was where they conducted their business and where they played.

By my day about half of the legislators were from Maricopa County and did not have to stay in a hotel. Even the guy from Casa Grande could drive home after work each night. One Tucson legislator used to fly home to Tucson every night on Cochise Airlines. So there was a relatively small bunch of us rural guys who tended to hang out together because we couldn't go home at night. Those of us who weren't interested in the social ramble used to go to hockey and basketball games together, have dinner together, and sometimes even sit around the lobby of the Adams Hotel together. For us rural transients, the Adams was still a kind of headquarters. These gatherings included legislators of both parties. It was there that I first met the outstanding governmental skills at the feet of George Cunningham.

Jacquie joined me in Phoenix for social events a few times each session. Sandra Day O'Connor was a member of the Senate and every spring she would throw a party at her house in Phoenix for legislators and spouses. We all gave each other gag gifts and there was a general spirit of non-partisan goodwill at her get-togethers. But serving in the legislature was mostly a lot of hard work, especially if you believed in doing your homework: reading the voluminous information needed to make good decisions on legislation, and doing the routine spadework needed to get good laws passed. It soon became apparent which members were there to work and which ones were not. I prided myself on being one who did his homework. I was a quick study of the legislative process and soon was considered competent in writing legislation. Actually getting legislation passed in the Republican controlled legislature was a more difficult matter and I had limited success there in my first term. But I was able to impact legislation and move some votes.

One example came in March 1969, when the Senate debated a proposed "Stop-and-Frisk" bill. This legislation would allow police to stop and search anyone who appeared suspicious. Coming, as it did, amid the social upheavals that accompanied the civil rights struggles and anti-war protests of that period, it was promoted as a law-and-order bill. Some of us feared that it would be used disproportionately against minority youth. On the floor of the Senate the bill looked like it might pass without objection. I rose and said that I had intended only to run the anchor leg of the race to argue against this dangerous bill, "but since no one else has started the race I will run all four laps rather than not run at all." The story about it in the *Phoenix Gazette* goes on to say,

> With traditional McNulty eloquence, the Bisbee senator asked his colleagues: "Do you really want this bill to become law in this state? Do you really want this to govern the relationship between your-selves—never mind your constituents for the moment—but between yourselves and officers of the law?"
> McNulty insisted that, "we're walking off from some rather severe social implications," and declared, "this law would not improve the quality of police work, but it would decrease the quality of justice."

Senators Kret and Conlan, powerful Republicans from Maricopa County, argued that I should have more confidence in the police and that abuse of the law would be "once in a million cases." Senator Campbell, an African-American senator from Phoenix who the *Gazette* described as "a Negro," said Stop-and-Frisk might really be viewed as "a nigger beware law." Campbell predicted that white police would use the law to stop cars carrying young Mexicans and blacks who did not fit the standards of the policemen.

Some school children who were in the gallery on a visit to the Capitol applauded and cheered Senator Campbell. Senator Holley then objected, saying, "I resent the outburst from the audience and their applause. If they are to come here, then they should restrain themselves." Senator Cardella of Tucson said, "The question of Stop and Frisk goes to the heart of some of the basic freedoms of this country." He added that it is "a sick thought" to believe that anyone who is against the bill is not a good American. The *Gazette* pointed out that no one objected when McNulty loudly applauded this comment. The debate on racial profiling (long before anyone had heard the term) led to a vote in which the bill was defeated by a margin of one and sent back to committee.

I was never reluctant to express my opinions, but I always tried to do it in such a way that my opponents on the other side of the aisle did not end up hating me. To disagree without being disagreeable is a fine skill for a politician who wants to get things done. It allowed me to form effective working relationships with legislators of both parties without compromising my political beliefs. I got along well with Gov. Jack Williams, for example. On a personal level, he could be very charming. I disagreed with many of his positions on issues, however, and usually voted against him.

I resisted the natural temptation to indulge in angry or emotional words when arguing an issue. Politicians often say things in the heat of the moment they think are deathless truths, but in fact are usually just nonsense or tedious restatements of arguments already made. I didn't go to the capital prepared to launch any holy wars. I thought that everyone was entitled to the benefit of the doubt. This approach allowed me to participate in the drafting of laws and to work with colleagues on both sides of the aisle. I was allowed to chair meetings of the Senate Committee of the Whole a few times, an honor that was rarely extended to Democrats by the Republican leader, Senator Jacquin of Tucson.

I often drove to Phoenix for the legislative week, leaving Bisbee at 5:30 a.m. on Monday morning and arriving at the Capitol by 8:30 a.m. Sometimes I flew to Phoenix from Bisbee and my old dad would drive me to the airport and pick me up at the end of the week, just like in the old days in Boston. The legislature went into recess on Thursday afternoon to leave Friday open for the business of the Appropriations Committee. So initially, my week as a legislator would end on Thursday afternoon and I would return to Bisbee that night. This gave me Friday to clear my desk at the law firm and weekends for hand-shaking with the constituents.

Time with the family was squeezed into these busy weekends. When I went on the Appropriations Committee in my third term, their Friday meetings cut my weekends at home down to one day since I still had to generate enough business to hold up my responsibilities to the law firm. The legislative sessions lasted from January until May or June. Each of my six legislative sessions was longer than the one before and set a new record for longest session. Then there were the special sessions called during the summer. Fortunately, I had the support of some splendid law partners in Martin Gentry, Matthew Borowiec, and Steve Desens, who helped to carry some of my legal load during the legislative sessions. Without them and Elizabeth Daume, my secretary for over forty years, I wouldn't have been able to keep all those balls in the air at once.

But the real hero who made it possible for me to have a political career was Jacquie. She kept the home fires burning by herself and was both mother and father to the kids while I was off in Phoenix legislating. Our second daughter, Amy Eleanor, had been born on February 15, 1967, so there were three McNulty kids when I was elected to the Senate. Once again we had driven from Bisbee to Tucson so Jacquie could have the baby at Tucson Medical Center. We got her checked in and comfortable and then talked to the doctor who told us we had plenty of time, so Michael, my dad, and I went down the road to the Pancake House for some breakfast. We were sitting there waiting for our pancakes when Mo Udall walked in with an entourage. He sat down with us and helped celebrate the pending arrival of little Amy with pancakes and coffee. Both Jacquie and Amy came through in fine form, and our family was complete.

In the summer of 1970 I was selected to attend the Eagleton Institute Summer School of Rutgers University. The Eagleton Institute was a New Brunswick, New Jersey, foundation which ran a seminar on state government and politics every summer. They used reports from newspaper people around the country to advise them as to which legislators were the comers, the people who brought real effort and maybe even a little intelligence to the process. One person was chosen from each state senate. That year we were all flown to San Marcos

Island in Florida where we were lodged with our wives for ten days or so in a resort.

We listened to presentations by a variety of political bigshots who were flown in from around the country. We engaged in discussions and debates about government at a reasonably erudite level. The Institute maintained records of folks who had attended in the past and a surprising number became governors, senators, and congressmen. I attended the program with the agreement that I would run for a second term, something I probably would not have done otherwise. The Eagleton Institute did not want to waste the opportunity on someone who would not be a legislator in the next session. I did run for reelection in 1970, but after that I had no further obligation.

I won the Democratic primary of September 1970 by a wide margin and ran unopposed in the general election. In February 1971, I was able to get an amendment passed to a bill overhauling the Corporation Commission. My amendment put the new cable television providers under the jurisdiction of the Arizona Corporation Commission. There were only twelve senators on the Democratic side of the aisle that year so Republican support was necessary. An account of the vote by Dick Casey in the *Tucson Daily Citizen* bears the headline, "Best Liked Senator? McNulty's Success Based on Respect."

> When it comes to verbal give and take in the Arizona Legislature, Sen. James F. McNulty Jr. has few peers. Now in his second term, the Bisbee Democrat has earned the respect of his colleagues not only as a gifted speaker with a wry, Irish sense of humor, but as a highly intelligent legislator. Being a Democrat, McNulty often finds himself lacking sufficient support to win any strictly political arguments, but nonetheless he is respected personally, even by Republicans.

Further into the story Casey writes,

> McNulty shies away from publicity—he is always willing to give the credit and the spotlight to someone else. "Just leave me alone," said McNulty good-naturedly when asked for an interview. He even tried to convince the reporter the time might better be spent interviewing another legislator.

Casey also observed that,

> McNulty is also held in esteem by veteran Democratic minority leader
> Harold Giss of Yuma, now in his 23rd year as a legislator and
> regarded as probably the most knowledgeable person on state
> government matters. It is Giss who does most of the painstakingly
> meticulous work on bills and primarily for that reason has remained
> in his position as minority floor leader.
>
> But McNulty is now regarded as Giss's near equal when it comes
> to correcting faulty legislation. And McNulty's floor arguments are
> beginning to carry more weight with Republicans who tend to mis-
> trust Giss. "It's sure good to have you here," Giss kiddingly yet seri-
> ously commented to McNulty in a recent committee meeting when
> the two were picking apart a bill. "I used to have to do all this by
> myself."

In April 1971, I argued against a Republican tax incentive plan to
attract the Greyhound Corporation's new headquarters to Phoenix. I
questioned the booster ethic that was turning Phoenix and Tucson into
urban leviathans that were consuming desert landscapes and creating
air quality problems. I raised the issue of "quality of life" and suggested
that measures to promote economic growth should be focused on rural
areas instead of the booming metropolis of Phoenix. I was also on a
conference committee that finalized what was then the state's strongest
anti-pollution law, a landmark piece of legislation.

During my time in the senate I worked closely with Republican Senator Sandra Day O'Connor on several issues. Together, we led the fight
to create the Local Alcoholism Reception Centers known as the LARC
program. This bill provided that instead of being jailed for public drunk-
enness, people would be taken to the local LARC center where they
would be detoxified and then put into treatment for alcoholism. Police
authorities across the state were, initially, skeptical of the plan and it
took a coalition of Democrats and Republicans to get it through the
Senate.

Senator O'Connor and I also worked together to get a bill passed
which overhauled the child custody laws. It set up a procedure that
divided custody battles into two sections. The first looked at the child's
current circumstances and determined whether a parent's rights should
be terminated and the child removed. The second determined the best

placement of the child. This prevented children from being used as pawns in parental custody disputes. I was able to write some law in Arizona in areas such as the aforementioned, but despite much diligent work I wasn't able to crack the Republicans' manipulation of the redistricting process to benefit their own incumbents.

Senate President Bill Jacquin, who was a very moderate Republican and one of the ablest legislators I have ever known, allowed me to come up with a redistricting plan of my own as an alternative to the Republican scheme. He gave me some staff to work on the project including a lawyer, an intern, and a statistical analyst. The deal was that the intern would be trained on the subject of redistricting so that there would be some expertise among the senate staff which could be applied to future redistricting efforts. It was a huge job, but we eventually produced a redistricting plan and posted it in the lobby of the Senate. About a week later Jacquin told me to take it down, saying, "Some of my guys like your bill better than mine." I said, "Wonderful. It shows you have some smart people taking orders from you."

But when push came to shove, our bill was sidelined in committee and the Republican redistricting bill was passed. It put me into the same Senate district as my Democratic friend and colleague, Sen. Charles Awalt. Awalt was a successful businessman from Safford who had been elected from Graham and Greenlee counties. In the redistricting of 1971 Cochise County was added to Graham and Greenlee and we both found ourselves in the new Senate District 8. If I was to run again in 1972, I would have to run against my friend Awalt and no matter who won, one of us would not be returning to the Arizona State Senate. Statewide, the Republicans put eight Democratic Senators into four districts with that redistricting bill.

In 1971 the Republicans also rammed through a congressional redistricting plan on a strictly partisan vote, which put them in control of three of the state's four congressional districts. Only Mo Udall's district, consisting of southeastern Arizona including Pima County, remained viable for a Democratic candidate. The other three were gerrymandered so that they all included parts of Maricopa County, where the Republican majority was enough to outnumber Democratic voters in the rural areas. This had the same effect as the redistricting of my senate district which had put Bisbee and the Arizona-Sonora Desert Museum in the same district. It resulted in a clutter of constituents whose interests were unrelated and who were separated by culture and distance. I called the action a "raw, naked grab for power" in the press and on the Senate floor. Paul Fannin and Barry Goldwater, both popular Republicans from Maricopa County, were Arizona's Senators, and our only Democratic Congressman was Mo Udall. The takeover of Arizona by the Republicans and Maricopa County was nearly complete. Pima County and southeastern Arizona were the last bastions of Democratic power in the state and, for us, there was a clear sense of withering. We were forced to question what we were doing right and what we could do better.

I decided not to run against Awalt for reelection to the Senate in 1972 for a variety of reasons. Awalt's political orientation and his positions on most issues were pretty close to mine, and he had more time and more money to devote to the cause. By this time I was interested in a congressional job and had decided to begin a gentle, informal campaign. Mo Udall thought that Barry Goldwater might be vulnerable and had some ideas about running for U.S. Senate. I announced that I would not run for reelection to the state senate. Mo commissioned a poll which told him that unseating Goldwater would be next to impossible and changed his mind about running against him. Watergate hit a few months later and the prospects brightened, but by then it was too late to get a campaign going. I wanted to put some time into my family and my law practice. I had even tried to resign from the position of attorney to the Sulphur Springs Valley Electrical Cooperative in 1971 because of the demands of serving in the legislature. They refused to accept the resignation, however, and I wound up staying on.

I endorsed Awalt, who won handily and returned to the senate for the session which began in January 1973. I put my energy into legal work and the family. Jacquie and I even took a long vacation in New England. Even though I was not in the legislature, I continued to work with my old colleagues there on certain pieces of legislation. The cable television issue reappeared in that session with a bill that would create an Office of Cable Television within the Arizona Corporation Commission and strengthen the enforcement of cable television regulations. I testified before the Municipal Affairs Committee on behalf of the new bill and lobbied for its passage. It passed over the objections of most Maricopa County lawmakers.

In the spring of 1973 Charles Awalt became ill. He confided to an old friend, Sen. Bill Hardt of Globe, that he had cancer, but carried on his work as usual. Newspapers observed that he looked gaunt and sick at the Democratic caucus held on June 6, but when asked about his condition, Awalt said only that he had been thrown from a horse and had busted a couple of ribs. He died at the end of June. I was encouraged to seek appointment to his seat, but I was in no hurry to return to the fray. My reaction as printed in the *Tucson Daily Citizen* was, "I have always felt that the fanatic search for political office demeans the office itself." According to state law, the vacancy would be filled by the district's county boards of supervisors, in this case, Cochise, Graham, and Greenlee Counties. Some folks wanted to appoint Awalt's widow, Kathleen. Several current or former legislators jockeyed for the appointment including Sen. John Mickelson of Safford, Mayor Milt Reay, also of Safford, Rep. Ed Sawyer of the same little Mormon town, and Jim Elliott of Douglas, whom I first went to the Senate with in 1968.

Shortly after Awalt's death, I received a call from Bill Jacquin who said, "The Supervisors of Greenlee, Graham, and Cochise Counties are going to meet this afternoon and appoint you to the Senate. Will you serve?" I said, "Do I get the committee appointments my predecessor had?" Jacquin agreed that I would get Awalt's seats on the Joint Legislative Budget Committee, Municipal Affairs, and the Appropriations Committee, as well as keeping my old assignment on Judiciary. I said yes.

The Senate was in session the following day and after Jacquin called the meeting to order he announced that the first order of business was the passing of a member of the body. They then had a splendid eulogy for Awalt. Jacquin next announced, "The Supervisors of Graham, Greenlee, and Cochise Counties have nominated former Senator James McNulty to fill the vacancy in Senate District 8. I have contacted him and he has indicated his willingness to serve. I hereby appoint a committee of two to escort Senator McNulty into the chamber. Senator O'Connor and Senator Stump (Minority leader Bob Stump of Tolleson), please go to the Senate Chambers and bring Mr. McNulty forward." As I was ushered onto the floor of the Senate I thought to myself, "This must be what it feels like when you get remarried."

I had enjoyed most of a year away from the legislature and had used the time to catch up on my work at the law firm and spend some vacation time with the family. Refreshed by this, I now plunged into my busiest period in the Senate and served the last year and a half of Awalt's term. In October 1973, we had a special session that ran until the regular session began at the beginning of 1974. During that special session we made some useful reforms to Arizona's school financing system and to the composition of the state's school districts. My work week did not end until Friday afternoons since I was now on Appropriations and the Joint Legislative Budget Committee. A young journalist at the University of Arizona named Peggy Hughes wrote a story for the *Bisbee Review* after interviewing me in Phoenix during that last year in the State Senate. She described my office on the third floor of the Senate Building in Phoenix this way:

> Personal idiosyncrasies are the only decorations. There is a sign saying, "Don't blame me, I'm from Massachusetts" behind McNulty's desk. The formica-topped aluminum-rimmed desks, linoleum floor, white walls and fluorescent lights make it look like a business temporarily set up in a warehouse. Stacks of paper clutter the desk and shelves. The sound of nearby ringing phones, typewriters, and conversations are the only background music.

To avoid any potential hint of conflict of interest, I had made it a practice to file a balance statement on my personal finances with the Senate Clerk each year during my service in the Arizona State Senate, although there was no requirement to do so. In my last year I took this voluntary financial disclosure one step further and posted a copy of my income tax return in the press room of the Senate Building. I have always believed that the finances of public office holders should be transparent and mine certainly always have been. The only thing the press learned in my returns that interested them was the fact that I tithed. The returns I posted showed donations of $4,777 to charities in 1973. Payment for Arizona legislators at that time was $6,000 per year plus a living allowance of about $1,500 for the rural folks who had to find lodging during the session. The theory was that keeping legislators kind of starved down would curtail certain excesses, but I never saw any evidence that this worked.

The low pay, heavy work load, and tremendous responsibility of public office are only a few of the drawbacks of political life, and certainly not the worst. People who aspire to public office are often asked if they have the "fire in their belly." The question is sobering. It compels the candidate to examine his or her willingness to endure everything from outright insults to contemptuous dismissals of their candidacy. Public service has its own unique dimensions. On the one hand, it requires arrogance on the part of the candidate, an arrogance which the candidate is wise to resist and obliged to conceal. This concealed arrogance suggests to the candidate that he or she, and none of the opponents, is the best person for the job. Without it, he or she would not be a candidate. Simultaneously, the candidates must eat regular slices of humble pie to advance their candidacy. This results in an internal balancing act which requires you to conceal your ambition while presenting yourself as the certain winner. The candidate uses the political arena not only to acquaint the voters with their own qualifications, but even more frequently to launch attacks on the opponent and initiate battles with them. The large amounts of money which go into the campaigns are used not only to build the candidate up, they also pay for the vilification of the opponent.

Such processes claim victims, but they are often those who, in fairness, should not be affected. The principal victim is the candidate's family. They can be greatly bruised in the rough exchange of political attack and counterattack. The families are also expected to appear on behalf of the candidate, a task for which they have been only slightly prepared. But the principal dilemma is the deprivation of time spent with the family. When do you see your wife and kids (especially the kids) when you have the demands of winning and occupying a political office? You can squeeze out some extra time by sleeping very little, but most of the energy and time required for a successful political career comes out of time that otherwise would be spent with the family. It can be found nowhere else. The children always appear somewhat surprised when the legislator makes an appearance in the family home. My kids always wanted to go somewhere on an outing or do something special after Mass on Sundays. Many were the times when we did, but many also were the times when I had to say no.

During the short day or two the politician has at home each week during the legislative session he can not ignore his constituents or the press. Politicians cannot afford to pass on an opportunity for a thirty-second sound bite on the evening news. Then there's the delegation of veterans who have a longstanding appointment and must be placated. There is the dedication of the new post office in Thatcher or the new school building in Nogales. There is the luncheon with the union guys and after that you have to drive to Willcox to accept an award from some group who would be horribly insulted if you failed to show. Sometimes spouses will join the office-holder for these rubber chicken affairs, but many spouses simply have no stomach for the whole process, partly because of the unkind comments to which they are sometimes subjected. When incumbents are running for reelection the demands on their time intensify as they must run their campaigns in addition to everything else.

The demands on one's time, the socializing that is an unavoidable part of the job, and the strains on the family sometimes result in tragic situations. Alcohol is an ever-present commodity in politics and more than one politician has surrendered to temptations of sexual dalliances or corruption. Divorce and family dissolution may be the greatest danger. Sometimes, in my most fanciful moods, I think that a rule should be passed which bars any adult under the age of forty from service in the Congress. By that age they are less subject to sexual peccadilloes and garden variety greed. Their children are mostly grown and their attention can be focused on the job without neglecting anyone.

So why do people do it? Why do they devote the time and energy necessary to be a serious candidate? Why do they subject themselves and their families to the abuse and the risk of a very public failure? For too many, it's mainly the glamour and the power. You get your name in the newspaper a lot and people treat you like you are really important. You walk into the Senate in the morning and the pages say, "Good morning, Senator. Can I bring you a newspaper, Senator? How about a cup of coffee, sir?" The whole process is one that engenders the sport and art of ass-kissing and always will. At first you think you are removed from the effects of that, but you are not. Sooner or later you begin to sense that maybe you really are special. Maybe you really do bring some unusual talents to this assembly. Maybe fate has cast you up on top of things because of your inherent ability, intelligence, wisdom, or any other appropriate adjective.

This is, ultimately, dangerous. You have to come down to earth every once in a while and keep some sense of balance about your role. You have to get beyond the ass-kissing: find out what people's motives are, which lobbyists tell the truth and which ones blow smoke. You need to consult with people, ask questions, and listen to their ideas. Keeping your mouth shut most of the time is key to all of this. And, as Mo Udall used to put it, "the less you say, the less you have to take back."

The reputation of the Arizona Legislature has suffered in the last few years because of scandals like the Alternative Fuel Bill fiasco, which cost the state millions of dollars. My impression of the men and women of the Arizona State Legislature, however, was that they were no more and no less honest and ethical than the population at large. We had ninety people in the legislature and I believe a sample of ninety plumbers or ninety lawyers would contain about the same percentage of those who were "learned" in their trade and those who were not, or those who were driven by high moral standards and those who were not. As in the federal congress, you have some people with great talents: people who have served their country bravely in wartime, people with extensive and excellent education, people who have been enormously successful in the business or professional worlds. Some of the members of the Arizona State Legislature did not reach this level of achievement or ability, but many others did.

As a legislator, you didn't want to get completely carried away with pragmatism, but you did have to make the system work. Legislators cannot allow the work of the state to break down: the lights have to come on and the public has to have certain governmental services. This reality motivates legislators to get the work done despite their differences.

A legislator by definition is someone who proposes some words to become law and bind society to certain standards. We rarely think of it in this vein, but, strictly speaking, that is the job. In the federal congress, more than half of the legislators are trained in the law. In state legislatures the ratio is lower, particularly in the Rocky Mountain West. Despite the low reputation of lawyers with the typical cynic on the street, this can create problems. The legislatures of several Rocky Mountain states have solved this by creating legislative counsels which are made up of trained lawyers. The legislator who is not trained in the law goes to them and says, "I want a law that stops this practice or that practice," and the lawyers draft the law. Many folks believe we'd be better off to get lawyers out of government. Some even think we ought to get them out of the legal system. But, in my humble opinion, this kind of thinking is silly. Nobody comes better grounded in the fundamentals of legislative work than a lawyer.

The drafting of a law is a touchy business. The law, in a free society, is a minimum tolerable code of social conduct. If a citizen falls below that standard the rest of us, society in general, will invoke sanctions. The law is only the least that you can do. No one should boast that they obey the law, because it is a standard of minimum performance: it is simply what you are supposed to do. Or, as Saint Augustine said, "In doing what we ought we deserve no praise, because it is our duty."

Sometimes legislators make the mistake of falling back on morality and metaphysics when drafting laws. But morality can not be legislated. The law provides a floor below which the citizen must not sink, but morality is not limited. I once had a client who was trying to collect a bad debt. He glanced at the bookshelf loaded with the twenty or so bound volumes of the Arizona Revised Statutes and asked, "Isn't there a law in there somewhere that says you have to pay your bills?" I had to tell him that there was not. There are plenty of laws that say what you can do to somebody who doesn't pay their bills, but there is no law saying you have to do it. A legislator needs to have a special understanding of all of this.

In the Bible, the lawmakers were highly revered, beginning with Moses. Over the millennia the law and civilization have gone hand in hand: the Code of Hammurabi, the Ten Commandments, the Talmud, the U.S. Constitution. In the history of American lawmaking you have giants like John Adams who served as president and afterward went back to the House of Representatives where he was a highly respected legislator. Writing laws is a task of enormous and solemn responsibility. But when you start making laws you soon find that honorable men and women disagree, sometimes strongly, on grounds of principle. That brings the legislator to the very personal business of argument, persuasion, and compromise, where tact and mutual respect carry the day. Politics does seem to be becoming more and more vituperative, however, and I worry about this mean streak in political discourse.

All over the world the democratic processes are becoming increasingly vicious and confrontational. When I was in the U.S. Congress I heard many oldtimers say the same thing, "This place is getting really mean!" I once witnessed, in that august deliberative body, a zealous young conservative recklessly and viciously attack another young congressman from a rural district in Texas. The young Texan listened to the tirade, and when it finally ended he rose and asked to be recognized. He responded to his attacker with one sentence, "What makes you so mean?" There was silence in the House for a moment and the zealot did not speak for a good while thereafter. Nobody missed him.

Back in the Cold War days we had a strategic principle which folks called Mutually Assured Destruction, or MAD for short. MAD meant that the Russians and the Americans would both arm themselves to the teeth and confront each other right up to the breaking point of nuclear warfare. But they would not cross that line of mutually assured destruction no matter how vicious the ideological, geopolitical struggle became. In forty years of conflict they never did cross that line, although they stood at it toe-to-toe and nose-to-nose several times. But on September 11, 2001, that line was crossed. The unthinkable atrocity was not nuclear, and the Russians were not the author of it, but the effect was the same. It meant that now there is nothing so heinous that our enemies would not attempt to use it against us. If they have access to a nuclear weapon we know they won't hesitate. That is why the events of September 11, 2001, are so ominous. There are people in the world today who recognize no restraints on their actions.

I fear that the same lack of restraint, the same willingness to cross that line between decency and barbarism, is creeping into the political process. An increasingly vituperative political climate can only impede the ability to make good law that serves the citizens well. A democratic political system, in order to work, requires a certain minimum level of civility and mutual respect among participants. Without it, the system becomes dysfunctional. The members of the Arizona State Legislature, during my time there, included the whole range of human character from the high-minded visionary to the venal blowhard. But, in my experience, Arizona legislators often voted to do the right thing even if it was the hard thing politically. It wasn't always exactly a tidal wave of like-minded action, but it happened and it still happens today. The lights still come on when Arizonans flip the switch.

CHAPTER EIGHT

The Long Road to Washington

DOWN IN THE MINING CAMPS they have a saying about the shift-work that keeps the mines running twenty-four hours a day. "You need three people," the oldtimers declare, "one coming, one working, and one going." There was always one crew getting ready to work, one crew in the mine working, and one crew that had just finished working. This is also a pretty good way to describe the business of politics. If you were serious about a political career you found yourself somewhere in that triangular equation. You were either working to win an office, you were occupying one, or you were vacating an office (ideally to win a better one) while making the slot available for someone else. Before I left the Arizona State Senate at the end of 1974 I was vigilant for my next political opportunity. I didn't have to wait long.

Mo Udall devoted himself completely to politics and he was constantly on the lookout for his next move. I was in very close touch with Mo and his crew in Washington. Orren Beaty, who had been Stew Udall's right hand man at the Interior Department, was now working for Mo on political strategy. As stated previously, Mo had sensed that Barry Goldwater might be vulnerable in 1974. Goldwater still seemed to carry a chip on his shoulder dating back to his 1964 loss to Lyndon Johnson and it affected his performance in the Senate.

In August 1975, Richard Nixon resigned in disgrace leaving Gerald Ford as the incumbent Republican president. The Republican Party had been tarnished by the worst political scandal of the century. Mo Udall had begun his presidential run before Watergate, but when the scandal hit, it obviously enhanced the Democrats' chances for winning the White House. Morris K. Udall announced his candidacy for the president of the United States from New Hampshire in November 1974. By this time he had earned the respect of his Congressional colleagues through honesty, humor, and hard work, and he wielded a great deal of influence and seniority within the House of Representatives. His southern Arizona base of power was secure.

Orren Beaty, Mo, and I talked frequently about the political landscape that was emerging out of the wreckage of Watergate and considered the various potential scenarios. Watergate had also influenced the Arizona political environment and some prominent Phoenix Republicans were among the indicted. In the elections of 1974 Arizona voters expressed their displeasure with the party of Richard Nixon by electing Democrats like Raul Castro to the governorship and Bruce Babbitt as Attorney General.

In January 1975, I was being mentioned as a potential candidate for Republican Paul Fannin's Senate seat in the 1976 elections. Mo was well into his presidential campaign but he too considered running for Fannin's Senate seat in the event that his presidential bid failed. I did not really think I could win the Senate job, and I certainly had no intentions of running against Morris Udall for it. I had learned that lesson back in the student body elections of 1947. But I felt that I had an excellent chance of winning in Congressional District 2 if Mo moved up. Even if he lost to Carter, he was a logical candidate for a cabinet appointment such as Secretary of the Interior. A vice-presidential nomination was not outside the range of possibilities. I felt that my best move was to fill in behind Udall's presidential bid by running for his congressional seat. I announced my candidacy for the job in December 1975, stating that I would withdraw from the race in the event that Mo did not win the Democratic nomination for president.

Dennis DeConcini, Pima County Attorney and son of Supreme Court Justice Evo DeConcini, was another major player in Pima County Democratic politics who was alert to these same potential political opportunities. Dennis had managed Raul Castro's successful gubernatorial campaign. He was another bright and ambitious product of the University of Arizona Law School and he came from a southern Arizona political dynasty nearly as well known as the Udalls. Udall and DeConcini both put out feelers for a Senate bid and both were mentioned in the press as potential Democratic candidates. DeConcini was well aware that a Udall

Senate candidacy would trump his own, and he pressed Mo to make a decision. I think that Mo felt that Dennis was pushing him and the two kind of had it out.

At the beginning of March 1976, Mo and his wife Ella were in Tucson staying at the Westward Look Resort taking a break from the primaries that began in February. While he was there he announced that, in the event his presidential bid failed, he would run for his old Congressional seat and not the Senate. This cleared the way for DeConcini, who made his formal announcement of candidacy almost immediately. DeConcini won the Democratic nomination and did not have to face an incumbent in the general election since Fannin decided not to run for a third term.

My congressional aspirations, on the other hand, were still dependent on the outcome of Udall's presidential campaign. My candidacy could only succeed if Mo started winning a few presidential primaries here and there, yet I had to get my campaign geared up and running without delay. District 2 included Cochise, Santa Cruz, Pima, and a little of Pinal County, with most of the votes in Tucson. Coming from little Bisbee, I was faced with the obstacle of making myself known to the voters of Pima and Pinal Counties. The expenditure of shoe leather and tires on the car was the only way to compensate for my geographic disadvantage and build name recognition. I began spending one day a week in Tucson in the fall of 1975 and was in the Old Pueblo most of the time after I announced. Fortunately, educational goals had taken the entire family to the University of Arizona at this time. Michael was in his third year of law school, Cynthia was enrolled in a post-graduate anatomy course in the medical school, and Jacquie (with Amy in tow) was completing her Master's degree in political science. The McNulty students occupied three apartment units in Tucson. We also maintained our home in Bisbee, and I continued to work at my law office there as time allowed. I remember being on the road a great deal during these months, but I was at Jacquie's apartment in Tucson more than I was in Bisbee.

We put together an organization composed largely of young, liberal believers in the cause. Jody Sullivan was my campaign manager and she brought experience in local Tucson political races to the effort. Jody had a great sense of humor and she took the bad with the good, which is an essential skill in politics. Her husband, Paul Sullivan, was the Pima County Assessor and he helped with advice on political strategy and the intricacies of Pima County politics. Another campaign theoretician was Mike Foudy, who got his start in politics as part of my high school advisory board and campaign staff in Bisbee during the 1968 state senate campaign. Frank Felix, one of Tucson's state senators, was campaign chairman. George Steele, an officer at the Valley National Bank, acted as our campaign treasurer. We met on a regular basis and assigned tasks. With the family helping out and a large and able campaign staff, we could have our people at multiple events all over the district at any given time.

This political endeavor was different from my previous ones only in scale. It was another incremental step in the evolution of my campaigns. We had plenty of eager young volunteers, but we still didn't have much money. I raised $11,000 and spent about $9,000 before the party was over. I stuck with my rule that the campaign will not spend money it does not have. That can be a tough sell. People who have been in the business of politics for a while want you to eviscerate yourself in the name of the campaign. When winning is the only thing, the financial ruin of a candidate is a real possibility. I considered this an ever-present threat, and was always extremely conservative in my spending. In the 1976 Congressional campaign I decided to give my candidacy a little boost with a pledge to return 75 percent of any donations I received if I dropped out of the race before September.

I spent Saturdays doing "the walk": knocking on doors and introducing myself to the voters of Tucson. We would get our gang together early in the morning and blanket a specific neighborhood. Jody Sullivan would put together lists for us using precinct registers. Everybody would get a card showing folks' names, party registrations, and occupations for a particular block. We also did get-acquainted meetings in peoples' homes and back yards. This was pretty expensive in terms of time spent and the good you did yourself. Even if the host had a nice big back yard you would rarely get more than twenty-five voters. In all these voter contacts we would ask for signatures on our nomination petition and solicit donations. Occasionally, my staff would put me on the telephone and I would call people off a list and ask if they would like to make a contribution. Today we are simply inundated with those solicitations at election time, but in those days lots of people did make a donation. In the rural parts of the district we did the traditional visits to the county courthouses and city halls. Most of my attention had to go to Tucson, however, as that is where the votes were and where I was a relative unknown.

There was a constant uncertainty that hovered over the 1976 campaign and it became more pressing as Mo Udall's presidential campaign faltered. Mo looked strong in the first few primaries and did place second twice, but he did not win in any. I remember how elated he was the night of the Wisconsin primary because, when he retired for the evening, it looked like he had won. The next morning he got up to find out that the ballot count was finished and he had placed second. Tom Volgy had announced his candidacy for the District 2 congressional seat fairly late in the game and he was to be my opponent in the primary. He too had promised to pull out if Mo found it necessary to run for his old job. Mo continued to lose one primary after another and, despite my fervent support for my old friend and mentor, I soon had to face up to the fact that Jimmy Carter was winning far more delegates. I could not, in good conscience, continue to ask for people's time and money in support of my candidacy because I knew that I would be withdrawing from the race in favor of Mo.

On April 7, 1976, I wrote a letter to Mo which begins,

> Dear Morris:
>   Chuck it. Chuck it now.
>   You have gone further than any Representative in this century. And you did it with intelligence, guts, and class. You might still win; but you might be pinched into oblivion like Messrs. Bayh and Harris.

I went on to urge him to throw his support to Humphrey and run again for his District 2 congressional seat. I told him he could win in District 2, "without ever leaving Rehoboth Beach," and he might wind up as chairman of the Interior Committee with a powerful ally in the White House. A vice-presidential nomination or a cabinet appointment for Mo were still not outside the range of possibilities. I wrote to him again on April 28 and told him that I thought he should go ahead and announce for the District 2 race:

Dear Morris:

I may be wrong, but I'm often inconsistent too.

I previously told you that an announcement by you for the House of Representatives would be interpreted as a sign of some weakness in your presidential effort by the press. I still think that. But I don't think it's all that much worse than what they are saying now anyway.

...The big thing, though, is that these things are all over in about five weeks. Given things as they are, I tend to think that it might be wise for you to get lined out for a run at the House of Representatives. Rather than have some reporter find nomination petitions being circulated, I think you might just simply causally announce that you were going to keep the House option open.

...Forge ahead but hedge your bets.

I wrote again on May 7 and told Morris to, "Get back here and announce for the House of Representatives." I also noted that *Newsweek* had reported he had signed a personal promissory note for $30,000 to support his campaign and added, "I know it's your money, but I hope you don't do much more of that." The morning after the Michigan primary, which Mo lost, I called him from the Plaza Hotel in Tucson. I told him that the jig was up and that I didn't see any point in my staying in the District 2 congressional race. Mo was taking a respectable number of delegates to the convention with him, however, and he was not yet accepting defeat. He feared that my withdrawal would undermine his presidential efforts. I was known to be a close personal friend as well as a political ally and the press would assume I had inside knowledge of Mo's intentions. They would interpret my withdrawal as evidence that Mo was about to give up the presidential effort and run for his old congressional seat. It was an interpretation that was not entirely without merit, but I really didn't think the national press would even notice anything that I did. Mo told me that I should stay in the race because if I dropped out Volgy might stay in, or somebody else might pop up and decide to run. I told him that I'd look foolish if I stayed at this much longer. I said that I was clearly a stalking horse anyway and that proclaiming that Udall still has a good chance of winning the presidential nomination is not an opinion that is widely shared. Mo was very reluctant to give his okay, but I was determined that I wasn't going to continue my campaign.

On May 10, I penned another letter to Udall which I began by reporting on a meeting with representatives of the United Steel Workers
where labor's endorsement of Jimmy Carter was discussed and Udall's
candidacy was spoken of in the past tense. The letter includes the following:

> Thanks for the telephone call last week. I have two dozen appoint-
> ments over the next six weeks, but that is just a microcosm of your
> effort. For the most part, the 50 trips made to Tucson since New
> Year's Day have been interesting, although tiring at times. But with
> the current circumstances, there is an element of play-acting involved.
> I find that extremely wearing.
>
> Consequently, barring some miracle, I intend to announce my
> withdrawal in your favor on Friday, May 21st. I don't know any
> other way to go. I don't want to cancel appointments without reason.
> I don't want simply to not show. I don't want to continue as I am.
>
> I urge you to mark only one certain date in your calendar, Home-
> coming Breakfast at the University of Arizona this fall. We'll have
> lots of laughs. It will be a happy, non-competitive assembly where
> no one needs to prove anything.
>
> Sincerely yours,
> James F. McNulty, Jr.

No miracle occurred to change my plans, so I held a press conference in Tucson and announced my withdrawal from the race on May
21, 1976. I said that I still thought it was possible that Mo might be on
the national ticket in November, but that I was less certain of this than
when I had announced my candidacy. I added that I would not be comfortable continuing to solicit funds and make appearances when it looked
increasingly likely that Mo would be running for his District 2 congressional seat again. I received a last-minute rush of calls from Mo's aides
and allies urging me not to drop out, some saying that Jimmy Carter
would use my withdrawal against Mo. Volgy held on for a while longer
and there was some unpleasantness about my withdrawal. But I knew
that the party was over and that fact soon became clear to all, including
Volgy and Mo. Volgy withdrew and Mo filed as a candidate for his
District 2 Congressional seat well before the July 9 deadline.

I did not feel bruised by the events of that campaign. Actually, I rather enjoyed the whole thing. And my withdrawal did not affect my friendship with Mo. He wanted me to stay in the race for perfectly understandable reasons: politicians regard their first task as getting elected, and their second is staying that way. This is how their interests are accommodated. I still believe that if Mo had moved up and my congressional campaign had continued in 1976, I would have been the near-certain winner of the election.

I had made over a hundred visits throughout District 2 in that short campaign and had made myself known to the voters of Pima County and Tucson. I proceeded to refund 75 percent ($8,250) of the donations I had received to the contributors, an action that many found astounding. What made this a little easier was the surprising fact that about a fifth of the checks sent out as refunds were returned back to us by the contributors. I also received many small donations to help defray the cost of the refund, and ended up paying only some of it myself. I did not, however, make any large financial transfusion of my own money to this or any other campaign I ever ran. I received letters saying, "I never thought I'd see the day when I'd receive a return refund from a political donation." There was even one fellow, an oldtime union guy named Eddie Adams, who rose in several gatherings to proclaim, "You people should acknowledge something that in my life I thought I would never see. Money returned from a politician!"

I was with Mo Udall in the middle of July 1976 in Madison Square Garden just before he walked to the podium to make his concession speech at the Democratic National Convention. Udall was upbeat, he had accepted his defeat by Carter and he wore his good humor like armor. His wife, Ella, and a few others were also there in the dressing room. It is hard to deal with such defeats and politicians normally wind up hating their victorious rivals. To be a candidate you have to believe passionately that you are the one right person for the job, which means the rival is not. There were some hard feelings between our camp and the Carter forces, but we were facing an election and had to pull together. I don't think Mo felt any animosity towards Carter. One of his best lines ever was, "You can really learn humility by running against Jimmy Carter in thirteen primaries and losing every one of them." Mo never wished anybody ill. Never. The opposite, however, is not true. Some pretty mean stuff was said about him over the years.

I was soon appointed as Southern Arizona Campaign Manager for the Carter/Mondale organization and I did what I could to get them elected. I also, as always, worked for Mo in his 1976 congressional race against Republican Laird Gutterson in District 2. Mo wound up with some pretty substantial debt for his two campaigns in 1976, and, according to what he told me, Jimmy Carter decided that he would help. Such promises, made in the heat of the political fray, are generally not enforceable more than two hours after they are uttered. Carter did, however, appear at a gala fund-raiser for Mo in Phoenix which I attended.

As Southern Arizona Coordinator for his campaign, I had an opportunity to speak to Carter briefly. He had spent some time in the Georgia Legislature, so we chatted about our experiences in state legislative work. Carter had a very earnest manner and he was an easy man to talk to. He had that talent of making you feel like you had his full and complete attention when he focused those blue eyes on you. He was probably the most religious man we have had in the White House, with the possible exception of Abraham Lincoln. Lincoln, however, practiced a very informal type of religion whereas Carter's faith was more formal. From that period forward Morris Udall was much in demand, telling his stories, projecting his good-natured viewpoint. He won the chairmanship of the Interior Committee and exercised more influence than ever on Capitol Hill.

Dennis DeConcini's election to the United States Senate in 1976 was assisted by the fact that the two Republican candidates thoroughly disabled one another in the primary. John Conlan and Sam Steiger were the Republican contenders and there were some pretty nasty charges traded between the two. Sam Steiger was and is an extremely forthright fellow who does not conceal his opinions. He is a wonderful guy, despite the fact that he sometimes indulges in outrageous antics like shooting a hapless burro or painting an outlaw pedestrian crossing on a Prescott street in the dead of night. In 1976 Steiger believed, probably correctly, that Conlan was indulging in an underhanded campaign to smear him in the press. Some negative stories had appeared in print and Steiger was convinced that they had been planted by Conlan. Steiger, who was really steamed over all this, held a press conference in the lobby of the Westward Ho in Phoenix to fend off the charges by Conlan. The Phoenix television and newspaper people rushed down there to document the spectacle.

As Steiger was speaking he heard a door close on the mezzanine above the lobby. He looked up and caught a glimpse of what he was sure was Conlan. Sam ran up the staircase and got to the door that Conlan had disappeared into, but it was locked. With the press looking on with open mouths, Sam stood there pounding on the door and screaming, "Come on out of there! If you can say something about me out on the street you can be a man and say it to my face!" It was good, clean, red-blooded Arizona politics and this kind of thing did not hurt DeConcini's chances a bit when he ran against Steiger in the general election.

After his marathon presidential campaign an exhausted Mo Udall returned with Ella to their home in Washington. Mo had been surrounded constantly by Secret Service men for the past year and he had never had to touch a suitcase during that time or deal with the other trivialities of life from which great men are spared. Suddenly he was a regular congressman again with some time on his hands. The day after their return to a more normal existence Ella said to Mo, "Well, that ordeal is behind us, what should we do now?" She suggested that they do some work on the house, which had been neglected during the long presidential campaign. Mo agreed. He got a ladder and a neighbor and the two of them went up on the roof to do some kind of repair. Mo fell off the roof and broke one arm and injured the other so that both arms had to be immobilized in casts.

I remember him telling me at the time that a man certainly learns what his needs are when he has broken both of his arms. His Parkinson's disease was not diagnosed until 1979, and it did not seem to affect him in the 1976 campaign. But the illness was certainly a terrible burden to bear for anyone, and even more difficult for a man in a demanding job like chairman of the House Interior Committee. Mo did some of his greatest legislative work while struggling against the debilitating effects of that ghastly disease.

At the end of 1976 I was appointed to the State Salary Commission. Every other year this committee came into being, held some hearings, and then made recommendations on new salaries for elected state officials of the legislative and executive branches. There were only five people on the committee and they were usually past members of the state legislature. It was modeled after a federal program adopted by Congress to stop the annual agonizing, ugly fights about wages for members of that body.

The commission had been set up during my time in the State Senate and we had quite a fight with Gov. Jack Williams about it. Originally, Williams had agreed that the commission would submit their recommendations on salaries for both the legislative and executive office holders of the state and they would be approved or rejected by the legislature with the governor holding the usual veto prerogative. But at the last minute, Williams decided that he couldn't allow legislators to set their own salaries and threatened to veto the bill. We held a conference to decide whether or not to attempt an override, but the Republicans had no stomach for such a venture. In the end the law that was passed specified that the commission's salary recommendations for elected officials of the executive branch would be approved or rejected by the legislature and the governor. Their recommendations on legislative salaries, however, would be submitted to a vote of the people.

We reviewed the jobs, the credentials of the office holders, their conduct of the office, and the information on the duties of each office which were submitted by the various departments. We made our recommendations which included raising the woefully inadequate salaries of Arizona legislators from $6,000 to $9,600 a year, a figure that would have still left them among the lowest paid in the western states. We went through the entire process, including trips around the state to promote our recommendations. As is usually the case, the raises we recommended for the legislators were never enacted, although the other elected officials received their raises. In the twenty or so years that this salary commission operated, legislative salaries were seldom actually increased through this mechanism. Arizona legislators remain woefully underpaid to this day.

Governor Castro was appointed Ambassador to Argentina by Jimmy Carter at the close of 1977, and longtime Secretary of State Wesley H. Bolin became Governor of Arizona through the constitutional line of succession. Tragically, he died in office a few weeks later. As Attorney General, Bruce Babbitt was next in line so he was sworn in as governor, albeit by a rather strange set of circumstances. He was a very intelligent guy and one of the capable young Democratic up-and-comers at the time. He was from a well known family of pioneer northern Arizona ranchers and merchants. Bruce was a liberal Democrat, but he had to be careful not to come across as too liberal when he ran for reelection against Evan Mecham, who gave him quite a race. I was co-chairman of his reelection campaign in 1978 and was able to keep my southern Arizona troops in line for him. Thankfully, Babbitt was able to win that election despite the fact that a majority of the voters in the state were Republicans.

The 1976 and 1978 elections resulted in some encouraging Democratic victories. Arizonans elected Democrats like Dennis DeConcini and Bruce Babbitt to statewide offices. Neither was from Maricopa County. Back in 1968 when I first went to the State Senate, the one-man, one-vote rulings had recently come out and they were changing the way electoral districts were drawn. In the early 1960s, the Supreme Court ruled in a series of three cases over the next few years. The relevant cases included *Baker v. Carr* where the Tennessee legislature had divided that state up into congressional districts of widely varying numbers of voters. *Reynolds v. Sims* was an Alabama case which ruled that the new rule was applicable to the various state houses of representatives and the various state senates. The third opinion was *Lucas v. General Assembly*, a Colorado case in which the state legislature had submitted to the voters a redistricting plan that did not comply with the "one-man, one-vote" rule.

We rural folks really thought this was the end. Phoenix had 55 percent of the population of the state and a majority of registered voters were Republicans. On a purely arithmetic basis, the one-man, one-vote rulings meant that Phoenix Republicans would call the shots in Safford, Clifton, Payson, and all of the rural areas of the state. We worried that the little burgs would lose their cherished local control. Theoretically, one-man, one-vote puts Maricopa County firmly in the driver's seat and makes the rest of us irrelevant. But it didn't always work out that way and the elections of 1976 and 1978 are evidence of this. I think what saved us is that in Arizona the Republicans generally managed to gin up a few candidates who were anathema to the middle of the road voters. Evan Mecham would be one good example. Republican candidates had the votes going into the contest, but high-handedness and over-reliance on right-wing truisms often scared off some of the moderate voters.

Mo Udall had a pretty tough race in 1978, and as usual I was one of his lieutenants. By then a negative reaction to his presidential bid seemed to have set in and Mo was deeply concerned about the upcoming election. He was very conscious of his declining support after his defeat in the presidential race. The Republicans ran a fairly strong candidate in Thomas Richey and Udall's percentage went down to 53 percent that year with 44 percent going to Richey. I remember being on the phone with Mo on election night as we sweated out the count. I gave him reports on the early numbers I was receiving from Douglas and Cochise County which were, of course, Democratic strongholds. It wasn't until the next election that we got back to the margins that Udall normally enjoyed.

By election time in 1978 I had made a decision on my own next political move and was well advanced into the quest. I had my sights on what was, for a Democrat, the Holy Grail of Arizona politics: Barry Goldwater's seat in the United States Senate. He would be up for reelection in 1980 and I had a lot of work to do.

For the first time in my political career it was decided that a poll should be commissioned to test my chances against Goldwater. I met with my advisors and we agreed we'd spend most of the money in the campaign kitty on a poll. Peter Hart was recommended to us for the work. He was a preeminent national political pollster and we hired him for what seemed to me at the time an enormous amount of money, I think it was around $15,000. He went to work and about a month later he called and said, "I'm coming to Phoenix to give you the report and discuss it with you." About five of us met with Hart at an advisor's home in Phoenix. He handed out a bound report that must have been an inch and a half thick and I turned straight to the last page.

There, under the heading "Conclusions," it stated that "Barry Goldwater is the most vulnerable United States Senator in the Congress today." The report identified the issues and the areas of the state that needed to be addressed to beat him. Most folks believed that Goldwater was practically unbeatable and the poll gave my candidacy added credibility. Unlike the poll Udall commissioned in 1974, this one indicated that Goldwater could be beat, although it did not say it would be easy.

I showed the poll results to labor leaders and others whose backing I was seeking. Many of the leaders who saw it were still skeptical about my chances. They said that I didn't have the money or the name recognition in Phoenix necessary to win the job. But the poll improved my ability to raise money and gave me the encouragement I needed so I made the final decision to run for the U.S. Senate. My formal announcement of candidacy came on November 21, 1979.

I made my announcement at press conferences in three towns that day: first at a breakfast in Bisbee, then at a press conference in Tucson, and finally in the early afternoon at the Adams Hotel in Phoenix. In my speech I said:

> I am here today to announce my candidacy for the U.S. Senate. I do not claim to have all the solutions. But I am saying that we, the people, have the ability to establish national goals and to achieve them. I am ready to serve you in Washington. I want to try to bring this creature we call government back to its proper relationship with the governed. I do not believe I can do it alone, but I believe I can provide a wholesome stewardship.
>
> I face a formidable race for a high office. I ask all who can do so in good conscience to support me in every helpful way. With your commitment and mine we can bring about a new relationship between the governing and the governed, a climate of honor and truth and responsibility.

By the time I announced Jacquie, Amy, and I had already been living in Phoenix for two months. We bought a home in north Phoenix and enrolled Amy, who was twelve, in Madison Meadows Elementary School. Cynthia was also in Phoenix attending the American Graduate School of International Management. Michael, by this time, was working on the staff of the joint House-Senate Office of Technology Assessment in Washington, having finished a stint as an administrative assistant for Mo Udall. Living in Phoenix was one of the prices that had to be paid in order to overcome my perennial geographic disadvantage. Just as in 1976, I was a relative unknown who had to introduce himself to a whole new set of voters. The majority of those voters were in Phoenix and the best way to meet them was to be there.

In the first week of December 1979 I traveled to Washington, D.C., to line up support for my candidacy. I met with the leadership of various national labor unions and other interest groups such as representatives of the citrus and cattle industries. Throughout the Senate race, I kept up a schedule that had me back at my desk in the law office in Bisbee two days every other week. I stayed at our house there when in town, but it was a pretty empty place.

My mother died at the age of 91 years in May of that year. She was diagnosed with congestive heart failure years before and had been declining. My mother really is the one who ignited my earliest interest in politics, and I probably learned more about the subject from her than from anyone else. For her, politics was at the core of the welfare of the community, and participation was both a duty and an honor. I still can see her standing outside the polling place in the Boston drizzle with her hat and her purse. Greeting every neighbor by name, very formal and polite, but always with a flash of humor and an unspoken political reminder. In her own way and on her own level, she knew how to shake the electoral tree as well as anyone. After the funeral in Bisbee I went straight back to campaigning. She would have wanted me to continue the quest, and I did so without flagging. My dad soldiered on alone in their house in Bisbee, but it was not easy for him.

In a U.S. Senate campaign the entire state is included in the itinerary. I started early and worked late, traveling by car and small plane to every corner of Arizona. I kept getting a cordial reception, but most folks didn't think I had a chance. The Kiwanis Clubs shared that opinion, but they hadn't seen Barry Goldwater in three years, he hadn't done much in Washington during that time, and he didn't answer letters. So they were not entirely averse to my message when I spoke at their meetings. I think Barry was still reacting to his loss way back in the 1964 presidential contest. He had taken to answering questions more bluntly than political good sense would have suggested, and he had missed over a third of the roll call votes in the last four sessions of the Senate. I started to receive more contributions and we wound up receiving about $115,000. This was big money for me, but it was pocket change for a senate race even in 1980.

After I had announced and been at it a while, a multi-millionaire Phoenix developer by the name of Bill Schulz called a press conference and said that he was going to run for the Democratic nomination for the U.S. Senate. Schulz had been nibbling around the edges of political life in the state and had toyed with three or four different big jobs. He had made a lot of money building apartments during the boom years for real estate developers in Phoenix and he wanted to do something political with it. Apparently, he decided that I didn't have any money, and that he could essentially come in and buy the nomination. Today we have seen a proliferation of this attitude all over the country. Schulz was aware of the results of my poll and I think it factored into his decision to run. He proclaimed that he was prepared to spend a million dollars on the campaign. I huddled with my group of advisors, and we concluded that there was no way we could match his spending, but we had the advantage in experience and eloquence.

The third contender in the Democratic senate primary race of 1980 was an orthopedic surgeon from Globe named Frank DePaoli. DePaoli was a decorated Vietnam vet who had been urged to run by some union people in Globe. Frank had some unusual ideas and seemed to be off on a frolic of his own during this race. He and I became good friends during the campaign and the word was soon out that, when organizing the seating at dinner parties, McNulty and DePaoli could be seated together, but Schulz should be put at another table.

My campaign chairman was the venerable Ernest McFarland, who had already been an Arizona governor and senator, and who was still a major factor in Democratic affairs. Gary Saulson, Peter Zimmerman, and Caryn Thompson were the staff of my campaign in 1980. I got valuable support from DeConcini, Morris Udall, and other Arizona Democratic notables. I was also able to get the endorsements of some national Democratic Party figures, including Sen. Gary Hart of Colorado who was already being mentioned as a presidential candidate. He arrived in Phoenix on October 25 and held a press conference where he promoted my candidacy.

Despite these endorsements I was the clear underdog in the race and, for the only time in my political career, I was not able to get the endorsement of my old friends in the labor unions. The head of the Arizona Federation of Teachers got up in the crucial meeting of the Committee on Political Education (COPE) of the Arizona AFL-CIO to speak on my behalf, and Darwin Aycock, head of the state AFL-CIO stood by me in the subsequent vote, but they ended up voting to endorse

Schulz despite my strong record as an advocate of the causes of labor and education. The teachers and the unions both withheld their backing out of fear of the well-financed Schulz juggernaut.

I got very little television coverage in my 1976 congressional race because there was hardly a reason to put my face on TV in a campaign that was over before the primary. But television was something I did have to contend with in the 1980 senate race. Learning how to do television is something you have to work at, and in that campaign I was thrown into the TV business at the deep end. There was a whole retinue of people involved in the taping sessions and we would do a take four or five times before they were satisfied. All for maybe twenty seconds of air time. The same applied to the interviews which were distilled into the newsbites on which television news thrives. I invited Schulz to debate me on television, but he seemed reluctant to take me on in an exchange of ideas and he declined. He did, however, appear at a few major events with me and DePaoli during the campaign.

One of these was a blockbuster appearance in Tucson which was to include the three of us, but, as I recall, DePaoli didn't show up. The place was packed with rabid, fervent Tucson liberals who were lining up behind me looking to do great things. In my speech I concluded that the people of the Democratic Party, when looking at this senate race and this man Goldwater, should realize that what this challenge requires is a fast horse that can run a hard race. "You need a strong horse," I said, "not a rich jockey!" I must admit I had some fun with these kind of things. My backers expressed their agreement noisily, and then it was Schulz's turn to speak. He did his best, but the fellow was at a terrible disadvantage with that crowd. His two main issues were controlling the costs of Reagan's military build-up and instituting a tighter monetary policy. I was pushing policies that would help small business people, and advocating a less paranoid and more constructive relationship with the Soviets. My trip to the Soviet Union had led me to believe that their capacity to threaten us was a good deal less than what we feared.

The Central Arizona Project was still an important issue and opposition to it was political suicide. Growth ruled the day in Arizona, and the drive to dam the rivers and fill the desert valleys with housing developments prevailed. I can even remember political quarrels about allowing counties to create planning and zoning commissions, which at one time were thought to be the work of the devil by conservatives and developers. In the election of 1980 I tried to outline the parameters of the environmental problems related to uncontrolled growth. The environmentalists were very vocal and they had some clout. They gave my campaign some generous contributions and some valuable support.

A few weeks before the primary Schulz started buying massive amounts of television time and blanketing the state with his political advertising. You couldn't turn on a TV between Kayenta and Sasabe without seeing his face. Schulz spent about $1,000,000 in that primary race, almost entirely out of his own pocket. I spent $115,000. Schulz ended up with 54 percent of the vote, I got 35 percent, and DePaoli had 10 percent. I took Cochise County, and that was it. I remember going down to my headquarters the next morning and finding Sandra Day O'Connor there among my grieving campaign workers. She said some kind words that meant a great deal to me that morning.

Jacquie, Amy, and I loaded up the car and moved back to our home in Bisbee the next day. I threw my support to Schulz for the general election and he came close to winning the contest, but Barry Goldwater eked out a narrow win and held on to his senate seat. Jacquie had enjoyed some aspects of our time in Phoenix; she knew a lot of people from our days at the University of Arizona who lived there. But it was somewhat of a drain on the stamina. Amy had started her freshman year at Xavier High School, but we moved back to Bisbee immediately and sold the Phoenix house. I had spent twenty-eight years in the shadow of the Mule Mountains and Bisbee was the place that felt like home. I was, however, beginning to wonder if a person from a scenic, historic little town of 8,000 souls in the far southeastern corner of the state could be elected to the United States Congress.

Back in December of 1979, when my senate campaign was just being launched, Bruce Babbitt had flown into Tucson to speak at a Democratic Party Christmas affair held at the old Ramada Inn. After we were all settled in, the speeches started and when Babbitt rose his comments included some very laudatory words about me and my senate candidacy. A few months later Schulz and DePaoli entered the race and Bruce changed his tune. The newspaper guys immediately descended on him and asked, "Do you stand by your endorsement of McNulty?" Babbitt responded that, as titular head of the Arizona Democratic Party, he had to remain neutral in the senate primary contest. The *Arizona Daily Star* asked me for a comment and I simply agreed that the role of governor requires neutrality in these situations. Dennis DeConcini called me when he read the story and said, "Boy, you really let him off the hook!"

After the election was over Governor Babbitt called me in Bisbee and expressed his regrets about my defeat. He then offered me a choice of consolation prizes: either a seat on the Appellate Court or membership on the Arizona Board of Regents. I told Bruce, "The Appellate Court vacancy is not in my area of the state, but the Board of Regents, that is a job which interests me very much." Babbitt agreed to my appointment but almost immediately the Phoenix establishment began lobbying him hard to choose an Arizona State University alum. It was that ancient ASU/UA rivalry raising its ugly head yet again. There were Sun Devil types who felt that the University of Arizona was growing too much, to the detriment of their alma mater in Tempe. A number of people like Don Pitt and Stanley Feldman were mentioned for the job. About a week later Bruce called again and asked, "Are you going to be in Phoenix in the next 24 hours?" I wasn't, but Bruce said that he'd really like to see me in his office at the Capitol by tomorrow. So I got in the car and drove to Phoenix. Babbitt asked me if I was going to use the Board of Regents job to get myself elected to the Congress. I responded that the way it looked, I was not going to be a candidate, "but if things change and I have a shot, you better believe I will run for Congress." Bruce went ahead and sent my name over to the Arizona State Senate.

Both Arizona State University and the University of Arizona had long traditions of supporting their intercollegiate athletic teams in a variety of ways, some of which were questionable to say the least. Stories had appeared in the press about boosters dispensing cash to star players from the trunks of their cars, athletes getting passing grades without showing up for class or doing any work, and a host of other irregularities. The academic achievements of our student athletes was, in general, inadequate. The president of the Board of Regents, Tom Chandler, put me on the Intercollegiate Athletic Committee as chairman and we started a program to convince everyone that the abuses happening in the athletic programs, particularly at the UA and ASU, were no longer going to be tolerated.

I called a meeting with the head coaches of the basketball and football programs of both schools for 7:00 a.m. on a Tuesday morning at the Board of Regents office in Phoenix. The president of the Board of Regents ordered them to attend and they were not happy about it. The UA basketball coach, Fred Snowden, was there along with ASU's Ned Wulk and the head coaches of the two football programs. I reviewed with them some of the problematic practices that we were aware of, and informed them all that such practices were to cease forthwith. Wulk rose to leave, and I asked if he understood. "We heard you," was his sullen reply.

We required the athletic departments to begin tracking the grade averages of scholarship athletes as well as their graduation rates, and to report these figures to us. Where athletes were not succeeding academically, we wanted to know why. The athletic departments at the three Arizona universities got tutoring programs going and started monitoring the academic performance of their athletes closely. Today this is standard procedure in the National Collegiate Athletic Association, but we were doing it long before it was required by them. I believe that we turned around an ugly trend and since that time the athletic programs at the three schools have had good records and decent people running them.

During my two years on the Board of Regents we had to select new presidents for both Arizona State University and the University of Arizona, and I served on the selection committee. This was a long and tedious process and a kind of medieval ritual where we sorted through some two hundred applicants to arrive at a list of about fifteen whom we interviewed and re-interviewed. Then we thrashed around for a while deciding on the names of the five finalists which we submitted to the Board of Regents. The ultimate result was the hiring of President J. Russell Nelson at ASU and President Henry Koffler at the University of Arizona. I was extremely impressed with the enormous talent of the applicants, particularly for the UA job, and the experience reinforced my admiration for the University. I am not uncritical of my alma mater, but I am proud of it, despite some of the disciplinary situations that we had to deal with. The most notable of these was probably the professor at the UA who cooked marijuana cookies for his students. We suspended him without pay for two years.

In 1981 I was keeping one eye on the latest round of gerrymandering of the Arizona congressional districts which was triggered by the 1980 census. The Republican-dominated legislature had become quite sophisticated at using computers to draw up districts in which they thought they could win. They input data from every census tract, every enumeration district, every precinct in the state. Then the machine could be given an instruction such as, "create discrete districts that protect incumbents with at least 54 percent of their party's votes." In a few seconds the computer would spit out a map that looked like an inkblot image, a real work of art. It was all completely legal, of course, and the new Arizona Congressional District 5 was drawn in 1981 to the specifications of a Tucson Republican who was chairman of the Arizona State Senate Judiciary Committee.

When I looked at the new district it was clear to me that there was a chance for a Democrat to win it. By this point in my career I knew myself well enough to know that I had a talent for legislative work. The judiciary did not interest me particularly and neither did jobs in the executive branch. I had been brought up in an environment that valued politics and considered it essential to the health of the community. My previous candidacies are evidence enough of my longstanding goal of serving in the United States Congress. The opportunity I saw in District 5 was hard to resist.

In March 1982, I was putting out feelers, but had not yet made my final decision to enter the race. Then, on St. Patrick's Day, my father passed away of cancer of the esophagus. We buried him next to my mother in Bisbee. I don't know if I would have run for Congress if my father had not died at that moment. But when he passed away I just decided that now was the time. I consulted with party leaders, including State Committee Chairman Sam Goddard. On the last day of March 1982, only four months away from the election, I said, "Here I go." I had no money, no campaign manager, and had not rented space for a headquarters, but then nobody else had any of those things yet either, so it was fair enough.

The redistricting that created District 5 had affected Mo Udall, but like any other powerful incumbent he had stayed on top of it. With their 1981 redistricting the Republicans split his base in Tucson into two districts and the Democrats sued. By 1984 all this had been resolved in court with a compromise that resulted in a very safe district for Mo.

The Republicans essentially packed as many Democrats into his district as possible so that they had a good chance to take the others. The new District 5 that was created in 1982 covered the southeastern corner of the state including all of Greenlee and Cochise Counties, and parts of Santa Cruz, Graham, Pinal, and Apache Counties. It extended north-west to take in substantial parts of Pima County and Tucson. Mo's district was generally to the north and west of mine and included most of Pinal County, but Tucson was divided between the two jurisdictions with the majority of it lying in Mo's District 2.

Priscilla Kuhn, a longtime Tucson activist, signed on as my campaign manager. She was very tuned in to social legislation being considered in the federal congress and she was a hard worker. George Steele was my treasurer once again. I didn't have a campaign chairman as such, because I felt that I knew as much about the game of politics in Arizona as anyone, so I just ran the show myself with input from my advisors. We opened our campaign headquarters at 509 N. Craycroft Rd. on Saturday, May 29. Soleng Tom, a landlord from South Tucson, was my opponent in the primary, although he got into the race very late. He didn't do much campaigning and only took about 18 percent of the primary vote which made my 80 percent look pretty good.

I had a much more serious opponent for the general election in Jim Kolbe. Kolbe was a bright young Republican land developer from Patagonia. His family had roots in Chicago and Kolbe was a graduate of Northwestern University who had served in the Arizona legislature. Kolbe is a hard worker and he spent years preparing for this campaign, but he always impressed me as a worried man who tends to play his cards very close to the vest. He likes to keep tight control over things, which is one legitimate way of doing things, but it has never been my style.

We spent $343,000 in that campaign but were still outspent by the Republicans who raised about $500,000. We produced some short television commercials that were reasonably well received. The Republicans had identified Arizona's District 5 as one of the key races in the nation that year and Kolbe used a lot of material prepared by the Republican National Committee in his campaign. They had the professional quality people and equipment needed to make these spots and they did a good job. But I knew they were getting a little desperate when they put out a spot that said something like, "This race is not about who

Ruben Ortega (left), outcounty coordinator for the McNulty for Congress campaign, confers with the candidate. PHOTO BY TIM FULLER

is good looking and who has the best smile." Anybody who would worry about getting into a beauty contest with me has to be a little insecure. I reacted by saying that this race was certainly no beauty contest. This is about as harsh as that campaign got.

I walked through the neighborhoods of the district as I had done before, sometimes actually breaking into a run when moving over to the next block. One of the campaign workers would provide me with a three-by-five index card at the beginning of every morning which listed my schedule for the day. Any day that was full from dawn to late in the evening was a good day campaigning. I performed all of the normal campaign activities that I had perfected over the past twenty years and worked hard at it. Pollution from mine and smelter emissions was a big issue and, despite the fact that my base was in a mining community, I felt that placing limits on such pollution would serve the greater good. This time I got the strong endorsement of the unions and the teachers as well as the backing of a unified state Democratic Party. Bruce Babbitt was supportive, as were Mo Udall and Dennis DeConcini. They were all up for reelection and were all working hard and spending big bucks

As the vote total rolls in for victory, Priscilla Duddleston prepares for a boisterous evening. PHOTO BY TIM FULLER

to get Democrats to the polls. A number of state legislators also appeared with me at various events. We made a big get-out-the-vote effort in the weeks before the election and we got an excellent Democratic turnout.

The District 5 race had been identified by the leaders of both parties as a contest that could be won by either side. Kolbe got the help of some top figures in the Reagan administration including Agriculture Secretary John Block and Vice President George H. W. Bush who both flew in to endorse him during the campaign. I had some national Democratic Party figures fly into Arizona to endorse me including Congressmen Claude Pepper and Dick Gephardt, and Senator Paul Simon. Mo Udall helped recruit Sen. Bill Bradley who agreed to fly in for a fund-raiser at the airport in Tucson. When I asked Bradley what I could do for him as a gesture of thanks he said, "My fee is a full massage from Joe Proski." Proski was the legendary trainer for the Phoenix Suns and was much in demand by NBA stars all over the country. Bradley, of course, had been an NBA player himself, and knew Proski. I made the arrangements. Senator Bradley flew into Tucson on September 3 and spoke for about forty contributors at the Inn at the Airport. He then got on a flight to Phoenix where he got his massage and then went straight back to the airport and flew east.

The League of Women Voters sponsored their usual debate which was held at a motel along the freeway. Kolbe gave his opening statement first and when he spoke he was a little fidgety. He did his four minutes and it was my turn. I began by saying, "I'm Jim McNulty, the Irish guy from Bisbee who got 80 percent of the vote in the primary election." I tried to stimulate some enthusiasm, have a little fun, and get them to smile. Next came an opportunity for the candidates to question one another. We sparred over a few issues but I scored some real points when I brought up his position on curtailing retirement benefits for state legislators. I pointed out that he had never done anything to indicate he held this belief while he was in the state legislature himself: he had never filed a bill or criticized the retirement system. "Why then do you take this position now, and why does it contradict your previous words and actions?" I asked. When we were running against each other two years later we were preparing for another debate when the Kolbe advisors informed us that they would not be doing any questions and answers directly between the candidates that year.

The media had projected a very close election and on election night all eyes were watching as the vote trickled in. We spent the evening at a Democratic Party victory bash at the Jewish Community Center, but it was hard to enjoy since the District 5 race was very close. I started the evening with a good margin but the count got closer as the evening progressed. After midnight I was still ahead, largely because of the returns coming in from the mining camps. Phelps Dodge had closed their mine in Morenci and unemployment in Greenlee County had reached 60 percent. I received 2,417 votes to Kolbe's 710 in Greenlee County. At about 1:00 a.m. somebody phoned in a vote from the San Manuel/Oracle area where the strong union presence gave us another very en-

The McNulty family on inauguration day in January 1983: (left to right) Amy, Cynthia, Jim, Michael, and Jacquie.

couraging margin. Shortly afterward, I stepped in front of the microphones and said, "I've won. The race is over. I'm going to bed." It was late and I was tired.

The pundits still thought the race was too close to call, but Jacquie and I drove back to our room at the Arizona Inn and the kids went back to their homes. I told the desk clerk that I needed some rest and that he was not to put any calls through to our room. But I guess Kolbe must have bulldozed him because the phone rang at about 4:00 a.m. It was Kolbe, of course, and he was in a pretty sour mood. I guess I would have been too if I'd been in his shoes. With as much good grace as he could muster, he said, "I just wanted to congratulate you. It looks like you won." I thanked him and said, "It's been a good race." It really was a pretty good race because it had focused primarily on issues; there was a minimum of namecalling and obvious malice. The official vote count was 82,938 for McNulty and 80,531 for Kolbe.

The next morning I had an early meeting of the Board of Directors of the electric co-op down in Benson. I got up at the crack of dawn and drove down there, much to the amazement of the other directors who had heard the news of my election. I stayed for part of the meeting and then drove back to my campaign headquarters in Tucson. Morris Udall was there along with all the key people in my campaign. Mo made a speech and I made a speech and then we all adjourned to get back to work. There was much to be done. I began working to put my law business in good order and clear the deck for my next job.

We also got started on the job of hiring a congressional staff. I put together a screening committee consisting of Michael McNulty, Art Chapa, and Tom Chandler. We advertised in the papers asking those interested in working in Congress to contact us. I think we got about seven hundred applications by the time my committee told me to shut it off or find another committee. Many very talented young folks wanted to come on board so we stretched our staff budget as far as we could. All this enterprise relied on the talent of such young people as Mo Portley, David Duncan, and Paul Tang. We had a lot of diversity in the group and some really great people including my administrative assistant Jim Altenstadter and Dr. John Crow, who was a political science professor at the University of Arizona. We hired Jim Barry, who is now Pima County Administrator Chuck Huckelberry's assistant. We also hired Ruben Ortega, Allison Hughes, Margaret Steele, Cilla Duddleston, Jody Sullivan, Carla Blackwell, Linda Lewis, and Priscilla Kuhn. In Washington, June Foster, a former employee of Mo Udall, was hired as executive secretary. Linda Wright, wife of Bruce, succeeded June.

Jacquie, Amy, and I traveled to Washington at New Year's to enroll Amy in Georgetown Visitation High School. We also settled into a two-story Federal-style home at 38th and Woodley. George Steele put us in touch with the banker we used. The home proved to be in a perfect neighborhood—close to the National Cathedral, on the bus route to school, on an easy driving route to work, and it included many services that were needed in daily living—especially during snowstorms.

It had taken eight years, but I was finally moving into the third corner of the triangular equation of politics. I was ready to go down into the mine and begin working my shift.

CHAPTER NINE

Working My Shift

MY SERVICE AS A UNITED STATES CONGRESSMAN was the most exciting job I ever had. There were important calls to be made which had national and global consequences. There were big questions of war and peace in places like the Middle East and Central America. There were priorities to set, budgets to pass, and votes to cast on serious economic matters. There was also important work to be done for the people of Arizona. I loved it.

I served on the Public Works Committee and the Interior Committee which was chaired by Morris K. Udall. Mo helped get me started in the Congress and working together with him there was a real pleasure for both of us. We thought alike on so many things that we didn't need to ponder each other's positions. I knew his people and he knew mine. Other members soon learned that sometimes I was the one delivering the message, but it came from Mo. It wasn't all cookies and cream between Mo and me all the time, but in our time together in Washington, we were able to get some things done.

We stood our watch for the Central Arizona Project, as did every Arizona congressman since the days of Carl Hayden. A project on the scale of the C.A.P. could never be pushed through Congress today. It was one of the last big national water projects and it required the work of whole generations of powerful Arizona congressmen to become reality. By the time I was in Washington this marathon lobbying project had been ritualized into an annual pilgrimage to the House Appropriations subcommittee that controlled interior projects. The governor would fly in, and, together with Arizona's congressional delegation, would make an appearance before the subcommittee. In fact, Congressman Udall and Congressman Tom Bevill of Alabama, who was a senior member of the House Appropriations Committee and chairman of the Energy and

Water Development Subcommittee, made most of those decisions quietly over lunch and it was pretty much pro forma after that.

We also passed a bill which authorized the replacement of the turbines in Hoover Dam with much larger ones with far greater generating capacity. Millions of dollars worth of additional electricity were produced which created the question of where it was going to flow. We were able to strike an excellent deal for the State of Arizona, but not without a major fight. Some big-city interests, led by Sen. Barbara Boxer of California, sponsored an amendment which would have required the additional electricity to be auctioned off to the highest bidder. It was not easy to argue with this, and "The Boxer Rebellion" was a real threat.

Udall and I, of course, wanted this new block of power to be distributed to Colorado River states including Arizona, as had always been done in the past. Senator Boxer essentially told us, "Oh no you don't! You have had that cushy deal for the last several decades and now it's our turn." Mo, who was floor manager for the bill, was suffering from Parkinson's disease by this time. He couldn't run around the chamber as he had before, so I often acted as his gofer. As the vote was being taken we were sitting together watching the tally on the electronic board that shows every representative's name with a green light or a red light next to it to indicate their vote for or against. We each had our lists and we checked names off or added them back in as votes were cast and changed. When the Chair was ready to make the announcement, "All time is up," the vote was tied which would have resulted in the defeat of our counter-amendment.

Congress does not like to keep revisiting these hard-fought battles so we knew that this vote would establish the method for dealing with new electricity from federal reclamation projects long into the future. Mo studied the board for a moment, then turned to me and said, "Go get Bob Garcia." As I sprinted up the stairs in search of Rep. Garcia, Mo discreetly signaled the Chair to delay announcing the result for a few minutes. I found Congressman Garcia of New York and said, "Mo wants to see you right now. It's important." Garcia represented the Bronx and had no great interest in western power issues. He replied, "If Mo Udall wants me, he's got me. Let's go!"

We ran down to the well of the House and Mo said, "Bob, I see you voted "no" on this measure. Is it something about which you have a real

Jim McNulty pictured at a Capitol Hill reception in his honor with fellow Arizona Congressmen John Rhodes (left) and Morris K. Udall.

conviction, or could you change your mind?" Garcia indicated that he was willing to consider changing his vote. Mo told him that it was a bill about electricity from the Southwest and for the Southwest and that it wouldn't impact his constituents. Bob said, "Mo, if you say it's okay, then I know it is," and he took out the little card which indicates that a congressman has changed his vote. The card was signed and submitted, the red light next to Garcia's name on the board changed to green, and the clerk intoned, "Mr. Garcia changes his vote from no to aye." Udall waved at the chairman of the Committee of the Whole who then banged his gavel and announced, "By your vote of 199 to 197 you have passed...." The Boxer Rebellion was quelled.

Citizens complain justifiably that Congress dawdles and delays endlessly, but Congress can move plenty fast when it wants to. Another example of this came when I helped override a Reagan veto. The Congress had passed a bill appropriating about $36 million for research on the management of water resources to be conducted by land grant colleges. I had worked on its passage in the House and Senate. We never had an inkling that President Reagan would turn it down, but he decided federal support was not necessary and vetoed it. The land grant schools were furious. It was a small amount of money ($115,000 of it supported research at the University of Arizona) and less than had been appropriated in past years. The schools involved had a record of operating excellent research projects under the program. The sponsor of the bill in the Senate was a fellow from South Dakota named James Abdnor who was up for reelection.

South Dakota didn't have much, and doesn't to this day, but they did have a good land grant college which did this type of hydrological research. Water is critical to their survival, just as it is here in Arizona. Senator Abdnor and I got together and decided that we just might be able to override. Abdnor was a die-hard Republican and he had come close to persuading Reagan to sign the bill. He hated to challenge the leader of his party with an override attempt, but he felt he had no choice. He didn't want it done in an ugly or partisan manner which would embarrass Reagan unduly, which was fine with me. The president had been advised to veto the bill by Secretary of the Interior Bill Clark and by David Stockman, who had been Nixon's Budget Director and was thought by some to be astute on budgetary matters. Abdnor had good connections so we powwowed and came up with a strategy with the view that the president, if he saw such a thing mobilizing, wouldn't stay with his threatened veto. It would have been risking too much for too little.

After a couple of months with neither side backing down it was agreed that Mr. Abdnor would move that the Senate, where his party was in the majority, override the president's veto. He informed me that the time was nigh, and I broke in on a House leadership meeting to let them know that the Senate was about to act on the matter. We were in the caucus office where the party leadership met in private session, usually on Thursdays. I told Speaker Tip O'Neill that I wanted a spot on the calendar for an override vote. Majority Leader Jim Wright of Texas had the job of setting the agenda and he said, "Well, there are other things that are more important. We'll get to it soon."

I had brought my legislative director, Dr. John Crow, to the meeting

Bob Stump, congressman from northwestern Arizona and a friend of Jim's when they served in the Arizona Senate, greet daughter Cynthia at the 1983 inauguration.

Bill Richardson was elected to the House from New Mexico in 1982. He also served as Secretary of Energy under President Clinton and later as Governor of New Mexico.

Senator Barry Goldwater and his staff member Judy Eisenhower greet Jim at a Department of the Interior reception in 1983.

and we had done our homework. Crow told them that he had done some research which showed that the likelihood of a veto being over-ridden decreases rapidly as time elapses after the motion is made. Once the motion has been made the administration and its party really swing into action to avoid the embarrassment of having the president's veto overturned. In fact, we had learned that the White House had started a telephone blitz at nine o'clock that morning and it was already gathering steam among the Republicans in the House.

Senator Abdnor had gotten his override motion through the Senate in short order and it was our turn. Wright was persuaded somewhat by Dr. Crow's argument that if we were going to win this override vote we had to move *now*. He relented and indicated that he would "think about" scheduling it for a vote, "first thing tomorrow." Tip O'Neill, who had listened closely to Dr. Crow's advice, said, "Think about it nothing! We

A group of Irish-Americans celebrating St. Patrick's Day at the Irish Embassy in Washington, 1983: (left to right) Rep. Austin, Rep. McNulty, President Ronald Reagan, and Rep. Bill Coyne.

can do it right now! We're going on the floor at eleven o'clock and it will be the first item considered."

Fortunately, many Republican congressmen from the West had strong ties to their local land grant colleges and they were in favor of the program. I stood up in the House and made the motion to override, arguing the need for immediate action. I used some intentionally non-threatening language and said, "I think the president simply got some poor advice on this matter." Within fifteen minutes we had voted and the motion was passed, demonstrating the speed with which Congress can act. Such an event affords an opportunity for some partisan crowing, and one Democratic congressman chided me for letting the president "down too easy" in my remarks. But we got the vote and that was the important thing. I was told that it was only the second time in the twentieth century that a freshman congressman had led a successful veto override. All but one Democrat voted with us along with a substantial number of Republicans and the result was 309 to 81. The pundits called

Jim McNulty and Tip O'Neill in the Speaker's office.

it a clear victory for western agriculture. A few months later, when another override loomed, the administration invoked the specter of the defeat on the Water Resources Research Bill to motivate the Republican leadership to prevent a recurrence.

The main quarrel in Washington during the two years I was there centered on the fact that we had a president who had run in the name of frugality in government, yet, once in office, had been a wildly reckless spender. The Congress wouldn't approve some of his defense bills and he wouldn't approve some of their domestic spending. Both sides cited frugality in government as their primary motivation and the result was virtual gridlock in the budgetary process. The government ran on one continuing resolution after another during the 98th Congress.

These continuing resolutions usually came up on very short notice. The Speaker would get up and say, "At midnight tonight the oil runs dry!" He would urge us all to chomp our gum and stamp our feet and then go vote, "Yes," which would keep everything going for maybe another ten days. Every once in a while the members would get really steamed-up over this continuing impasse. Once, when we had one of these continuing resolutions coming to a vote, the Republicans and some of the wild-haired Democrats rebelled against the leadership. "Let's just send them a lesson!" they whispered. And they defeated the resolution. Then a sober voice in the back row said, "Everybody has had their fun. You can all now go home and say, 'Not me, I voted against it!' At 3:00 this afternoon we will vote on it again. And we will vote the right way this time. Any questions?" And at 3:00 p.m. fifty or sixty representatives who had voted against the resolution a few hours earlier voted in favor and passed it.

All this resulted in the first government shutdown in history when the oil was actually allowed to run dry for a while. The Reagan administration engineered this event because they thought the people would rise up in righteous wrath against the Democrats. But the reaction was quite different. Most folks saw that the Republicans had forced the shutdown and they got most of the blame.

Another event that occurred during my time in Washington was the bitter and violent strike against Phelps Dodge that began on July 1, 1983, in Bisbee, Clifton, Douglas, and Ajo. It rapidly degenerated. Strikebreakers were sent in, angry strikers blocked access to the mines, people got roughed up and a child was wounded by an errant bullet in Ajo. Governor Babbitt sent in the National Guard and Clifton took on the aspect of an occupied zone. In late September a monsoon-generated flood of biblical proportions and timing turned the San Francisco River into a raging torrent and destroyed about a third of Clifton.

Bruce Babbitt took a terrible beating in the press when the pictures of armed soldiers menacing strikers and their wives hit the media. The strike dragged on and in July of 1984, one year after it had begun, a force of two hundred officers of the Department of Public Safety broke up a union rally with tear gas and nonlethal projectiles. It was an ugly mess and families were being torn apart: some went back to work without a contract, others moved. In May 1984 I decided to undertake the impossible by setting up a secret meeting between Lynn Williams, who was the national president of the Steelworkers Union which was leading the strike, and George Munroe, C.E.O. of Phelps Dodge.

*Jim McNulty on the floor of the House with (left to right) Rep. Bob Carr,
Rep. Sid Yates, Speaker Tip O'Neill, and Rep. Claude Pepper.*

I first broached the idea to Jack Sheehan, who was the chief Washington lobbyist for the United Steelworkers of America. The Steelworkers had supported me in 1982 so I had made it a point to introduce
myself to Sheehan when I first arrived in Washington, and had seen him
on the Hill occasionally. I told him that I wanted to see if we could put
Lynn Williams and George Munroe in the same room at the same time
without anyone else being present except for me. Several weeks later as
things continued to heat up in Clifton, Mr. Sheehan phoned and advised me that Mr. Williams was in Washington and was willing to come
and talk to me. The stipulation was that there would be no publicity
whatsoever. That promise was kept.

Shortly, Mr. Sheehan and Mr. Williams arrived and I brought them
into my private office. I did not advise my staff of the appointment or
introduce my guests to anyone. Mr. Williams sat down and began by
asking what kind of monster this Munroe fellow was. I told him I knew

Munroe and called him by his first name, but that our acquaintance was purely social. I had met George at the annual parties thrown by the Phelps Dodge bigshots in Bisbee. The Munroe I knew was very urbane with an excellent sense of humor and did not wear his ideology on his sleeve. Mr. Williams was not wholly convinced but decided that there would probably be nothing to lose. He also wanted to be assured that there would be no publicity of the matter.

I wrote a confidential letter to George Munroe and advised him of my idea. Within twenty-four hours Munroe was on the phone asking me what I was up to. I told him, "I'm trying to settle this strike and put all my neighbors back to work." He said he was in New York but asked if he could come down to see me that afternoon. About three hours later he arrived with one other person and, as I had with Sheehan and Williams, I took them directly into my private office without any formalities.

It was clear that Munroe did not want to meet with Williams. The man who accompanied him was fervid about it and denounced the leaders of the strike as thugs and hoodlums. The two offered no hope of a settlement. I asked what harm could come from an unpublicized meeting between the two principals? While the Phelps Dodge men did not speak harshly of Mr. Williams, they did insist that the strikers were beyond reason or salvation and that Phelps Dodge was not going to negotiate with them. They left as quietly as they had come, and I concluded the entire matter by relaying the news to Sheehan that Munroe would not meet with Williams. He professed no surprise.

People from the *MacNeil-Lehrer Report* had gotten wind of the effort and called my office with a request to interview me regarding the strike. The whole thing had been an attempt to open a back-door channel of communications and was predicated on privacy so I declined their request to appear on the show. Eventually the strikebreakers at Phelps Dodge voted to decertify the unions. The mines at Ajo and Douglas were closed and little Greenlee County remains economically depressed to this day.

With a slim majority in the 1982 election and an opponent who spent my entire term preparing for his next run against me, I felt the need to spend as much time back in my district as possible. Mo wanted me to accompany him on a junket to go salmon fishing in Alaska at one point but I declined because I felt I could not afford the time away from the constituents. I felt keenly the pressure of the approaching 1984 elections. I knew it was important to be in my district as much as possible. After I left Washington at the end of 1984, I checked my calendars and tallied forty-three weekends spent in Arizona during the two years. Meanwhile, the courts were fooling around with the boundaries of Arizona's congressional districts again as a result of a redistricting lawsuit brought by the Democratic Party. This led to some real friction between Morris Udall and me.

Mo and I had some deep disagreements about the redistricting that would impact the 1984 elections. He claimed that his District 2, as drawn for 1982, gave him too narrow a margin. He was able to get a bigger chunk of Tucson put into District 2. Apache Bend, which had a large Republican registration, was moved into my District 5. I tried to get more of Santa Cruz County to compensate, but was unsuccessful. I told Mo the new district lines were going to be very harmful to my efforts and the quarrel continued for months, but he continued to insist he simply had to have the boundaries that had been proposed. The irony of all this is that the Republicans didn't even field a candidate in District 2 in 1984 and Mo only had a Communist to run against. Mo received almost 88 percent of the vote.

The 1984 race against Jim Kolbe was another high-priority contest for both national political parties. District 5 was still seen as eminently winnable by either side and the national organizations of both parties rallied for their candidates. Phil Gramm had stood up on the floor of the House and denounced me and a few others and this served to identify us as the primary targets in the 1984 elections. Scott Nelson, Western Regional Director for the Democratic National Committee, flew in to Tucson in March and said that the District 5 contest was "one of our top two or three races in the Democratic Party." He promised us as much help "as our resources will permit." He cautioned, however, that it wouldn't match the help Kolbe was getting from the Republican National Committee.

Somewhat to my surprise, I was the recipient of more campaign money in 1984 than I would have guessed. This was despite the fact that I had introduced H.R. 1799, a bill which would drastically reduce the amount Political Action Committees (PACs) could give congressional

Congressman McNulty and Congressman Udall, southeastern Arizona's Democratic team in Congress.

candidates. I received endorsements and donations from organizations including the VFW, the Vietnam Veterans of America, the AFL-CIO, the Women's Political Caucus, the National Council of Senior Citizens, a number of labor unions, and the League of Conservation Voters, which is an alliance of the big environmental organizations. Kolbe was endorsed and supported by the Business and Industry PAC, the Independent Petroleum Producers, the U.S. Chamber of Commerce, the Association of Small Businesses, the National Rifle Association, and the National Council on Defense, among others. I spent $523,359 to Kolbe's $573,644 in the 1984 election. News reports said it was the fifth most expensive contest for the House of Representatives that year.

Most of the people who had worked on my 1982 campaign were back again for the 1984 race. Priscilla Kuhn, who had been running my Tucson office, still played the key operational role and George Steele stayed on as treasurer. Prill and George were two of the reasons why my

Tom Foley, a Democratic leader in the House of Representatives from Washington state, sponsored a campaign event in Tucson.

staff was the envy of many of my friends in Congress. George had spent most of his adult life in the small towns of Arizona as a manager for the Valley National Bank and had risen to a high position. He took on the responsibility for doing all the reporting to the Federal Election Commission and his work was impeccable. He could also be very demanding when it came to matters of accounting. I often got hotel bills back with a note from him instructing me to provide this or that additional piece of information. We would say, "Yes sir," and do whatever he required. Tom Chandler was back as campaign chairman, along with experienced folks like Allison Hughes, Linda Lewis, Art Chapa, Jim Barry, Carla Blackwell, and many others. Rich Moret acted as our official media maven and my son Michael was very involved.

Pundits had labeled the 1982 race a contest between "the two gentlemen-Jims." The 1984 race, however, had a very different tone. This time around Kolbe had my voting record in the House of Representatives to run against and he was not shy about it. Walter Mondale was at the top of the Democratic ticket that year in an uphill struggle against the popular Ronald Reagan. The economy had improved somewhat and unemployment was not at the crisis levels we saw during the 1982 election. Some consider incumbency an advantage, and in many ways it is, but Kolbe did a pretty good job of turning it into a disadvantage by distorting my positions on issues ranging from defense spending and fiscal matters to crime and support of the copper industry. In general he painted me as a tax-and-spend liberal who was soft on the revolutionaries in Central America and on murderers and rapists here. This last charge was the result of my opposition to the death penalty, which he used aggressively as Election Day neared.

These messages were conveyed in various ways, including the planting of shills or hecklers in my audiences. I would make a speech at a Kiwanis Club and when I asked for questions this guy would jump up and recite some loaded question that was intended to embarrass me. This same fellow kept showing up at clubs all over the district. I would simply answer his question and then say, "You should tell the people here that you follow me around to these appearances and that you aren't a member of Kiwanis, are you? You aren't a member of any of these clubs." But the fellow had the skin of a rhinoceros and I just figured it was part of the process. When Gary Hart appeared with me at a rally in Tucson some young Kolbe supporters were there wearing large dunce caps and carrying McNulty signs . Morons for McNulty. At a parade in Bisbee some young Republicans trotted alongside the car I was riding in and passed out Kolbe literature. As political chicanery goes, this stuff is pretty mild. But this kind of nonsense was rare in the 1982 contest.

I was endorsed by the *Arizona Daily Star* in an editorial that appeared on October 27. The piece summarizes my case for reelection quite concisely and I reprinted it in one of my last mailings. I am offering it to the reader here because it provides an accurate record of the candidates' positions on most of the salient issues of the 1984 District 5 congressional contest:

Dist. 5 Congress: McNulty
Capable incumbent has an excellent first-term record

The public has seen only two years of the excellent work Rep. Jim McNulty can do. With a second term, the likable Democrat will go on capably representing his newly created 5th Congressional District.

McNulty faces a familiar opponent, Jim Kolbe, a former Arizona legislator, in a rematch of the 1982 race.

In his freshman term, McNulty wrote key amendments and legislation, impressing his colleagues and serving the interests of the voters. He successfully led an override of President Reagan's veto of a bill important to Southern Arizona. It called for the study of water law, an area of survival for Arizona, and was probably the only time a freshman congressman ever managed to beat back a veto by a president from an opposing party.

McNulty pushed an amendment based on cost-saving provisions of the Grace Commission, a move that would save the government $25 million a year on the costs of military construction projects. He took the action despite opposition by his own Democratic leadership, showing he acts on his convictions, despite party loyalty.

McNulty's opponent, Republican Jim Kolbe, has some enlightened views of social issues that are disdained by many in his party. He and McNulty both share approval of the Equal Rights Amendment, affirmative action, and disapproval of the Simpson-Mazzoli immigration bill.

They part company on several other vital issues. Both candidates oppose the MX missile but Kolbe's charge that McNulty opposes all weapons is in error. McNulty voted for the Trident Submarine, the Cruise and Pershing missiles and recently for a $295 billion military bill.

McNulty voted for a verifiable freeze of nuclear weapons production. His opponent said he does not favor "freezing an unstable position." How "unstable" is the United States' fighting capability? The Soviet Union has 8,240 strategic nuclear weapons. The United States has 11,190. Both arsenals represent overkill since it only takes a few thousand warheads to totally destroy each nation.

Both McNulty and Kolbe want a balanced budget but their methods differ radically. Kolbe wants a constitutional amendment, a painstaking campaign of many years length. McNulty wants Congress, the body that approves or rejects federal budgets, to draft a bill to do the job.

Kolbe, unlike McNulty, supports short-term military aid to Central America and has accused the incumbent of consistently voting against any aid, including economic aid, to stop the move toward totalitarianism in Nicaragua.

McNulty is against military aid, including U.S. support of the

Nicaraguan "contra" forces. But he has voted four times in support of economic aid for the region, including a $5.8 billion appropriation of economic aid for all of Central America.

The race for District 5 has been marred by repeated distortions of McNulty's congressional voting record by his opponent. McNulty described his campaign appropriately when he said he wants to be judged on the basis of his record in Congress and not on literature put out by the Kolbe camp that tries to misrepresent the congressman's stands.

On issue after issue, McNulty comes down on the side of common sense. His congressional record is solid, and he deserves a repeat engagement in the Capitol.

A couple of weeks before the election the Republicans sent out a mailing styled as an "Issues Quiz" which purported to outline the candidates' positions on seven issues. It was sent to the rural areas of the district where my margin had carried the day in 1982. The mailer contained at least one obvious error as well as misrepresentations of my positions on crime and support for the agricultural industry. We knew from our tracking polls that the race was extremely close and we felt that we had to set the record straight.

It was decided that Tom Chandler would convene a press conference to refute the misinformation. He identified the outright error regarding my rating by the American Farm Bureau Federation and explained the complete story of my record on crime and punishment. In my comments to reporters I echoed Tom's opinion that the Kolbe forces were guilty of misrepresenting my positions. We started airing a television ad showing Kolbe as Pinocchio with a nose that grew ever longer. *The Tucson Citizen*, which had endorsed Kolbe in 1982, backed me in 1984. On October 24, Ted Craig wrote an editorial in the *Citizen* titled, "Congressional Rematch Takes Low Road This Time." It includes these observations on the tone of the contest in 1984:

> It's a different campaign this time. Now we see a Kolbe who never stopped running after his defeat, a man who seems obsessed by a desire to enter Congress at any cost. He is supported by the full dollar power and venom of his national party which has zeroed in on some potentially vulnerable first term congressmen who won close elections in 1982.

The tactics directed from the national level are not nearly the same as those previously followed by Kolbe. Now the campaign appears to be a lot more anti-McNulty than pro-Kolbe. It's not as though Kolbe could claim that he was motivated originally by a desire to serve the public by ousting a liability from office; there was no one in the new office when he started running. But now he follows the throw-the-scoundrel-out line as the national party serves up mud by the bucketfuls.

The voting public is being hit by a barrage of charges designed to make McNulty look like a menace to the human race in general and the good folk of this congressional district in particular. A radio commercial depicts this decent man as a two-faced, deceitful individual who, when on Arizona television, poses as the admirable person he's always been, but when he goes back to Washington—watch out! He does terrible things, knuckling under to Big Labor, chumming around with Tip O'Neill, voting with the Democrats. He is accused of being "soft on crime" and, incredibly, while seeking voters in copper country, of selling the copper industry down the river to foreign interests. It's a silly idea, but you never know what the voters might believe.

Thomas Chandler, a Tucson attorney and head of McNulty's campaign, last week called what he said was his first press conference in 46 years of political life and expressed his outrage at a mail-out from the GOP's national headquarters....

I can sympathize with his outrage. I too have been turned off by the unbelievable assaults on McNulty, a respected small-town (Bisbee) lawyer, former legislator, former member of the Arizona Board of Regents. Anyone who knows McNulty has to be appalled at the smears directed at a man who has added a rare touch of intellect and wit to our Congress.

On Election Day, November 6, 1984, I began the day with a 5:30 a.m. rally at Democratic Headquarters to motivate the troops for our final push to get out the vote. From there I drove down to Bisbee to vote and do some last-minute campaigning. By evening the family and I had assembled in a room at the Carpenters Union Hall in Tucson where the Democrats were gathering for their election night festivities. I had been watching the tracking polls for months by this time and I had seen Kolbe's numbers inching up, point by point. I told the family that we very well

Jim McNulty in a quiet moment before an appearance in downtown Tucson during the 1984 campaign.

might lose this one, "and if we do, I want to see stiff upper lips and no blubbering."

My supporters were encouraged by the early results, but in my experience the initial hours of a close election don't mean much. Sometimes politicians like to find a silver lining and you hear them say things like, "Hold everything! Those outside precincts are coming in and now here's that critical Holbrook vote!" With the current procedures and computer counting methods you really don't know what you're getting as the vote counts come in. There are always the guys who sit around and analyze the forty-six votes in Chinle precinct, but I don't think it does much good these days.

It turned out to be another long night. The Democratic faithful in the hall watched the news of Ronald Reagan's landslide victory over Walter Mondale with resignation and reserved their hopes for the District 5 congressional race. Kolbe soon pulled ahead by a tiny margin and maintained a slim lead for the first few hours. But by midnight his lead was widening and by 1:00 a.m. he was on top by 6,000 votes. I made my concession speech at 1:30 a.m. with the family standing beside me. I told the assembled faithful that Kolbe had won and that I had no regrets about my term in Congress or my campaign. "Chins up!" I said, "We have a right to walk off the stage proudly." I poured champagne for campaign workers and family and deflected questions about my future and the reasons for the loss.

When it was all said and done Kolbe received 116,075 votes to my 109,871. It would be easy enough to blame it on the Reagan landslide, but the president's huge margin coincided with only a very small movement to the Republican side in the District 5 congressional race. Economic conditions had improved since 1982 and the voter turnout was bigger since it was a presidential election year. Babbitt and DeConcini were not running so I did not benefit from their get-out-the-vote drives as I had in 1982. There are dozens of possible reasons for the loss, but the truth is a race that close can boil down to the candidate's haircut. Any position you take or vote you cast in Congress can alienate enough single-issue voters to make the difference. If I had it to do over again I don't think I would change a thing I did in those two years.

During the time I served in the Congress my general disposition was to refrain from spending money recklessly, to keep a strong defense without beggaring ourselves, to have a tax system that is reasonably fair, to have a foreign policy that was decently enlightened, and to have some sense of compassion for those who have the very least in our society. I believed that people who could work ought to do so, but I also protected food programs for children and hot lunch programs for kids from low-income families. I always fought for education. I voted against the MX missile and I was very uneasy about our infatuation with nuclear instruments of war. I didn't believe that our policies in Central America or Lebanon were sensible and I voted that way. I thought that the hundreds of millions of dollars we sent to the Contras in Nicaragua was a waste of our tax money which only led to a bloodier stalemate.

During these years of the Reagan Revolution the crucial underlying issue for lawmakers, in my opinion, was how far apart are we willing to allow the opposite poles of political opinion to stretch? In my view, they were already as far apart as the society could tolerate without becoming dysfunctional and I was not willing to contribute to stretching them any further. The Reagan administration was able to convince middle-class America that it was supporting a whole race of malingerers and scofflaws. They fed the people the idea that they were being discriminated against by ne'er-do-wells. Out of that came a very utilitarian and ultimately unhealthy political atmosphere which defined government as the enemy. There are certainly lots of problems, but we are not going to solve them by being angry at the institutions that are at hand to deal with them, however imperfect they may be.

Fiscally, the Reagan years were the most reckless in the history of the nation. We doubled our national debt in five and a half years. It took us two hundred years to create the first trillion dollars of debt, and it took Reagan and the Congress only five and a half years to create the second trillion. We pumped more money into the Defense Department than they could intelligently spend. It wasn't that the Department of Defense was run by crooks, it was simply that pumping a billion dollars a day into the military was beyond their capacity to absorb in a sensible, useful way.

*   *   *

WHEN I WENT TO WASHINGTON IN 1982, I decided to keep a record of my experiences there. I wrote frankly as an inside observer of the legislative process as it existed in the 98th Congress. It seemed to me that such a first-hand account might be of interest someday, and so a selection of my observations is appended to this memoir in the section titled, "Letters from Washington."

CHAPTER TEN

Life After Congress?

AFTER THE 1984 ELECTION JACQUIE AND I RETURNED to our home in Bisbee, but only for a few months. I interviewed with the firm of Bilby, Thompson, Shoenhair and Warnock in Tucson and they encouraged me to join them. I became a partner in March 1985 and resumed my career as an attorney. Jacquie and I moved to Tucson and bought a townhouse in the historic Snob Hollow barrio just north of downtown. In May 1989, the Bilby firm completed a merger with Snell and Wilmer which I had helped to negotiate. I became a partner in the Tucson office of Snell and Wilmer and continued my legal work with them. I made my last career change in May 1993 when I joined the firm of Brown and Bain as a partner. My son Michael was the local managing partner in the firm so I finished my legal career working alongside him in another good law firm.

After the 1984 election I donated the balance in my campaign treasury to the Pima County Democratic Party and remained active in the party at both the local and state level. I did not foreclose on the possibility of another run at Congress. I watched the developing field of Democratic candidates for District 5 as the 1986 contest approached, but in the end decided not to put the family and myself through the political wringer again. I called a press conference and announced that I wasn't going to be a candidate that year, leaving open the possibility of a run sometime in the future. Today, aided by the wisdom of hindsight, I believe I should have run in 1986 and that I might have won.

Jacquie and I did some traveling after we left Washington, including a return visit to the Soviet Union in 1986. We went with a group from the University of Arizona organized by Dr. Del Phillips, who was Director of the UA Russian Institute. It was a three-week tour beginning in Leningrad, proceeding through Lithuania and Moldavia to Yalta and finally on to Moscow. Compared to 1962, I found a Russia that was better fed, better clothed and seemed more confident. There were more cars on real highways, more apartments and more public transportation. But the progress had been achieved through many small concessions by the state to consumer hopes. Together, these concessions weren't enough to give the citizens the sense that they had succeeded economically. The improvements were just enough to keep them sullen instead of openly rebellious.

I went to the Soviet Union armed with the names of eleven Refuseniks, people who had advised the Soviet Union that they would like to emigrate to Israel. The Soviet Union was very unforgiving of such treachery and treated those who chose this option harshly. If an American announced his disaffection with this country and his determination to live elsewhere, most Americans would say, "Good riddance!" and contribute to the cost of a one-way ticket. In the Soviet Union, leaving the motherland is regarded as an insult which undermines national prestige and is an ungrateful response for all the Soviet Union has done for the would-be émigré. I had five names in Leningrad, and one evening I departed the tour along with Tucsonan Larry Cheek who came along as my interpreter. From a pay-phone we called the four numbers we had, finding only one person who answered. Lena Keis's initial response to Larry was timid and guarded, but once she understood our purpose she provided vague directions to her apartment.

Lena Keis lived in a grimy apartment in a crumbling building in a drab neighborhood on a dilapidated street. Lena holds a degree in engineering and her husband George is trained as an electrical engineer. They applied to emigrate in 1980 and were both refused. Her parents were allowed to leave and her father had died in Israel. She was not allowed to attend the funeral. The family has been subjected to shabby treatment in the workplace, at school, and in general since they requested to emigrate. Lena had been fired from her job and was unemployed. George was working as an inspector of heavy trucks.

Although she was a fairly young and pretty woman, Lena was aging prematurely. We delivered some gifts we had brought from Tucson and she wept when we left. We also met with the family of Joseph Pekar in Moscow. This time a dedicated cab driver had delivered us through the warrens of enormous apartment buildings until we found the right door. I gave Pekar the balance of the gifts we had brought, asking him to

Former Arizona Regent Jim and his wife Jacquie attend one of many events at the University of Arizona.

distribute them to the three other Refusenik families we had on our Moscow list. As I was leaving, I asked Mr. Pekar what, if anything, future visitors could bring for him. He answered with a sad smile, "A visa."

Mo Udall soldiered on in Washington despite his struggle with Parkinson's disease and we remained close. In 1991 he fell down a staircase in his home. Such falls are one of the consequences of Parkinson's disease and they can trigger a sudden advance of the symptoms. This is what happened to Mo. He retired from the House of Representatives in May 1991, almost exactly thirty years after he was first elected to Congress in the special election of 1961. After the fall, Mo never recovered his ability to speak. Or at least I never saw him speak in any of my visits to the Veterans Hospital in Washington where he received such excellent care. In 1998 my old friend was named to the U.S. Capitol Historical Society Athletic Hall of Fame for his accomplishments on the bas-

A grandfather's fringe benefits: the San Diego Zoo.

ketball court. I accepted the award for him and gave a speech that concluded with these words:

> Mo endured personal misfortunes, none worse than his present physical condition. But within his gaunt ill frame, we know a penetrating intelligence still lives. We know that he catalogs yet more stories to entertain and amuse, but to bruise no one. We have been graced by his presence, and in days when Arizonans are feeling their self-esteem slightly sliding, we know that this man distinguished himself and honors us who chose him. The *Congressional Quarterly...* upon Mo's retirement spoke this judgment of the ages, "The dominant political forces at work today systematically devalue the two traits that made Mo's mark: a willingness to take risks and a commitment to larger institutions than himself." So let it be.

Of course I thought about running in the special election to fill Mo's seat in 1991. But by that time District 2 had been redrawn to include part of Maricopa County. Ed Pastor, a Democrat with his base in Maricopa County, had a clear geographic advantage. When there are several candidates in a primary, the one from Maricopa County is the winner. So, thinking that there was no place for me, I decided to do something different, something I had wanted to do for a while. At the ripe old age of sixty-seven, I joined the Peace Corps.

I was the second-oldest in a group of about sixty volunteers going through the preparations and training. Most of them were idealistic young folks who were in it for the experience of living in a third-world country. They called me Don Jaime and I thought they were admirable American kids. I thought the seventy-year-old fellow who was the only one senior to me was quite a guy too. After completing all the training and preparations I flew to Guatemala in September of 1992.

We were taken up into the mountains between Guatemala City and the town of Antigua where we were each installed with a local family. The Peace Corps had learned that boarding volunteers together retarded their ability to learn the language. So we spent our evenings with local families where we were immersed in the language and culture. They fed us and gave us a place to sleep. Some of the host families had electricity and running water, some didn't. Sanitation was very poor, especially up-country.

The local people were Maya Indians while the moneyed, political class were Hispanics who looked down on the Indians as subhumans. The discrimination they suffered and the conditions in which the Maya lived were a real eye-opener. Here, in the ruggedly beautiful mountains of Guatemala, I really saw firsthand the cruel political and economic realities that spawn revolution and war in Central America and elsewhere. The Maya made up over fifty percent of the population, yet had virtually no representation in the national legislative body. They had a multiplicity of different dialects which were mutually unintelligible so it was very difficult for them to act together. There were sporadic uprisings, not to mention an active guerrilla movement. The army turned murderous from time to time and Guatemala was a pretty dangerous place.

Our mission was to prepare for the planting of fruit orchards by selecting suitable sites and plant varieties. Once a few of us wanted to visit a village some distance away. We were told that we were forbidden to travel there because of guerrilla activity in the area. On another occasion some guerrillas jumped up out of the bush alongside the road

*Jim McNulty with his cheering section after his race in the 1998 National
Senior Olympics held in Tucson. Jim is standing with arm around
granddaughter Clare, along with (left to right) Jacquie, Michael, Cynthia
(wearing hat), son-in-law Brian Buller, daughter-in-law Linda McNulty,
and Amy, holding granddaughter Jacquie.*

and stopped the bus that was used to transport us into town for shopping. I was not on that trip, but those who were had their watches,
wallets, and passports collected by some very serious young masked
gunmen armed with AK-47's. It certainly would not do to lose any Peace
Corps volunteers, especially one who was an ex-congressman, so I was
somewhat limited in what I could see and do. But it was quite an experience for about two months until my intestinal tract became the nurs-
ery for some of the insidious intestinal parasites that call Guatemala
home.

I lost weight, and I didn't have much to spare. One night my dinner
consisted of two Vienna sausages. I developed pains in my gut and grew
weak and wobbly so they took me down to a hospital in Guatemala

City. We had all been trained to cook our food well and we were provided with bottled water to drink, but everybody lost weight down there and many got sick enough to be returned home. Many others quit because of the conditions so the attrition rate among volunteers was pretty high. I had really wanted to complete the entire two-year hitch in Guatemala, partly so I could perfect my Spanish. The illness was real, however, so I was forced to leave after only about two months in-country. Back at home and under Jacquie's care I took the appropriate medicines and gradually recovered.

In the winter of 1993 the World Peace Through Law Section of the Arizona State Bar sponsored a seminar with Father Desmond Wilson as keynote speaker. Father Wilson was an Irish human rights activist and recipient of the Oslo Peace Prize who had founded the Springhill Community House in Belfast. He told us about seven young men from his neighborhood who were being held on dubious murder charges and also about the Emergency Legislation which suspended certain civil and political rights in Northern Ireland during the unrest. He invited us to observe the trial of the Ballymurphy boys and bear witness to what was taking place in the legal system there. A series of meetings followed and in January 1994 we formed a delegation of concerned citizens who committed to traveling to Belfast to see firsthand the realities of the "Irish Troubles." The delegation, mostly composed of attorneys, finally left for Ireland at the end of October 1994.

We arrived at a time when the prevailing emotion seemed to be a cautious but still skeptical hope for peace. British soldiers were patrolling mainly Catholic neighborhoods with fully drawn automatic weapons, but they were now wearing berets rather than helmets. The trial of three of the Ballymurphy boys was still in progress and we attended the proceedings. During our stay they were finally freed on bond after three years in prison. We also met with leaders from six different political parties representing the entire spectrum of Irish political opinion. This was not my first trip to Ireland, and I felt very comfortable there. Although the downtown streets of Belfast were mainly empty after dark, we were still able to experience some of the Irish people's warmth and love of music.

In 1998 I decided that it might be fun to revisit the athletic glories of my youth. This desire on my part received the full approbation of my close and admired friend, Gayle Hopkins, the Associate to the Director of Athletics at the University of Arizona. I had never stopped running even though I was in my seventies. While I was in Washington I used to run in the neighborhood around the National Cathedral at least a few times a week. I trained on the track at the University of Arizona stadium and entered qualifying races in Phoenix, Las Vegas, and St. George, Utah, in a quest to make it to the national Senior Olympics which were held in Tucson that year. In the Tucson race I think I came in thirteenth in the 440 among a field of elders who could probably outrun a lot of teenagers. I also worked on the committee which organized the whole thing which was not nearly as much fun as competing in the races. Jacquie, as well as our children and grandchildren, were there cheering me on. The only thing that was missing was my old dad watching silently in the bleachers.

EPILOGUE

THE BARD SAYS THAT THE PAST IS MERELY PROLOGUE. That's my case, too. And so I wind up here bringing all this business to a good-natured conclusion. I have more reason than most to accelerate into the last stoplight. I have been diagnosed as having a mild case of "essential tremors." At the moment, the biggest handicap is that my already wretched penmanship has been rendered even worse and I have been learning how to do things with my left hand. I still run or swim every night for some modest exercise and my diet is robust to say the least. I am seventy-six and still enjoy the artistic and athletic offerings that abound here in Tucson.

I retired from the practice of law at the close of 2000, but still keep my office on the nineteenth floor of the City Center Building in the suite of the Brown and Bain law firm. I can walk from our home in Snob Hollow to my office in about fifteen minutes. That is where you will find me during business hours on most days when I am not busy doing something with Jacquie.

My involvement with various community organizations continues. Last week this meant sorting through some fifty excellent applications to select recipients for grants from the Marmis Foundation and the Jewish Community Center. It also meant attending difficult meetings of an advisory committee to the Diocese of Tucson which is trying to develop policy to deal with the sexual abuse tragedy within the Church. And there are always the luncheons, dinners, fund-raisers, and social events to attend. My plate is full and I certainly do not lack for useful work to do and new challenges.

The preparation of this book has been one of those challenges for nearly a year now. The process has been arduous enough and has summoned up some ghosts. It has also brought back many poignant snapshots from childhood and youth. Life in St. Theresa's Parish was crowded, frugal, and difficult, but such considerations were not burdensome to us. Our spiritual needs were taken care of and then some. My mother was always on the lookout for conduct and language she described as "fresh." My dad was always ready to take us down to the cinema at South Station where, for ten cents, we could watch football highlights for an hour, completely enthralled. We were as many as six people living in a two-bedroom flat which is smaller than our townhouse in Snob Hollow today. I also recall the tender way my grandmother Gallogly used to hold my hands in hers when we sat and talked. Family, Church, health, education, political freedom: those were the things that really mattered then and still do today.

Life for Jacquie and me is enriched by our own children and grandchildren. Michael and his wife, Linda, both practicing attorneys, live here in Tucson with their daughter Clare, who shows great artistic promise. Amy is making a career in retail, and her husband, Brian Buller, is looking for a career in Federal law enforcement. They are also Tucson residents along with their two girls: Jacqueline, and Jill. Cynthia, who owns an environmental business, lives in Scottsdale, about an hour and a half away. I want to acknowledge my nephews, Michael and Joel, who live in California. When all the children and grandchildren are around for holidays and special events, our home is a noisy, happy place. There is nowhere I would rather be.

In addition to producing some splendid grandchildren, my offspring have collected more than their share of academic degrees, as did my sisters. My sister Nancy wound up with a Master's degree in Spanish Literature followed by a career in the U.S. Agency for International Development with postings in places like Senegal, Colombia, Argentina, and Rome. She moved to Tucson in 1997 and died here in 2000. My younger sister, Anne, graduated from Boston University then earned an advanced degree in Library Science. She worked for the California Junior College System for twenty-five years and is currently retired in Albany, California. I freely admit to taking pride in my family, and often reflect on the decision made by my immigrant ancestors which made all of our accomplishments possible. Their risky choice to leave the green and stony hills of County Leitrim and County Sligo to make a new home in America opened the door for all of us.

Faith is another constant in my life, as it was for my immigrant ancestors. After a lifetime spent in the spiritual embrace of the Catholic Church, I believe that the Church does provide many of the answers to the fundamental questions of life. It is an institution with a two thousand year history that provides answers to most moral questions and inspires our spiritual life. The Church offers certainty in a world of uncertainty and bears none ill. It suffers criticism gently and never closes the door to any constructive application. Over time it has endured many blows, but it always revivifies itself and its members. The Church will always have problems to confront, and today is certainly no exception.

As I write this, the most pressing problem is the scandalous behavior of a few priests who have betrayed a sacred trust and done harm to children and young people. Another intransigent problem is, quite simply put, the relationship between women and the legal scholars of the Church. Can a woman be ordained for the priesthood? Should priests be allowed to marry? Should the Church continue to circumscribe birth control? The women of the world have largely ignored the dictates of the Church regarding procreation.

Sometimes I wonder how any institution could be so out of touch on such critical issues. I think it is a compliment to the Church that women have defied this decree without an excessive expression of anger or outrage. I believe that a distinction should be made between abortion, which the Church rightfully denounces, and birth control. The Church has handled this issue badly. There are other ancient dispositions of the Church which are out of step with the ordinary practices of Catholics today. But I know from long observation that believers in peaceful change can be effective working within the Church and that this is the only way to achieve the uniformity which the Catholic Church values so highly.

An abiding pride in my Irish heritage remains as another major theme of my life. My thinking about the conflict between the English and the Irish has evolved, however, and I have concluded that the United Kingdom is not a wicked creature on the world stage. I have even become somewhat of an Anglophile in my old age. The United Kingdom of today is a decent and civilized nation with a demonstrated record of peaceful pursuit. England is unfailingly loyal to America and should not be burdened with minor league efforts to destroy it that are in total contradiction to the religious principles and sense of justice of the vast majority. I am hopeful that the forces necessary to finally bring the long slaughter in Ireland to an end are nearly in place and the troubles in Ireland are and should be a matter of diminishing concern.

A large share of the burden of this effort rightfully falls on the Irish in America who have, for too long, fallen into the practice of demonstrating loyalties and fierce emotions more appropriate to a football game than to constructive political discourse. There are greater concerns at stake than tribal loyalty. Responsible people will put aside everything that urges violence and mayhem. I ask all Irish people to forswear the guerrilla tactics of years gone by and abandon the sophomoric efforts to launch quasi-wars that are both sinful and futile.

I have not lost my attraction to politics. When I pick up the *Arizona Daily Star* and read about the developing field of candidates for the Democratic nomination in the new District 7, for example, I analyze the information from the viewpoint of a potential candidate. I suppose we all filter things through the sieve of our own experience. Most of my adult life has been lived from one election to the next. It has been fueled by my love for the excitement of high office and big decisions. When I look at the names of candidates and their polling numbers, I see opportunity. When there are four or five people running, somebody may slip in there with 30 percent, and win. Sometimes I think that if I didn't have this tremor business, I could go out there and do it again today.

I gradually grew accustomed to the unnecessary and sometimes embarrassing attention I received as a man who had, albeit briefly, served in the House of Representatives. I learned to enjoy some aspects of it, like leading the parade on St. Patrick's Day or Labor Day. I have perfected the preparation and delivery of eulogies, a task I am called for all too often these days. I still can't walk down Stone Avenue downtown without stopping several times to greet old friends. In 1996, after returning from a Wildcat basketball game, I wrote the following paragraphs about the phenomenon of being an ex-public figure:

It was intermission in Tucson at sold-out McKale Center with the Wildcats in still another comfortable lead against a PAC Ten rival. Several rows below me was a prosperous looking young man, probably a professional, whose eyes had met mine twice. When our eyes met a third time he rose and climbed the four rows up to my seat and introduced himself. He pumped my hand warmly and said, "You will always be my Congressman." It was a touching moment.

It happens a dozen times a year or so since I left office some twelve years ago. Clerks in stores or seat mates at concerts, even casual street traffic, all are sources of like sentiments from people I do not know. It is tiny, but it is very powerful. It is probably meaningless in any cosmic sense. But to me it is nurturing and as valuable as life itself. I don't handle them well, but these short conversations live on in my memory.

In his excellent diary of a congressional campaign Simon Bullitt muses on the reaction of candidates to the vicissitudes of the campaign trail. The candidate is inappropriately discouraged by a rude or even mildly uncomplimentary remark. And moments later he or she exults in a kind word all out of proportion to its meaning. There's a greater sense of continuity of public life than commonly believed. We're mesmerized by the vulgarity of politics, the trashiness and the expensive vilification. And, surprisingly, there are some people who don't forget you, even after a decade or more.

I have regularly been invited to places where the host or hostess simply wants to introduce "former Congressman McNulty" to all her friends, acquaintances, business associates, and relatives in order to somehow impress them. The public treats these scenes with a degree of solemnity that is both kind and amusing.

I am long since inured to the certainty that my obituary will dwell on my brief federal service. I was not sufficiently well-loved to be reelected, but not so useless as to be completely forgotten, which would deny me these precious reminders of another life, the most exciting I ever had.

These events are also a chance to speak more forthrightly than I could previously. Now I can indulge in the prerogative of an old man to express himself without fear. For example, I love nothing better than to identify myself to an audience as a left-wing, pinko, liberal, Irish Catholic Democrat. And proud of it! That would have generated real rage at one time but now I am invulnerable to it. Now I can have some fun and my advisors have nothing to fear.

These unsolicited words of kindness from strangers are always unexpected and brief. But they are a regular, powerful reminder that I must have been doing some good things to still enjoy these admittedly tiny gestures of faith, admiration, and goodwill which survive after all these years.

Letters from Washington

WHEN I ARRIVED IN WASHINGTON at the close of 1982, I decided to maintain a record of my observations of the federal Congress. It seemed to me that a regular firsthand account, if done faithfully, might be of interest someday. I wasn't trying to pursue any particular political objective, in fact I rarely if ever mention bills I sponsored or votes I cast in the entries reproduced below. Instead, I wrote frankly as an inside observer of the legislative process as it existed in the 98th Congress. It was my intention to treat my subject with a soft hand. I tried not to bruise a soul if it could be avoided and I sought to maintain a humorous thread throughout.

I wrote most of the following passages in my office on the third floor of the Longworth House Office Building, frequently early on Monday mornings. They were written quickly because things were happening very quickly, and I wanted to capture the events while the experiences were fresh. I used the names of others rarely, and my own does not appear anywhere in the letters. Borrowing from the Gaelic, I signed each of the letters with the pseudonym "A. N. Ooltayg." A rough translation would suggest that the musings are the product of a son of Ulster.

DECEMBER 20, 1982

The Class of '82 in the 98th Congress is smart, well-educated, and impressively experienced in government. It is also young, long-haired, blow-dried, and heavy on Slavic surnames. It is rightly adjudged cool to Reaganomics and wrongly considered a reincarnation of pre-World War II New Deal attitudes.

Both the Democratic and Republican newcomers have been fed lavishly, entertained mightily, and soft-soaped expertly. Loyalty has been engineered craftily and advice has been given attractively and unremittingly. Each member had a brief onset of remorse: one inquired out loud if he was the only person in the room who had wondered "why the hell I wanted this job."

They have brought ideas and independence but more in the vein of hard-headed and quiet rationality than the outward rebelliousness of a prior generation. They are not going to suffer the pure ideologies of the current administration further. But they aren't comfortable with what one called the "give-away-the-farm" theories of their predecessors, particularly their Democratic predecessors, whom they see as being long on heart but short on head.

They don't like the enormous unemployment and they don't like the high long-term interest rates. They don't like the huge deficits and they don't like the federal government's budgeting process, assuming there is one. They want the system to work and they are not outwardly hostile to capitalism. They are seemingly sensitive to justice for women and minorities, but they talk in terms of excellence, performance, and accountability that, carried too far, hold little promise for those least well off.

They want to do widely dissimilar things ranging from the elimination of the Capitol's elevator operators (the elevators are automated and require no operators) to dispensing to the other America a big chunk of the federal government now in place in the District of Columbia. Some wonder out loud if we can afford a bicameral federal legislature, noting that lots of sophisticated democracies do no worse with but one body.

They are uneasy at the pace of legislative life, disquieted by the hurly-burly floor action and the surface evidence of near chaos on the so-called debates. There are a total of eighty-one of them: fifty-four Democrats and twenty-seven Republicans. Mortality tables tell us that forty of them will never be reelected to the Congress. Which forty are they?

For a substantial minority of the eighty-one, the pay scale is a come-down. And the cost of living is a come-up, or, more accurately, a fly-up. One member claimed that housing prices were not exorbitant, "they were only extortionate." Some have already spoken from the well of the floor. Mighty few were listening, but the speeches had all of the agreeable excitement of a baptism.

Ahead lies some pretty interesting action. There is no doubt that the Democratic leadership intends to fling Texas Representative Phil Gramm from the eighth story of the Capitol for heinous defection. The view is that the subsequent collision of Mr. Gramm with the earth is not proximately related to the flinging. Then there will be a lesson in democracy, or perhaps a lesson in excessive democracy, when the House votes interminably on filling committee positions. That raises the heavy question suggested by Mr. Rostenkowski's claim that the November election was an instruction from the voters to stop dilly-dallying and govern. More later.

A. N. Ooltayg

JANUARY 4, 1983

The new Congress has been sworn in, organized, advised of its prerogatives, and dismissed. Four days after the Congress began, it left for a two-week "District Work Period." The phrase is intended to describe a process better known as "campaigning."

The swearing-in was accompanied by nearly all of the members (416 out of the 435), and by about eighty children, some as young as six months. The practice of allowing children on the floor for the swearing-in was recently begun and is probably worthy of an earlier age Hanoverian parliament. For the spectators, the choices were to describe the scene as boring or as one of bedlam. No other choices seemed to be permitted.

Some anticipated moments of high drama never materialized. Representative Gramm of Texas resigned from the House because he was either a "snitch" or a man of "high principles," depending on one's disposition. His legislative execution was thus made moot and was followed immediately by his announcement of candidacy from the other party for the seat he had just resigned.

Committee assignments consumed the balance of the week and the period probably represented a high point, if not in work, at least in motion by the House of Representatives over the next two years. Then, studious newcomers went off to a think tank and the veterans left to inspect matters of interest to the American taxpayer in such places as Brazil and Australia.

Meanwhile, bad news dominates all discussion. Deficits grow larger and long-term interest rates do not grow much smaller. The president seems increasingly isolated as fewer and fewer members of his party are willing to endorse his economic program unqualifiedly and most of the Democrats have long since jumped ship.

The worsening economy has substantially aggravated problems with Social Security, and it is highly likely that this spicy meatball will be on everyone's menu in short order, a meal no politician contemplates with pleasure. The anguish of budget making and appropriating for the year that is now more than 25 percent gone. Under the rules, the year that begins next October 1st should be substantially handled by May 15th. Will they do it? Tune in again.

A. N. Ooltayg

JANUARY 26, 1983

On Monday the state of the union address as history was the subject of a funny television parody. But on Tuesday the president refused to oblige and instead read an eleven-page address of curiously low wattage that somehow measured the job as much as it did his performance. The high point was a cheer, principally from Democrats and at least partly derisive, for the president's strongly expressed intention to improve the economy by attacking unemployment. Mr. Reagan handled it with good nature and actually emerged one up from the exchange.

The White House simultaneously published a press release which candidly stated that the deficit for fiscal year 1984 would be $189 billion. All the other estimates for the current year are for a deficit of $200 billion and the previous year showed a deficit of $110 billion. The total increase in the national debt of $500 billion in thirty-six months is a matter of profound concern to all, notwithstanding the generally conciliatory words of the president and the generally gentle reception of it by the members.

The week was further marked by the appearance of Secretary of the Interior James Watt before the Interior Committee in what had all the aspects of a full-scale bear-baiting session. A ranking member advised Mr. Watt that the record of the Interior Department was "an abomination." Partisans lost no time in advising the secretary that he was possibly "the best Secretary of the Interior the country ever had." Considerable room for other options lay between the poles.

The secretary advised Arizona that the slippage in delivery of water from the Central Arizona Project could be "two to three years." Chairman Udall thought that was a worst-case scenario, but it still surfaced the possibility that the water might be as late as 1991 to 1993 in arriving in Tucson.

Meanwhile, the committees organize the sub-committees and the sub-committees take their initial uncertain steps. The flavor of bi-partisanship is sharply in the air and, for a variety of reasons, fiscal policy is front and center. It is a new and interesting national enterprise. Maybe.

A. N. Ooltayg

FEBRUARY 8, 1983

Perplexing as it is to outsiders, the attitude of Washingtonians toward their professional football team is a robust fact of life. Members of Congress transport other members of Congress to the Capitol in wheelbarrows. The president gives every federal employee a two-hour respite to attend a parade honoring the Redskins. Numerous forgettable speeches are made under the unanimous consent rule.

The nation's capital, trying simultaneously to be a national capital and also a small town full of pride and sufficient unto itself, has the problems that could easily be predicted. The latter wish dominates at the moment, but the pot continues to boil on Capitol Hill as hearings on the Social Security overhaul continue. At the same time enormous efforts are being made to compel retrenchment in the enormous defense outlays and vast efforts are under way to put a public works bill in place.

....Current plans are to go to the floor with the Social Security bill on March 8th and to achieve the first budget resolution by March 15th. That will represent very heavy going, but everyone is dissatisfied with running the government by continuing resolution. Whether they are dissatisfied enough should be known fairly soon.

A. N. Ooltayg

FEBRUARY 22, 1983

Spring begins in Washington before it begins anywhere else. Its commencement is noted by the arrival of the constituents on Capitol Hill. All the heavy-duty citizen lobbying is concentrated in the first three months of each congressional session. Teachers and school board members and unions and manufacturers and benevolent associations and fraternal societies and a few organizations with no detectable purpose routinely arrive at the seat of government at the beginning of the year. The causes are many as viewed by title. But as viewed by means, the causes are but one: money.

Everyone with the tiniest conceivable slice of turf to preserve in terms of federal benevolence is present here in Washington with powerful reasons for the maintenance or even the increase of the status quo. And there are no supplicants who would simultaneously deny the necessity of trimming the budget, or lowering the deficit, or even balancing the budget. Most have plans for funding their program. The two current favorites are a national lottery and slashing foreign aid. The latter is a perennial frontrunner.

In addition to these constituencies, there are the groups that are apprehensive that their perquisites may be undergoing some severe scrutiny. Most of the elements of the health care system fall into this category. And, of course, all recipients of entitlement, pension, and retirement programs live here. The arguments fall into three categories: the moral, the just, and the political. The latter is generally accompanied by some veiled threat.

In the meantime, the nation's capital endured the third largest snowstorm of the century. If the Russians sought an end to the functioning of American civil authority and if they could summon up a twenty-inch snowstorm on demand, the Soviet military budget could be very nearly eliminated. The subways (where it does not snow) were closed during the snowstorm. But warmer days came swiftly and a fast pace was quickly restored. The Congress has been promised the opportunity to look the Social Security question squarely in the eye. The findings of the commission have made this perilous exercise less unattractive.

A. N. Ooltayg

MARCH 7, 1983

Washington is the land of the ultimate threat. Loss of career, position of power, or even of life (or at least, enormous physical harm), are beginning places. It may be, however, that the final punishment is simply the loss of cafeteria privileges on alternate Thursdays. This remedy has been suggested, only half in jest, after certain congressional miscreants have escaped even a symbolic slap on the wrist for their misdeeds. But usually, things begin with an ultimate threat.

The chairman of a major committee tells one of the maximum leaders that the chairman has doubts about a bill. Maximum Leader says, "I'd hate to have to take away your committee chairmanship." A member approaches a friend who has the power of assigning members to committees. The member urges a particular appointment with these words, "Put so-and-so on Merchant Marines or you are (expletive deleted) dead." The member thus addressed indicates that he did not even know that so-and-so was interested in that committee. No mind.

All of this tends to contribute to the surreal nature of the job. Most of the debates have been held in informal and un-witnessed settings. Minds are so thoroughly made up that hearings are scandalously ill-attended. A major committee with forty members may be hearing an important bill with as few as one person present. He or she is there because the process requires a chairperson.

The Congress has finally let out the clutch on some things. A new Civilian Conservation Corps has been passed. An expensive bill for the teaching of science and mathematics has been passed. Nearly $5 billion has been authorized for a jobs bill....

A. N. Ooltayg

MARCH 24, 1983

"Overkill is the name of the game around here." The Speaker made this pronouncement in a matter of fact tone. He is in the upper twenty-five of those with the most seniority in the House of Representatives and is known as an able, intelligent, and just man.

He is right. In a world where we begin with ultimate threats to deter action, it only figures that overkill would be the rule of thumb to produce action. So it is. No order is given once nor to fewer than four persons. No one assumes that yesterday's promise has any currency today. Members who have agreed seven times to take a certain position are intentionally quizzed for an eighth time, and a ninth time, and so on.

All of this tends to make an already frenetic world unreal. There is a tendency to be afflicted with unreality in the process under the best of circumstances. Overkill makes it more so. One might almost think that legislation is done by proclamation. Bills bear the name of seventy or one hundred, and in extreme cases, as many as 250 sponsors. Those same bills can't make their way out of committee. And refusal to sign a bill is tantamount to some veiled suggestion that it won't be voted for either. This is true even when the bill for which the signature is solicited contains one hundred pages of finely printed material.

And still a thread of common sense is maintained and, more often than not, prevails. But it does not do so easily. The tide of mail engulfs the offices. The members hire additional help and the taxpayers subsidize the cost of responding to tens of thousands of preprinted postcards.

Notwithstanding all of this, the Congress has passed a very substantial bill providing millions of dollars for jobs and improvement of public structures. It has made vast reforms in the Social Security system, it has signaled a clear breakthrough in the direction of improving the scientific and mathematical skills of the next generation, it has created a wholesome refuge for the unemployed youth of the nation, and it has preliminarily put in place a reasonably sensible budget. The Easter vacations are here and the members are gone, but much work really has been done.

A. N. Ooltayg

APRIL 8, 1983

The Easter recess concluded and was followed immediately by the post-Easter recess. The Speaker took the keys with him to China and overlooked telling anyone. Consequently, the members of Congress present during the week (who tended to be the new folks) stood around and griped about the loss of valuable campaigning time.

All of this was tempered by the rather good reception accorded members during the Easter break. A Boll Weevil who had seen new ways and voted for the budget proclaimed, triumphantly, that only one person in his southern state had rebuked him for his support of the budget. But elation does not last long in this business: grandson of nuclear freeze is just over the horizon. Then there are a couple of billion dollar credit bills. And looming near is the deadline on appropriations.

A young whippersnapper from Arizona is challenging both the Justice Department and the Defense Department with a bill to allow folks in the armed forces to sue for medical malpractice. The administration officials are downright huffy about it, especially when they learned that a speedy hearing of the proposal was scheduled. The Senate has been unable to agree on a budget and five Republican members have already spoken up for the repeal of the third year of the Reagan income tax cut....

...Washington is unduly wet and improvidently cold. There is some sense of too many things coming unstuck. The House thinks the administration is violating their prohibition against efforts to bring down the Nicaraguan administration. The people who cheered the appointment of George Shultz as Secretary of State are now beginning a subtle campaign writing him off for his failure to pull a rabbit from a hat. And the administration, which has claimed some inability to monitor the Russians as the reason for the MX program, has now published, in infinite detail, a book setting out at length the vast armed service capabilities of the Russians. You can obtain a copy for $6.50. It all goes to ask the question: will the center hold?

A. N. Ooltayg

APRIL 22, 1983

The return of the world tourists prompted around Congress what passes for a flurry of activity. The Senate Finance Committee voted down the president's budget seventeen to four. The president believes things are unraveling in Central America at a remarkable rate. That prompted a request for a special joint meeting of the House and Senate, the eighth since World War II. Nuclear freeze was debated for the fourth time and it is widely believed there are no new thoughts to be expressed on the subject. But there are still twenty plus amendments and the process, from a parliamentary standpoint, is the House's equivalent of the Senate's tolerance for filibuster.

The city is concluding one of the wettest months in its history. That may account for the Congress bogging down for the month. The most resolute act of the body was the enormous attendance at the funeral of Congressman Phil Burton, the Congress's answer to Brendan Behan, and a figure larger than life. His funeral eulogy appropriately noted the likelihood of his being busy already at the process of reapportioning the hereafter.

The Congress is scheduled to work all but four days in May and June and must get cracking on final budget resolutions. The administration is adamant about a 15 percent increase in defense spending. The House and Senate prefer far less. The administration is adamant about supporting the governments of Central American countries like El Salvador. The House and Senate are skeptical to a like degree and disenchanted with thinly veiled American sponsored insurgencies like the one in Nicaragua. The administration is absolutely opposed to trade retaliation against the Japanese, yet the House and Senate believe the Japanese are cheating our nation and its workers. Who resolves these? How? When? The next few months will demonstrate such resolution as is apt to be obtained.

A. N. Ooltayg

234 / Running Uphill

MAY 16, 1983

The nation's greatest game of chicken in this century continues. Not much noticed by the press and rarely discussed in those terms, the game is deadly and the stakes are enormous. The players are the administration on one side and the majority of the Congress on the other. And within that majority there are a substantial number of Republicans. All of this goes to the ultimate question as to who will be the first blinker/blinkee.

The administration is willing to tolerate the enormous deficits as a temporary price for the enormous tax cuts of 1981. The substantial undoing of the 1981 tax cuts by the 1982 tax increases lulled many into dreamland. In short, the administration fundamentally believes the monster of government must be starved and the majority, perhaps the substantial majority, of Congress believes the monster has been starved to a dangerous degree already. Some strange allies have emerged from all of this. Prominent heads of corporations and former Secretaries of the Treasury have warned against continued borrowing to finance tax decreases. And organizations from the most liberal labor unions to the most conservative professional associations have done the same.

But the appeal to mindless hostility toward the central government and to a fundamentalist wrath toward taxes have mobilized a modest number of formal forces but an enormous number of informal forces formed only around one goal. The deficit for the first six months was $121 billion. That was $11 billion more than the deficit for the entire fiscal year of 1983 when we nearly doubled the record for the biggest annual deficit ever incurred in the history of the country.

So who blinks first? Thus far neither party has wavered. By administration standards, the House is beyond redemption and the Senate approaches treason. By congressional standards, the administration has departed the real world and forsworn direction and influence, entitled only to a polite hearing before an out of hand dismissal. And a small band continues to dream of an American bipartisan fiscal policy.

A. N. Ooltayg

JUNE 6, 1983

Eighty-eighty time has arrived in Washington. The figures refer to the temperature and the relative humidity in no particular order. In fact, the relative humidity sometimes exceeds 80 percent and no member of humankind, vulnerable to assaults on his or her intelligence, would be found alive, dead, or comatose in the District in August. At the same time, the leadership has stepped up the workload. For several years the Congress has not passed any appropriations bills by the first of July. This time the House is going to try to compel votes on six of the Appropriations Committee's thirteen Subcommittees by that date. It has scheduled Energy and Water, Commerce, Justice and State, Treasury and Post Office, Agriculture, and HUD, with action hoped for by the magic date. If this much is successful, it will be a tribute of substance to a Congress that really did come to work, especially in the House.

Overlying everything are the stubborn, intractable positions taken by the Congress on the one hand, and the administration on the other. The Senate and the House are only $21 billion apart in projected needed revenue. The administration and the Congress are light years apart. As a diversion, the Republicans have mounted well-financed campaigns against the Democratic National Party, the Democratic Telethon, and selected Democratic House incumbents. Some of the rhetoric is more worthy of battles a year hence. Mencken claimed no one ever went broke underestimating the taste of the American public. Is there a political corollary? Is it also impossible to overestimate the capacity of the American public for unceasing political races? It is a distressing thought.

A. N. Ooltayg

June 20, 1983

"Congress doesn't need more space, it needs better work habits!" So spoke a cheeky freshman in intramural debate recently on the subject of moving the west wall of the Capitol building. To the surprise of many, the committee proposal for extending it was decisively defeated and it's on to restoration. But the freshman's criticism remains. The long ingrained habits of the Tuesday through Thursday club will not readily yield. Two-thirds of the members can be back in a local airport ninety minutes after leaving National Airport in Washington. And go they do. A member from a major American metropolis states matter of factly that he has not been in Washington on a Monday since he was sworn in.

The public contributes to all of this in an unintentional but positive fashion. The complaints that the members are not frequently enough back in their districts are convenient pegs for the two-nights-a-week-in-Washington gang to hang their hats on. In a recent exchange at the end of the week the Majority Leader was asked for the following week's schedule. He indicated bills would be considered under suspension on Monday but no votes would be taken. The emphasis was on the last clause. The Minority Leader was, apparently, not fully satisfied and asked, "When will the votes be taken?" The Majority Leader assured him there would be no votes before Tuesday. The Minority Leader was still not sufficiently reassured. "What time on Tuesday?" he asked. The Majority Leader indicated the votes would be late enough in the day to accommodate the members.

At the bottom of the colloquy was the conceded position that members would be furious if required to vote before early or mid-afternoon on Tuesday. Why? All the members want perfect voting records but they want those records accumulated over the shortest possible period of time. And so, in they come on Tuesday morning and out they go on Thursday evening. Proponents of the extension of the west wall of the Capitol said they needed more space because committee rooms were hard to reserve. One cynical member observed that if the Congress only worked one day a week the Capitol building would never have enough committee rooms.

Staffs work long hours. Leadership works long hours and the strivers work long hours. But the gritty political reality of the Tuesday through Thursday club syndrome lives on. And now that fundraising season is upon us in full force and now that most of these affairs are held on Tuesday, Wednesday, and Thursday evenings between 6:00 and 8:00 p.m., there will be plentiful anger if the leadership holds the House in session late.

What time does that leave? For the hard slogging it leaves four to six hours on Tuesdays beginning at noon. And it allows six to eight hours on Wednesdays and Thursdays with the sessions beginning at 10:00 a.m. And that isn't long enough. The first authors of this government wanted a House of Representatives that offered a quick fix to an unhappy electorate. The assumption was that substantial time would be spent among the folks. The further assumption was that the elected would listen and the electorate would talk. Now, the practice is that the elected are frequently among the people, but the speakers and the listeners have changed places. All pretty much to our disadvantage.

A. N. Ooltayg

JULY 1, 1983

For the Congress the major holidays represent a modern Diaspora. The speed and the size of the emigration compel wonder, if not awe. As usual, the congressional leadership demanded a week's work before the Fourth of July. And as usual, the membership was on tiptoes by mid-afternoon Thursday and long gone by sunset.

On the other hand, an admirable effort has been done in one field. Eight of the thirteen appropriations committees have brought measures to the floor that have been approved. And the total would be nine but for some gimmickry by the Rules Committee. Additionally, the Commerce appropriation has been considered, and that only leaves the perennially difficult Defense Appropriations Bill as a major effort. Last year at this same time not one of the thirteen bills had been passed by the House by Independence Day. The contrast is little short of startling.

In the meantime, the House and Senate have agreed on a budget which is a "budget buster" according to the administration. Curiously enough, it is simultaneously the vehicle for a smaller deficit than that proposed by the administration. In fact, the administration is bruised by the bipartisan nature of a budget approved in a Democratic House and a Republican Senate. The administration has threatened vetoes of appropriations bills and will have every opportunity to do just that in the next two weeks. If there is government by continuing resolution next year, it will be the function of the veto and not congressional paralysis.

...Well over three thousand bills have now been filed, and only about another thousand will materialize this year. However, every proposal is a potential statute through the adjournment of the Congress in 1984. Or, as has been previously said, no man or woman in this republic may consider his or her life or property out of risk while these learned folks meet. Mark Twain put it differently, stating, "There is no distinctly native American criminal class except Congress."

A. N. Ooltayg

July 21, 1983

July is an ugly month in Washington, at least from the standpoint of the climate. That is the good news because the bad news is that August is even uglier. House action, or inaction, has been as steamy as the climate and progress has been moderate.

The House spent a traumatic, ugly day censuring two errant members for moderate sins immoderately practiced. The public censuring occurred in the well of the house for the two miscreants and offered two unsettling moments reminiscent of the initial punishment inflicted on sinners aboard the Bounty. The significant aspect of their offense was the youthfulness of the objects of their affection, but the sniggering heard among the members measured the deed.

...In two weeks the legislative process will come to a total halt for thirty-one days. And thirty days after that the odds are strong that the Congress will function on a crisis basis. But while the Congress vacations (in fact campaigns), a fairly large-scale unqualified war is being waged in Central America without the benefit of declaration or even formal acknowledgment. What was once a pretense for intercepting arms is now in fact a full scale effort to overthrow a freely chosen government, a government whose establishment America approved. The authors and executors are determined there shall be no choices other than between Marxists and capitalists. Shrillness has begotten shrillness and the Congress will ultimately be presented with two sorry options.

A. N. Ooltayg

AUGUST 23, 1983

The House of Representatives gave up the ghost Thursday evening, August 4. The folks had put in two solid weeks of work and were beginning to generate a modest amount of self-pity, the hallmark of all society. By sundown on August 5, they were gone. Many would not be back until September 12: a recess of five weeks and two days. Given that amount of time, the innocent would assume the decks would be cleared for action on Monday, September 12.

Not so. Wrathful declarations were heard against "over-eager efforts" to schedule action on September 12. Even that one tiny day was begrudged and nothing will happen before Tuesday, September 13. The irony of it all is that Yom Kippur falls on Friday, September 16, and the House will recess at the close of business on September 15. The three-day work week is immortal!

Meanwhile, in an especially maladroit effort, the Republican National Committee defined thirteen Democrats as Communist wimps for voting against an amendment to the International Monetary Fund bill. The Republicans carefully avoided sending the press release to Peoria, Illinois, the home of Republican Leader Bob Michel, who voted in the same fashion as the thirteen Democrats. The bill, much treasured by the administration, passed by six votes and half the thirteen outraged Democrats have asked the president whether he prefers the bill or muzzling the Republican National Committee. Sounds interesting.

Five appropriations bills remain to be moved out of the House. The defense appropriation will be the most difficult as round three of the MX controversy approaches. And then time is running out on the Democrats' promise to increase tax revenues by $12 billion to keep faith with their budget. They did try, but the Senate rejected the ceiling set on the maximum income tax reduction. A lot of Democrats were relieved and will use that as an excuse to do nothing further.

Labor Day will see the return of these modern missionaries to the rest of the world. China, Europe, South America, Central America, and Africa will all have been the beneficiaries of congressional inspection. Men and women whose lives have shifted to the national scene find life at the Kiwanis Club in Willcox, Arizona, or the Garden Club in Emporia, Kansas, too bland. A terribly busy priest attempting to leave the confessional told a would-be penitent named Flannery to come back next week unless his sins were especially grave. On the way home Flannery meets Murphy who is himself on his way to confess his sins. Flannery warns Murphy away, saying, "Murphy, he's only hearing murder cases today." So with the veterans of the hill. Finally, they only hear murder cases.

A. N. Ooltayg

SEPTEMBER 23, 1983

The Congress returned from a five-week recess without any detectable enthusiasm. Waiting was a substantial caseload which was overshadowed by the savage execution of a commercial airplane and its 239 passengers. The constant expressions of wrath revealed by their intensity the inability to retaliate in any satisfyingly vengeful way. Even the president drew the wrath of the very conservative by his restrained approach.

Obedient to Murphy's Law, foreign affairs were threatening to go to hell in the Middle East as well. The deaths of Marines in Lebanon were prompting demand for the invocation of the War Powers Act. This would give the Congress the right to summon the troops home. But all exceptions have their own exceptions. The administration promptly invoked the Chauduri case as support for the proposition that the ability of the Congress as defined in the War Powers Act was effectively terminated. It is a common Washington event. All arguments are circular.

The fiscal year is about to end with the biggest deficit in the history of the nation. Not only that, the deficit will be twice as big as the next biggest deficit in the history of the nation. And to round out the circle, that latter deficit was itself a record and twice as big as the previous biggest deficit in the history of the nation. The numbers are: 1981, $50 billion; 1982, $100 billion; 1983, $200 billion. The good news is that the 1984 deficit may not even quite tie the 1983 deficit and be in the vicinity of "only" $185 billion. The stock market should be staggering but it reached a new high.

The end of the fiscal year is a week away and continuing resolutions will once more be born and hatched. This is the system which bases its intellectual integrity on the premise that everything that was done in the previous year was done both accurately and well. No audible guffaws, please.

New members are increasingly restless and getting the wind in their rigging. Two mildly confrontational meetings have been held with the leadership with no immediately observable results other than the spoiling of the digestion of a few. It is not a situation that will go away.

A. N. Ooltayg

October 7, 1983

The House completed its post-summer, pre–Columbus Day recess with an approval of the administration's determination to keep Marines in Lebanon for eighteen months. It was not without bitterness. A predictable legislative rule of thumb is that when a member begins a conversation, "I voted for the measure, but...," the member wishes he or she had voted otherwise. There was an unusually heavy use of the term the day after. Its appearance was most feisty at a Whip meeting where the Speaker was assaulted by a rueful supporter in terms of the supporter's dependence upon the Speaker's representations that he would "monitor the situation constantly and carefully."

The stage has been set in a debate which departed from all natural alliances. The measure was highlighted by the final appeal of the Speaker to support the president. A majority of the Democrats voted otherwise and the tumultuous applause that followed the Speaker's remarks came almost exclusively from the minority. The pattern persisted in the Senate where all but three Democrats voted against the measure. Seemingly, the administration would recognize the narrowness of its consensus.

The debate on occasion reached epic levels with memorable quotes coming from Representative Gibbons who claimed that our Lebanese forces were "too few to fight and too many to die." But the most dramatic remarks came from Arizona's John McCain who was held in a concrete box for six years as a prisoner of war in North Vietnam. McCain claimed the agreement was to preserve peace and asked rhetorically, "What peace?" The agreement was claimed to aid the Lebanese government and McCain asked, "What government?" Some Israeli supporters insisted support of the bill was necessary for the defense of Israel. Some claimed the possible death of U.S. Marines would be read by an American public as sacrifices on behalf of an Israel that has always vowed to do its own fighting and dying.

Residual bitterness persists and friends and foes alike pray for no more injuries, no more deaths.

A. N. Ooltayg

NOVEMBER 4, 1983

In case you haven't noticed, the school of thought that believes death is honored only by more deaths is back in business. Shameless waving of the bloody shirt has been the message of the past two weeks. In that period of time well over two hundred Marines were killed in an explosion that brought a four-story reinforced concrete building down on sleeping American Marines in Beirut. And a dozen more were killed in the overcoming of the nation of Grenada, an island of 133 square miles with the population of Schenectady, New York.

The futility of the Beirut enterprise and the irrationality of the Grenada invasion defied reasonable explanation. Consequently, the message of the president was that the deaths should "not be in vain." It was always thus. This is an appeal to another instinct. It throws away rational debate because rational debate produces a contrary conclusion. And it simultaneously puts on the defensive those who would otherwise argue rationally, because it simultaneously suggests that the patriotic course lies solely in the name of the emotional appeal to prevent vain death.

It would seem America should have learned a lesson about not allowing death to be in vain. The Vietnam experience scarred us for all time. And when the debate really grew ugly, the unscrupulous stirred up the damage from that conflict into a state of hatred against those who questioned it. But the opponents of this madness have their own problems. They fail adequately to distinguish between unbalanced national decisions on the one hand, and the faceless, decent, unknown American soldiers who carry out those decisions in a spirit of obedience and honor. Men and women who are, for the very reasons of their motivation, entitled to our undying respect, affection, and the redress of all that tangible things can redress. We must compartmentalize our enormous admiration for their sacrifice and address, as a separate consideration, the massiveness of our error.

Grenada has become a nearly accomplished fact and in less than seven days. That is more a mark of the size of the venture than the skill of the directors. Further argument will be nearly moot. It will be claimed that this marks a decisiveness in our outlook that would be reassuring to our allies. Curiously enough, our allies deserted us en masse in their public positions and in the United Nations votes. And our complaints about Afghanistan will henceforth bring sharp Grenadan rejoinders. So the thing is done and the argument is pretty much moot. All we can do now is honor the dead, heal the wounded, and care for the widows and orphans.

But we must realize that greatness can be manifested by restraint and that no death will have been in vain if it encourages us to re-examine our course and amend our direction.

A. N. Ooltayg

NOVEMBER 23, 1983

No western parliamentary democracy has invented a graceful way to conclude a legislative session, and Congress is no exception. It only rarely indulges in the antics of the state legislatures where clocks are stopped so that work can be completed within the deadlines mandated by law. But the actions of the federal Congress, while less dramatic, may be profoundly more expensive or radically new in direction.

America adjourned its parliament two weeks ago with less turbulence than in prior years, but not without a quota of heavy-duty last minute actions. In the final twenty-four hours the International Monetary Fund was underwritten to the tune of $8.4 billion, and housing for the poor and middle-income folks was underwritten for $16 billion. In all, on that final Friday the Senate passed sixty-seven bills, resolutions, and other Measures. The House passed twenty-four. Almost all of them were done by unanimous consent.

Ostensibly debating something called "Physicians Comparability Day" the Congress forgave a handful of doctors who were overpaid some

$30,000. In the same bill Congress exempted itself for two years from most of the monthly expense of the Civil Service system without yielding any substantial rights in the system. It simultaneously gave itself an interest-free two-year loan for the balance of the monthly payments. Congress had voted itself retroactively into both the Civil Service and Social Security systems in May, and then let itself pretty well off the hook in November.

The House asked unanimous consent to call up H.R. 3766 giving two uninhabited islands in Puget Sound, totaling less than eighty acres, to the Makah Indian Tribe. No one objected. Done! So it was with the Las Vegas Paiutes, whose reservation comprises 12.5 acres in Nevada. And so the Congress quit. All the cockamamie was in place. Smiling, the leaders of both houses talked in stupendously insignificant patter, and then asked the president for permission to adjourn. In fact, the Speaker and the Senate Majority Leader purposely included language in the adjournment motion that gave *them* the power to return, *sans* White House orders. Perhaps the provision reflected a measure of post-Grenadan uncertainty on both sides of the aisle.

On the year, Congress reformed Social Security, but repudiated its own budget. Both houses agreed last May to trim some spending and raise some taxes, for the current year and for three succeeding years. In the end, they did almost nothing in this regard. Congress gave the president eighteen more months in Lebanon and sixty days in Grenada. It debated endlessly and supported a nuclear freeze, sort of. But it approved MX missiles and disapproved of Japanese cars, at least in great quantities. It approved the IMF and paying dairy farmers not to produce milk. It watched a decline in inflation with pleasure and silence, watched continuing high interest rates with concern, and watched the enormous budget deficits with horror, and the administration's lack of concern about this with disbelief.

It did grit its teeth on nerve gas and force that out of the budget. And it did hold the line to some degree, keeping defense authorizations at an 8 percent growth rate, about half that proposed by the president. And it completed the appropriations process more quickly than has been done in twenty years. It was often inefficient and occasionally untidy. It started, stopped, bobbed, wove, and dribbled. It contradicted itself, rose to redemptive heights, was coarse and even vulgar. It was, in short, a faithful mirror of the humanity we call America.

A. N. Ooltayg

DECEMBER 20, 1983

Congress's calendar year ends in places like Big Timber and Bisbee and New York, of course. For the 535 members there are likely 535 separate New Year's rituals. In the frozen, snowy northern perimeter, in the gentle night coolness of Florida's Gulf Stream–washed east shore, or the crackling, breathtaking clarity of the Southwest desert nights, and in the very crowded, tumultuous masses of America's urban megablobs, the old year leaves.

The epicenter of national expression is beautiful and impotent. Magnificent and useless. All effective legislative power has been totally dispersed. And a president uncomfortable with the constitutional restraints of the national legislature waivers between filling the vacuum and the fear of stimulating congressional activity.

The buildings stand, permanent memorials to an unequaled spirit. But the shakers and movers are about their business elsewhere. And Christmas, a week away, gradually deflects wrath, discourages legislative initiative, and indulges slackness, tardiness, and a festive spirit. Good will slips in along the way and the ceremony shall ever be annually repeated. For the sober moments (there are some), thoughts go to the enormous national debt, the enormous annual deficits, the Congress's disgraceful failure to reconcile the budget, its pathetic defeat of a rule that would only allow debate on the problem. Lebanon, where we pattern our efforts in the direction most denounced by our foe, grows more deadly daily. The economy grows slightly better slightly more slowly. But ten million don't have work and allies who believe in selective free-trading practices are doing precious little by way of adjustment.

Presidential politics are both a bore and a drain of assets, both on a cosmic scale. The lighted west face of the nation's Capitol—the most famous and most recognized (and most loved) scene in the world—is framed with a still glistening snow. The republic lives!

A. N. Ooltayg

JANUARY 24, 1984

Congress reconvened in high good spirits at noon on Monday, January 23, and proceeded to talk for five hours in official session. Lots of good things were covered: the Super Bowl, the recklessness of the Democrats, the recklessness of the Republicans, etc. Distributed for the information of all and the amusement of many was the 1984 Calendar. It indicated that there were eight days of work in January and twelve days of vacation in February. March would be an all-carry, no-roll month but April would see a nine-day vacation and May would see a six-day vacation. June would be another rigorous month followed by July with twenty-two days of vacation and August with nineteen. September only calls for a five-day vacation.

So there goes the neighborhood. There will be primary elections all summer and fall and the big poll-taking is on November 6. Some of the gloomier pessimists have advertised that Congress has precisely one hundred workdays within which to adopt the budget and pass thirteen appropriations bills. And all the leaders on both sides of the aisle have forsworn any significant legislative program. The malaise that marked the last two days of the previous session now threatens an entire year.

The business of not getting down to business is increasingly unsettling. In a body where there is already an enormous gridlock of will, it is a mistake to generate another gridlock based on political one-upsmanship. One suggested way out of the maze might be the refusal of Congress to extend the debt limit unless it is accompanied by genuine reform. The alternative is bringing the government to a halt, but such strong medicine might well make sense to some of the game players.

Senator Magnuson of Washington used to talk about doing "kitchen work." He simply meant the homely, mundane things that have only one merit: keeping the system functioning. A mere 4,500 bills were introduced in 1983. That's good news. Some sessions have seen over 14,000 bills introduced. A couple hundred bills will be sent to the president. He has vowed there will be no tax increase and so in all likelihood there will not. He has commanded a reduction in spending but will furnish no blueprint that makes a major dent in a $180 billion deficit. His polls say he is doing just fine, thank you. The more it changes, the more it stays the same.

A. N. Ooltayg

JANUARY 30, 1984

January 25th found the president advising the Congress on the state of the union. It's good, he said; and even better than that, it's "back." He didn't say where or what it was back from, but in specifying where it was now we can safely surmise what and where it has been. The "where it has been" included insufficient prayer in school rooms and lack of income tax credits for the parents of parochial school kids. It is now back from a heavily crime-ridden society to a moderately crime-ridden society, back from fiscal wild hares, back from questionable patriotism, back from admiring left-wingers, and back from timidity in the face of terrorism.

The president believes terrorism is a football team, all wearing the same colored jerseys with numbers, a commodity to be overcome in a fair fight and not at all the deadly, furtive, suicidal, and frequently solitary folk of reality.

It was the kind of speech an incumbent president, bent on running for reelection, should make in the quadrennial year. It's good for him and only a little less so for the Congress. In times that are somewhat more satisfying, the nation has a reluctance to turn out incumbent members of Congress. But perhaps the president is comfortable with one body reasonably responsive to him. Perhaps he has given up on the House with its now less compliant Speaker and its 270–165 margin....

A. N. Ooltayg

FEBRUARY 10, 1984

The Congress reconvened on January 23 and worked its three-day week for a grand total of three weeks. It then chucked these fervid efforts on February 9 in favor of a resumption of resolve, not to be undertaken until February 21. The abiding subject was Lebanon and the shift against administration policy was so pronounced that the president elected to lead the parade in preference to being ridden from town on a rail. But, as a consolation to the bitter and corrosive anti-Communists, the president allowed nonstop Moslem-bashing at the hands of the largest naval guns of our largest battleship. Vengeance is ours in this regime and we will leave you something especially unpleasant as evidence of our displeasure upon your failure to accept our solution.

Domestically, the Congress prepared to settle into a profound and permanent state of siege mentality or a temporary effort to deal terrorism a fundamental blow, depending upon your outlook. In any event, visiting the Congress, seeing the Representatives and Senators, and listening to the debates will be an enterprise only for the most determined. Citizens will be required to memorize and then divulge their Social Security number at every step. Additionally, folks without visible identification will no longer walk the halls of Congress or the six office buildings or any of the rest of the Capitol. Security will be more strict than is currently used at American airports.

And for those that have been disturbed at a 50 percent increase in the national debt in thirty-six months, the first signs of reckoning may be at hand. The stock market has declined 10 percent in thirty days. No one has a respectful adjective for the newly submitted budget, not even the stalwarts of the administration. Moderate observers have characterized it as foolish, blatantly political, and frightfully expensive. The administration's request for next year is a deficit increase of another $180 billion. If so, and it seems highly likely, this administration will have increased by 70 percent a national debt that took two hundred years to accumulate. For 1984 the Congress, home of the big spenders, appropriated $3.5 billion more than the president requested. In a $900 billion budget, the profligate and the frugal may be hard to distinguish.

A. N. Ooltayg

FEBRUARY 27, 1984

Congress completed a week of work by passing three measures of overwhelmingly moderate importance. The attendance rate falls off sharply as contests for congressional seats begin to materialize all over the land. For some, a primary election is less than ninety days away. Being reelected will consume the principal time and concern of most members.

The second legislative session is always inferior to the first. The arguments are now old hat. The political jabbing dominates the questions, the comments, and the parliamentary maneuvering. A day doesn't pass that prayer in school and a balanced budget are not mentioned with passion, but without the slightest likelihood of serious consideration. The dark side of the democratic style, its mercilessness, is more evident. Selected for defeat (figurative slaughter) are the new, the old, the weak, and the disabled. Intrinsic measures of merit unrelated to considerations of political longevity are inconsequential to the process.

The abiding stubbornness of the president is constantly clearer. He is wholly without support for a military adventure in Beirut. The Marines are still there. His fiscal policies are unsupported by a shred of affirmation from the economic experts. His budget is described as political poppycock by his admirers and worse by all others. He is undismayed. Why should he be otherwise? His popularity with the folks remains high.

Even the semi-sacred defense budget is finding itself increasingly isolated. The plan to increase the authorizations by 18 percent from $265 billion to $312 billion has seen even the most enthusiastic supporters of the administration reduced to inarticulate moaning and some outright treason. But MX's, B-1's, and fighting satellites, like Dracula, don't ever really die, even with the legislative equivalent of a stake driven through their hearts.

A. N. Ooltayg

MAY 8, 1984

Our nation is in the process of restoring its self-image. It is an exciting time and a perilous time as well. The process must be influenced substantially by wisdom because our hunger for a former sense of well-being is so fierce we may buy into a jingoistic short-term fix. Our uncurious president senses the need but lacks the depth. He feels imperfectly our impulses for national reinforcement, but he has a shallow sense of our uniqueness, of the initial motives that formed us, and of our deliberate creation of a new society which was a fresh start for an entire nation.

Liberty is at our core, of course. But so is Ben Franklin's cold and challenging rejoinder to the woman who saluted him as he left the constitutional convention upon the completion of its business. "Do we have a nation, Mr. Franklin?" she asked. "You do, madam," said Franklin grimly. "The question is, can you keep it?"

The president understands slightly or not at all the process of making the system work. Flaunting opposition to abortion, endorsing prayer, rebuking the unfortunate, or defining the valuable as the impoverished are all banners which lead nowhere politically or pragmatically decent. The question is rarely one of our values, rather it is one of how to get there. As Americans we want to be optimistic, we want to get cracking on the problems and solve them. It's hard for us to accept the reality of problems which cannot be solved. Older cultures think us ingenuous in a cynical world. But America still smells like hope in the nostrils of a vast majority of this world's humans. No one dies trying to get out of America and millions clamor for admission. They can't all be wrong.

So how do we proceed between the threats of a hollow, rootless, superficial, phony patriotism on one hand and a compromise with anti-human philosophies utterly alien to our beginnings on the other? To begin with, we need wisdom. Then we need discrimination informed by education. Our uniqueness cannot be suffered to deteriorate into arrogance. The challenge is formidable, but the reward will indeed endure. Our nature is to be optimistic. We have undoubtedly been more so than some occasions would justify. But if we had to choose between the errors of exuberance and those of crabbed omission, give me the former.

The ingredients, then, what are they? First, we will insist that opportunity is forever present and that the *sense* of opportunity will be similarly nourished. We will emphasize the recognition of the rights of humans, notwithstanding clear limitations on this effort. We will honor the freedom of the mind and preserve the dignity of work and restore the infrastructure of community voluntary service. We will ceaselessly monitor the gap between the promise and the performance of this great nation—but in an abiding spirit of hope. We will reach, increasing our knowledge as we simultaneously shed our ignorance. We will dare to treasure innocence and, finally, we shall redeem ourselves by nurturing peace.

In the most famous hall in the world, the chamber of the United States House of Representatives, there is only one piece of writing. It is engraved on a tablet high above the Speaker's seat and it is rarely seen by visitors. It was written in the nineteenth century by Daniel Webster:

"Let us develop the resources of our land, call forth its powers, build up its institutions, promote all its great interests, and see whether we also in our day and generation may not perform something worthy to be remembered." Amen.

A. N. Ooltayg

MAY 23, 1984

In Washington these days all conversations begin with, "I know we've got to do something about the budget, but...." Some of the "buts" include the necessity of depreciating buildings over fifteen years, not twenty, thank you. The cozy interest break we get on industrial development bonds is another "but." Naturally, no one thinks that income tax rates should be increased, but almost everyone thinks "loopholes should be closed." You can count the president in on that last one: he has vowed in the same breath not to increase taxes and to close loopholes. Tricky business.

Of course, cutting wages is out and plans to reduce the current cost-of-living adjustment formula is a "but" of the first order. There is much sympathy to the belief that the 3.5 percent annual wage increase expectation should not be touched and is obviously another "but." Stretch out the time to buy a fancy weapon? Settle for a hundred geeziks instead of two hundred? Don't be silly, that adds to the overall cost. Both of those things are among the "buts."

Social Security is a big ticket, *but* we did something about it last year. Nearly a third of the budget goes to defense activity, *but* the Russians are coming out of the air ducts. User fees are too low, *but* all the users' industries are sick. There's too much uneaten food in the warehouses, *but* we've got to preserve the small farms. Health care costs are too high, *but* the doctors can take it out on you if you start monkeying with their compensation.

Spending is too high, *but* Elk Pinch, West Virginia, needs some help with its sewer. The District of Columbia subway is losing money, *but* it needs to be bigger. There aren't many fish left in the Great Lakes, *but* there never will be unless we put the wood to the lamprey eels. Acid rain needs to be dealt with in the Midwest, *but* only by allowing the folks on the Pacific Coast to pay higher utility bills. We need to save money, *but* we need $57 million for photovoltaic energy systems and $33 million for biomass fuel. We've got to get tough about bucks, *but* we need $3.9 billion for three hundred flood control and irrigation projects.

There are no unworthy projects, no projects that aren't critical for that matter. One member greets all visitors with a hearty, "Welcome! We'll do anything you want that doesn't cost money." All laugh and the petitioners begin, "I know we've got to do something about the budget, *but*...."

A. N. Ooltayg

July 20, 1984

Citizens of European democracies leave American national political conventions shaking their heads. Choose a national leader in a boxing ring? Select the world's most powerful nation's most powerful figure in the coliseum on lion-feeding day? The amateurs we call delegates have every opportunity and much encouragement to reveal their bloody worst. Tiny issues are clearly underneath Armageddon itself. There were fights, hysteria, and bad manners reported, not to say stimulated, by the news industry which thrives on action, on "color," on excitement, and on denunciation. If you want temperate, rational evaluation and debate, go to Oxford. Stay out of our way in San Francisco.

But the essence of it all is the underlying vitality, the spirit and commitment and sleeplessness of people knowing they are being hyped and then deliberately roused by the stem-winders. They are manipulated by the music, the banners, the lighting, the timing, and the balloons. "I'd sure miss it," says one. "We're strictly scenery," says another, adding, "God, how I love it!"

They spend their money, deplete their emotional reserves, eat badly, sleep rarely, insist on their importance and that of the process (in that order). They leave exhausted and brag ever after, all their lives, of having been one of the four thousand that forged a result. Then they go back to Chicago and Sauk Centre and gather themselves for the next epic: November.

They don't really have counterparts in the western world. In Germany or Britain the game isn't quite for all the candles. Only in America is the time, the effort, the shocking number of dollars, the zeal, and the desperation all of such a quality and quantity. We're going to reform one of these days, not now of course. We're going to shorten the agony, reform the process, be less infatuated with perfection. We're going to do all these things—just as soon as we adopt a new national sport.

A. N. Ooltayg

JULY 27, 1984

What with all the marbles up for grabs in one hundred days, the players are not apt to be dormant. And when they're not dormant, they're not apt to be scrupulous with reason. A president who sent four budgets to Congress in four years and never came closer to balance than $100 billion knows that a balanced budget amendment in the constitution five years hence will do the job. If he's wrong, at least he'll be off the payroll by then. For the president, a right to veto by line item might also do nicely. The founders didn't favor it, and the constitution says explicitly, "...Congress shall have the power to lay and collect taxes...(and) to pay the debts."

The same president responded to an unusual nomination speech that included a promise (or threat) to raise taxes by decrying the wickedness of such an idea. But the sense of wickedness was missing four days before when the president signed the 1984 Deficit Reduction Act, a law increasing taxes over three years by $51 billion. And three days later this president demanded a Social Security hike, even if one was not due under the law. Cost to the taxpayers in 1985: $1.7 billion.

Curiously, the same president thirty days earlier had revived fears about the soundness of the Social Security system. This notwithstanding his May 1983 boast that the system was made healthy into the next century by the Social Security Reform Act passed that month. The president in fairly recent years has entertained seriously a voluntary Social Security program. No living expert has affirmed that this is politically possible and no dispassionate observer has attested that the many goals of the current system could be preserved in a voluntary system. But the president yields slowly or not at all. His long suit has been the things he is not. Will that be sufficient in 1984?

A. N. Ooltayg

SEPTEMBER 4, 1984

The official 1984 calendar for the second session of the 98th Congress indicated that the House recess would end on September 4th and that the House would get down to business on that day. Such a schedule defies all past fact. A group that will not work more than three days per week will, of course, also not work less than three days per week, regarding a one- or two-day week as too insignificant for their majestic attentions. One suspicious member attended the leadership Whip meeting on Thursday, August 9th, and was informed by the Majority Leader that, "there would be votes on Wednesday, September 5th." Reminded of that indiscretion on September 5th, the Majority Leader inquired with mock concern, "Did I really say that?"

The lower House (so called because it occupied the first floor of the Federal Building in New York in 1789 while the Senate occupied the second floor) has, in fact, done well, especially with respect to appropriations measures. Ten of the thirteen required have gone on to the Senate and other places of greater glory. And, God help us, *The Wall Street Journal* accused the Congress of succumbing to "an outbreak of responsibility." One of the three remaining, Transportation, is locked up in a spitting contest with the Transportation Committee chairman on one side of the wet barrier and the Transportation Appropriations Subcommittee chairman on the other. The second is Defense Appropriations and that consumes a week under the best of circumstances. The third is the Foreign Aid Appropriation and that probably cannot be passed and will, in all likelihood, be the subject of a continuing resolution....

A. N. Ooltayg

SEPTEMBER 28, 1984

It has previously been noted that Western parliamentary democracies have not devised a graceful method for ending a legislative session. This is particularly true of the term's final legislative session. It is predictable in the U.S. Congress, which has increasingly adopted a strategy first employed by our state legislatures generally known as the "Christmas Tree." In this quaint practice every special interest dreams up, writes down, and gift wraps a present to itself. The quid pro quo is that every would-be benefactor is allowed to prepare his or her own present. Since the idea is for every party to respect the cupidity of every other party, there is, thus, no restraint on avarice. The ancient admonition that the American system was "all sail and no rudder" is particularly true in this procedure.

The House passed a 1,100-page continuing resolution spending $600 billion, but before it was through they had added Foreign Aid and an Omnibus Water Projects bill and, at the last minute, a sort of comprehensive crime package. The Democrats thought that was fun in that the president would be forced to accept the Water Projects bill if he wanted the Crime bill. The Republicans thought it was fun to get the Democrats voting against the motion to recommit, which was promptly swollen into a pro-crime stance.

But all things contain some good news. The president was finally and reluctantly pushed away from his demand for a $48 billion increase in defense appropriations. It was his budget which demanded an increase in defense spending from $265 billion to $313 billion. Curiously enough, the compromise was engineered exclusively by Majority Leader Jim Baker and Speaker Tip O'Neill. Both chiefs simply handed their troops the compromise as an accomplished fact and, perhaps out of relief, both bodies embraced it willingly.

Political dimensions are being cranked into every conceivable opportunity. Folks are regularly admonished to vote for this or that procedure on the ground that it will enormously embarrass the opposition. No way to run a railroad. As usual the quantity of matters rushed to the floor is staggering. After four weeks of institutional indifference, the members were alerted to thirty-two bills on suspension, ten conference reports, a budget resolution, and two continuing resolutions, all to be handled in two days. Despite a feeling that quantity is in an inverse relationship to quality, a feeling not altogether unjustified, there are critical matters which must be handled.

A. N. Ooltayg

OCTOBER 4, 1984

The federal government went out of business last night at midnight. But that didn't worry anybody. The Congress knew when the members went home last night that the country was going to go out of business. Some solace was gained from the knowledge that the Senate never would adjourn. In fact, the Senators began their work at noon on Wednesday and, nearly twenty-four hours later, they are still ostensibly working.

About an hour ago the chairman of the House Appropriations Committee stood up and said he had another continuing resolution. A continuing resolution has the virtue of keeping the machinery in motion temporarily and vice of allowing the legislators still another few months of days or hours to make up their minds. A spitting contest promptly ensued. The villains were the Democrats in the House of Representatives or the Republicans in the House of Representatives or the administration, or the whole Senate (undifferentiated), based on the direction of your own bile.

After some minutes of that fun, the chairman of the Appropriations Committee suggested that "further acrimony" would not be particularly useful and received a round of applause for his observation. This was done under the unanimous consent procedure whereby any one of 435 people can announce, "I object," and the game is over. A few folks reserved their right to object as a means of throwing a few darts, but in relatively short order everyone sat back and allowed the continuing resolution to pass by voice vote, a measure that maintained the federal government in business until 6:00 p.m. on Friday, October 5th. The republic is thus saved for that period of time.

Meanwhile, on the floor, a vigorous debate has now begun on a bill to help conserve the dwindling numbers of Atlantic striped bass. No point in letting time go unused and let no one say that these fellows don't get down to business and chew the tough ones when they appear. Meanwhile further, Yom Kippur begins at sundown on Friday and Columbus Day occurs on Monday and the whole bloody business may well be resumed on October 9th pending, of course, a few more continuing resolutions to keep the ship of state on course for that five days.

A. N. Ooltayg

INDEX

Running Uphill was produced by
Green Sand Press in Tucson, Arizona. It was
composed in 10.5/14 Classical Garamond
with Geometric Slabserif 703 display.
The designer and project manager was
Harrison Shaffer. Editorial assistance was
provided by Stacey Lynn and Robert Lloyd.
The books were printed and bound by
Sheridan Books in Ann Arbor, Michigan.